To Majid
with love & ...

Enjoy!

Alhine
28/5/10

Cyber Conflict and Global Politics

This volume examines theoretical and empirical issues relating to cyberconflict and its implications for global security and politics.

Taking a multidimensional approach to current debates in Internet politics, the book comprises essays by leading experts from across the world. The volume includes a comprehensive introduction to current debates in the field and their ramifications for global politics, and follows this with empirical case studies. These include cyberconflict, cyberwars, information warfare and hacktivism, in contexts such as Sri Lanka, Lebanon and Estonia, the European Social Forum, feminist cyber crusades and the use of the Internet as a weapon by ethnoreligious and sociopolitical movements. The volume presents the theoretical debates and case studies of cyberconflict in a coherent, progressive and truly multidisciplinary way.

The book will be of interest to students of cyberconflict, Internet politics, security studies and IR in general.

Athina Karatzogianni is a Lecturer in Media, Culture and Society at the University of Hull and author of *The Politics of Cyberconflict* (Routledge, 2006).

Contemporary security studies

Series Editors: James Gow and Rachel Kerr

King's College London

This series focuses on new research across the spectrum of international peace and security, in an era where each year throws up multiple examples of conflicts that present new security challenges in the world around them.

NATO's Secret Armies
Operation Gladio and terrorism in Western Europe
Daniele Ganser

The US, NATO and Military Burden-Sharing
Peter Kent Forster and Stephen J. Cimbala

Russian Governance in the Twenty-First Century
Geo-strategy, geopolitics and new governance
Irina Isakova

The Foreign Office and Finland 1938–1940
Diplomatic sideshow
Craig Gerrard

Rethinking the Nature of War
Edited by Isabelle Duyvesteyn and Jan Angstrom

Perception and Reality in the Modern Yugoslav Conflict
Myth, falsehood and deceit
1991–1995
Brendan O'Shea

The Political Economy of Peacebuilding in Post-Dayton Bosnia
Tim Donais

The Distracted Eagle
The rift between America and old Europe
Peter H. Merkl

The Iraq War
European perspectives on politics, strategy, and operations
Edited by Jan Hallenberg and Håkan Karlsson

Strategic Contest
Weapons proliferation and war in the greater Middle East
Richard L. Russell

Disease and Security
Natural plagues and biological
weapons in East Asia
Christian Enermark

Explaining War and Peace
Case studies and necessary condition
counterfactuals
Jack Levy and Gary Goertz

War, Image and Legitimacy
Viewing contemporary conflict
James Gow and Milena Michalski

Information Strategy and Warfare
A guide to theory and practice
John Arquilla and Douglas A. Borer

**Countering the Proliferation of
Weapons of Mass Destruction**
NATO and EU options in the
Mediterranean and the Middle East
Thanos P. Dokos

Security and the War on Terror
*Edited by Alex J. Bellamy,
Roland Bleiker, Sara E. Davies and
Richard Devetak*

The European Union and Strategy
An emerging actor
*Edited by Jan Hallenberg and
Kjell Engelbrekt*

**Causes and Consequences of
International Conflict**
Data, methods and theory
Edited by Glenn Palmer

**Russian Energy Policy and Military
Power**
Putin's quest for greatness
Pavel Baev

**The Baltic Question During the
Cold War**
*Edited by John Hiden, Vahur Made,
and David J. Smith*

**America, the EU and Strategic
Culture**
Renegotiating the transatlantic bargain
Asle Toje

Afghanistan, Arms and Conflict
Post-9/11 security and insurgency
Michael Bhatia and Mark Sedra

**Punishment, Justice and
International Relations**
Ethics and order after the Cold War
Anthony F. Lang, Jr.

**Intra-State Conflict, Governments
and Security**
Dilemmas of deterrence and assurance
*Edited by Stephen M. Saideman and
Marie-Joëlle J. Zahar*

Democracy and Security
Preferences, norms and policy-making
*Edited by Matthew Evangelista,
Harald Müller and Niklas Schörnig*

The Homeland Security Dilemma
Fear, failure and the future of
American security
Frank P. Harvey

**Military Transformation and
Strategy**
Revolutions in military affairs and
small states
Edited by Bernard Loo

**Peace Operations and International
Criminal Justice**
Building peace after mass atrocities
Majbritt Lyck

NATO, Security and Risk Management
From Kosovo to Khandahar
M.J. Williams

Cyber Conflict and Global Politics
Edited by Athina Karatzogianni

Cyber Conflict and Global Politics

Edited by Athina Karatzogianni

Routledge
Taylor & Francis Group

LONDON AND NEW YORK

First published 2009
by Routledge
2 Park Square, Milton Park, Abingdon, Oxon OX14 4RN

Simultaneously published in the USA and Canada
by Routledge
270 Madison Ave, New York, NY 10016

Routledge is an imprint of the Taylor & Francis Group, an informa business

© 2009 Selection and editorial matter, Athina Karatzogianni; individual
chapters, the contributors

Typeset in Times by Wearset Ltd, Boldon, Tyne and Wear
Printed and bound in Great Britain by TJI Digital, Padstow, Cornwall

British Library Cataloguing in Publication Data
A catalogue record for this book is available from the British Library

Library of Congress Cataloging in Publication Data
A catalog record for this book has been requested

ISBN10: 0-415-45970-2 (hbk)
ISBN10: 0-203-89076-0 (ebk)

ISBN13: 978-0-415-45970-9 (hbk)
ISBN13: 978-0-203-89076-9 (ebk)

Contents

Contributors

Michel Bauwens is a Belgian integral philosopher and Peer-to-Peer theorist. He has worked as an Internet consultant, information analyst for the United States Information Agency, information manager for British Petroleum (where he created one of the first virtual information centres), and is former editor-in-chief of the first European digital convergence magazine, the Dutch-language *Wave*. He is the author of a number of online essays, including a seminal thesis 'Peer to Peer and Human Evolution and The Political Economy of Peer Production'. He is editor of Pluralities-Integration|Pluralities/Integration newsletter. He now lives in Chiang Mai, Thailand, where he created the Foundation for P2P Alternatives.

Michael Dartnell is Visiting Associate Professor in the Department of Political Science at York University, Toronto. He is the author of *Insurgency Online: WebActivism and Global Conflict* (University of Toronto Press, 2006); *Action Directe: Ultra-left Terrorism in France, 1979–1987* (London: Frank Cass, 1995) as well as articles on information technologies and conflict/security, terrorism, political violence, and conflict. His current research focuses on the inter-connections of communication, Islam and Western notions of power.

Dimitrios Delibasis is a Counsel for International Security Affairs, and an Officer of the Greek Army Reserves. He has recently been awarded his Doctorate from the University of Westminster, which is on 'The Right of States to Individual Self-Defense in Information Warfare Operations'. He has also been for the last five years a Visiting Lecturer in the University of Westminster, School of Law's Public International Law subject panel where he has taught Public International Law. He is currently teaching Human Rights and he is also a member of the Hellenic Institute of Strategic Studies where he renders services as a Counsel (depending on relevant needs) and has also represented the institute at several conferences overseas.

Frazer Egerton is a final year PhD candidate in the department of International Politics at the University of Wales, Aberystwyth. He has taught in Nepal and South Korea and is currently editorial assistant on the *International Relations* journal.

Zinthiya Ganeshpanchan is a Research Fellow, Loughborough University, Midland Center for Criminology and Criminal Justice. Her main research interests are gender, violence and activism.

Hall Gardner is a geostrategist with a comparative historical orientation (American University of Paris). His focus is on the origins of war, yet more specifically on deliberating the phenomenon of war's eruption and its regional and global ramifications, with an eye toward conflict resolution. His research blends a historical and theoretical approach with contemporary international affairs, concentrating on questions involving NATO and European Union enlargement, the collapse of the Soviet Union and its impact upon China and Eurasia in general, as well as the global ramifications of the 'war on terrorism'. He is a member of the Committee on Atlantic Studies and of The World Political Forum. He is also on the Board of Advisors of the Cicero Foundation, the Global Water Fund, and Just World International. He is the author of *Averting Global War: Regional Challenges, Overextension and Options for American Strategy* (Palgrave, 2007).

Andrew Hoskins is Associate Professor in the Department of Sociology, University of Warwick. He is founding Editor-in-Chief of a new Sage interdisciplinary journal, *Memory Studies* (www.sagepub.co.uk/ms) and founding Co-editor of the new Sage journal, *Media, War and Conflict* (www.sagepub.co.uk/mwc). He is Principal Investigator of an AHRC funded three-year research project 'Conflicts of Memory: Mediating and Commemorating the 2005 London Bombings' (www.media-memory.com), and Principal Investigator of a two-year ESRC funded project 'Legitimising the Discourses of Radicalisation: Political Violence in the New Media Ecology'. Recent publications include: *Televising War: From Vietnam to Iraq* (Continuum, 2004); *Media and Memory* (Routledge, 2007); *Television and Terror: Conflicting Times and the Crisis of News Discourse* (with Ben O'Loughlin, Palgrave Macmillan, 2007); and *War and Media* (with Ben O'Loughlin, Polity, 2008).

Athina Karatzogianni is a Lecturer in Media, Culture and Society at the University of Hull and author of *The Politics of Cyberconflict* (Routledge, 2006). Athina writes on Internet politics, the broader appreciation of the theoretical implications of networked forms of communication and organization, and the cyberconflict agenda. Currently, she is developing work with Andrew Robinson on *Power, Conflict and Resistance in the Contemporary World* for the Routledge Advanced Series in International Relations and Global Politics, which sets out to reinterpret world systems theory, attempting to understand resistance and opposition movements in terms of a combination of networked rhizomes and the assertion of reactive ethnoreligious identities. Other research focuses on small states' online representations, the global periphery, and war coverage in Lebanon and Iraq.

Anastasia Kavada is a Post-doctoral Researcher in the School of Media, Arts and Design at the University of Westminster where she also received her doctorate in Media and Communication. Her research combines elements of communication and social movement theories, as well as theories of identity, networks and self-organization. She is a founding member of the editorial board of *Westminster Papers in Communication and Culture*. Current research interests also include the uses of social networking sites for political campaigning, as well as the connection between new communication technologies and changing political identities.

Graham Meikle is the author of *Interpreting News* (Palgrave Macmillan, 2008) and *Future Active: Media Activism and the Internet* (Routledge, 2002). He lectures in the Department of Film, Media and Journalism at Stirling University in Scotland.

Ben O'Loughlin is Lecturer in International Relations at Royal Holloway, University of London, where he is Associate Director of the New Political Communication Unit (newpolcom.rhul.ac.uk). He completed his doctorate in Politics at the University of Oxford in 2005, and has been Visiting Fellow at King's College London. He works on the two-year ESRC funded project 'Legitimising the Discourses of Radicalisation: Political Violence in the New Media Ecology'. Publications include *Television and Terror* (Palgrave, 2007) and *War and Media* (Polity, 2008), both co-authored with Andrew Hoskins.

Gary D. Rawnsley is Professor of Asian International Communications in the Institute of Communications Studies, University of Leeds. He has published widely on international propaganda, public diplomacy, election campaigning and the media in processes of democratization. Professor Rawnsley is currently completing a project on Radio Free Asia and its impact on China's Harmonious Society. He is also involved in research about the media and democratization (with responsibility for Taiwan and Korea), and the Central Motion Picture Studio in Taiwan. He is the author of 'Old Wine in New Bottles: Taiwan-China Information Warfare and Propaganda', *International Affairs*, vol. 81, no. 5 (2005), pp. 1061–78.

Maria Touri is a Lecturer in the Department of Media and Communication at the University of Leicester. Her research interests are mainly in the area of political communications and the role of the media in international relations. More broadly, she is interested in the effects of media framing on policy making and decision-making processes. Maria is involved in the analysis of news coverage, journalistic practices and the media logic in situations of conflict. Recently she started to examine the role of new media technologies and blogs in the context of conflict and international relations.

Harinda Vidanage is a doctoral student in Politics, in the department of Politics of the School of Social and Political Studies, University of Edinburgh. His thesis looks at the formation of political spaces and spatial attributes of power in intense political engagement in cyberspace by diasporic political activists with case study focused on the Sri Lankan Tamil diasporan activists. He has pioneered empirical research into cybercafés in Sri Lanka and its role in connecting diasporic Tamil communities with the publication being translated into several languages. He was a former American Institute for Lankan Studies (AILS) fellow, researching 'cyborg nationalism'. His main research interests are on political spaces in cyberspace, power and cyber security. Harinda Vidanage was the youngest adviser to the Sri Lankan Prime Minister on international affairs and headed the Prime Ministerial research division. Currently he is an honorary adviser to the Sri Lankan president on international affairs.

Preface

This edited volume is bringing fourteen cyberconflict experts together for the first time in one cross-disciplinary volume focusing on theoretical and empirical issues relating to cyberconflict (i.e. conflict in computer mediated environments) and the effect of the Internet and ICTs on global security, politics, war, media coverage and society.

I have been researching cyberconflict for the last eight years and at first it was pretty much a lonely struggle. My research monograph *The Politics of Cyberconflict* (2006) was an attempt to raise the theoretical and methodological problems new media create or exacerbate when they interfere with global politics and vice versa. In addition, I attempted to provide a framework of utilizing existing media, conflict and social movement theories to explain ethnoreligious and sociopolitical cyberconflicts. The study was a product of its time (2000–5), which was a transformative period for both global politics and ICTs. Further, as it was engaging with a novel phenomenon and diverse literatures, it makes admittedly a complicated read.

This volume unpacks and discusses in more detail several of the issues raised in my monograph. The contributors of this volume offer their own theoretical and methodological solutions to these issues, which relate to their research subject. Conflicts in cyberspace are multiplying and researchers in the area are following suit. The hope is to encourage more research and discussion, by unfolding some of the problems currently shaping new media and politics. Unless we understand how to theorize and regulate cyberconflict, and how to collect the relevant data more effectively and how to bring together diverse disciplines and literatures (information warfare, Internet security, sociology/cultural studies, global communications studies and global politics), we will continue to study the effects of ICTs on conflict with a monolithic, incomplete and non-constructive mentality.

I am indebted to many friends and colleagues. Amongst these are: my parents for their tough love; Tim Hawkins for having dinner without me many times; Andrew Robinson and George Michaelides for letting me throw ideas at them; my editors Andrew Humphrys and Emily Kindleysides and the reviewers at Routledge for their helpful suggestions; Waddick Doyle, Pat Lair and Julie Thomas for a great year at the American University of Paris (AUP), where my contributing chapter was written; my present colleagues Matthew Pateman and Daniel McNeil at Media, Culture and Society in Hull University for their support; and Jim Bryant and Steve Mills for inviting me to call for a conference on cyberconflict for the Conflict Research Society, which brought all of us together. Yet, my biggest debt is to the authors of this volume who trusted me with their work: Hall, Ben, Andrew, Maria, Michael, Gary, Dimitrios, Frazer, Harinda, Zinthiya, Graham, Anastasia and Michel. This book is dedicated to you, and all the researchers of cyberconflict and global politics and their readers.

Athina Karatzogianni
Hull University, UK
29 February 2008

1 Introduction

New media and the reconfiguration of power in global politics

Athina Karatzogianni

Neo-liberal governments and institutions face a counter-hegemonic account of globalization, to which they have responded in a confused and often contradictory manner. One of the interesting sides to the argument is that the information revolution is altering the nature of conflict by strengthening network forms of organization over hierarchical forms. In contrast to the closure of space, the violence and identity divide found in ethnoreligious discourses, sociopolitical movements seem to rely more on networking and rhizomatic structures. US power is increasingly faced with resistance movements operating on a network model and utilizing new information technologies.

These movements can be divided into two broad groups; ethnoreligious movements and sociopolitical movements. (Of course, there are cultural and lifestyle activism movements but I would not make it my concern here). To suppress both kinds of movements, the US state relies on a binary, repressive mode of identity-construction, which divides the world into 'them and us'. This approach is guaranteed to escalate rather than resolve conflict. Its effects include the corrosion of civil and human rights and, most importantly, the increasing isolation of the would-be power-holders amid a sea of swarming resistances and uncontrollable spaces and flows. From 'with us or against us', domination therefore evolves into 'with or without you' (Karatzogianni and Robinson 2004, 2009, forthcoming).

An example of the struggle to restrict and control the flow of anti-American propaganda is the effort by the US Defense Department to block soldiers from accessing sites like YouTube and MySpace on its networks and their decision to launch their own Multi-National Force–Iraq broadcasts. Having said that, the military personnel in Iraq have never been allowed access anyway. The ban really affects military personnel globally, who nevertheless can afford to access through private service providers anyway, use closed systems like Army Knowledge Online, or Internet cafes, bypassing the ban from the DoD Internet. What is ironic, but hardly surprising, is that this policy comes straight after a decision to create an official military do-it-yourself under the YouTube video-sharing mechanism. The logic is that if soldiers are blogging and vlogging, they should at least do it under military censorship and approval and channel their journalistic/ cameramen ambitions in a controlled and filtered manner.

Channelling videos in a controlled manner is much more preferable for the military than having soldiers jeopardizing the reputation of the multinational forces, as has been the case in the past. It also produces an image of a military that is consistent with the current developments and embraces the technologies used by advanced countries and their citizens worldwide. Yet, it remains doubtful that these videos will have an effect in the periphery of the world system, where many people have yet to make a phone call. On a different issue, families of soldiers in Iraq and elsewhere are used to censorship. Regrettably, I think what will take some time to get used to is watching their loved ones fighting a war in online videos.

Nevertheless, this is part of an unprecedented operational tactic to counter the propaganda, organization, mobilization and recruiting techniques of Islamist extremist groups. The paramount example of this is Al-Qaeda's web presence and that of its affiliates. The Al-Qaeda network and its ideology relies more on common religious affiliation and kinship networks than strict national identity, which fits well with the borderless and network character of the Internet. Significant is also the fact that the Internet has been used as a primary mobilizational tool, especially after the breakdown of cells in Afghanistan, Saudi Arabia and Pakistan. On the Internet, Al-Qaeda is replicating recruitment and training techniques and evading security services, because they cannot be physically intercepted, due to the virtuality of their networks. The Internet is used by radical Islamist groups under the ideological umbrella global 'ummah' as a propaganda tool via electronic magazines, training manuals and general recruitment sites, as well as a weapon for disruptions aiming at financing operations, or stealing data and blueprints (see Chapter 5, this volume).

Further, recognizing the medium and countering the enemy's web presence is not the only reason for this current development in media policy. The past decade the US military has been consistently advised by thinktanks to exploit new information technologies and create and sustain a more network-based approach to warfare, utilizing psychological and information warfare and 'winning the hearts and minds of the population'. Especially post 9/11 and with the war in Afghanistan and Iraq, the US military has finally recognized the need to utilize new media and social networking technologies to tap into a younger American audience, recruit and mobilize global public opinion under a more favourable light of how this war is fought and why (on the question of public opinion and radicalization see Chapter 3, this volume).

Until very recently, the US military has been uncomfortable and clueless of how to deal with the uncontrollable and anarchic dimensions of the web, if efforts at cracking down on milbloggers and banning digital cameras following the Abu Ghraib scandal are anything to go by (see Chapter 4, this volume). The institution of embedded journalists and the crackdown of unilaterals in Iraq ensured a patriotic media in the US, and elsewhere, however this could not compensate for the increasing relevance of Al-Jazeera English, BBC World and France 24, their online equivalents and 'alternative' media services and bloggers/vloggers (video) found on the web, indicating a transformation in the field of global communications due to the advent of the Internet and its affiliated technologies (see Chapter 2, this volume).

As the war continues, and domestic public support for the war decreases in the US, the military had no choice but to create a global outlet for its multinational forces to bypass the global media which have become increasingly impatient of the war and more critical of its future. The YouTube videos of soldiers engaging with the local population, playing football with children and saving a kidnapped Iraqi is an effort to humanize an inhuman war. Nine out of ten top videos on YouTube are indeed military operations, 'a boots on the ground perspective'. What you see in these videos are soldiers that are simultaneously comfortable and uncomfortable fighting a war in front of a camera. It is a pornography of the simultaneous pride and suffering of these soldiers and the Iraqi population to an increasingly insensitivized audience.

The utilization of YouTube by the military raises important questions revolving around how information is released in the public domain and why, how much censorship is taking place and what alternative sources of information are available. These questions have to be posed in an analysis of the anti-Iraq war/ pro-war, anti-Islamic pro-Islamic cyberconflicts we are witnessing today. The way a war is communicated is as important as the conduct of the war itself. Among many examples, the counter-propaganda YouTube effort by the Multi-National Force – Iraq confirms that individuals and protagonists can now send stories more quickly than military press releases and mainstream journalists, indicating that civilian and military bloggers will have an independent capability to access future conflict arenas and to provide real-time visual and audio coverage of battlefield events. This has consequences for news management, even by very powerful states like the US.

In analysing the March 2003 Iraq conflict, the Internet's role in the conflict was studied in terms of its effect on the organization and spread of the movement, and its impact on war coverage and war-related cyberconflicts. The latter involved hacking between anti-war and pro-war hacktivists (sociopolitical cyberconflict), but also between pro-Islamic and anti-Islamic hackers (ethnoreligious cyberconflict) (Karatzogianni 2006).

On the sociopolitical cyberconflict field, the Internet played a distinctive role in the spread of the peace movement, on war coverage and on war-related cyberconflicts, rendering the full potential of the new medium in politics and information undisputable. In the months preceding the actual war in Iraq, a plenitude of phenomena on and off the Internet emerged, which in previous international conflicts were only embryonic. Before and during the war in Iraq, mobilization structures appear to have been greatly affected by the Internet. Peace groups organized demonstrations and events through the Internet, to the effect that ten million people protested against the war globally, with the net speeding up mobilization remarkably. It helped mobilization in loose coalitions of small groups that organized very quickly, at the same time preserving the particularity of distinct groups in network forms of organization. Anti-war groups used email lists and websites, group text messages and chatrooms to organize protests, and in some cases, to engage in symbolic hacking against the opposite viewpoint. Accordingly, the anti-war movement succeeded in that respect at gradually building their own image of the Americans and their allies and framing their message (no WMD, dodgy dossiers, humanitarian concerns, etc.). The integration of the Internet into mainstream media, the effect of online material challenging official government sources and the mainstream media, and blogging, are threatening the status quo countries and their representations in the global public sphere.

In terms of censorship, the latest literature supports the idea that journalists were not only censored and manipulated, but also targeted in this conflict – which brings up the issue of whether the US could control information. Apparently, through psychological operations, they could manipulate the conflict and control the media, especially the American mainstream media (almost always submissive to the patriotic/nationalistic discourse after 9/11). However, the current change of US broadcasting in doubting the effectiveness of the administration's efforts, and the military's inability to control inconsistencies and fiascos from twenty-four-hour Internet coverage or to manipulate the American image in the Muslim world, has forced the military to reconsider its media tactics. All these developments are indications of where future conflict is going. The US military utilizes its younger generation of officers, some of which are part of the Internet generation, to reach audiences at home and abroad in an effort to win the information war running parallel in cyberspace to the overly media-manipulated conflict in the battleground.

One of the major differences between Vietnam and even the 1991 Gulf War, is that the Internet has revolutionized not only coverage but has acted as a resource and weapon for the opposing parties in conflicts, a tool for organization, mobilization and recruiting, even conflict resolution and hacktivism. In the 'first living room war', the Vietnam War, despite the fact that the network news deserve credit for the eventual disillusionment with the war, at the same time they were also responsible for creating, or at least reinforcing, the illusion of American omnipotence in the first place. An example of this was that American media delayed for two years the reporting of the My Lai massacre, not because of censorship, nor because the facts were not instantly available, but due to resistance to the story by the US media itself. That was because the massacre occurred in 1967, when the storyline was focused on 'good news' about a war which, editors were persuaded, the US was winning. There are some parallels to be found with the Gulf War in 1991, however the major difference is that due to the speeds of twenty-four-hour coverage and alternative reporting and blogging challenging the mainstream media in the online public sphere, the time the mainstream media waste on patriotism and disillusionment is remarkably decreased due to the checks and balances imposed by the Internet revolution.

A further part of the cyberconflict environment is cyberterrorism: computer-based attacks intended to intimidate or coerce governments or societies in pursuit of goals that are political, religious or ideological. According to Arquilla and Ronfeldt (2001c), conflicts increasingly revolve around knowledge and the use of soft power. This would come about with the help of information-age ideologies in which identities and loyalties shift from the nation-state to the transnational level of global civil society (see Chapter 8, this volume). Additionally, netwar is referred to as the low, societal type of struggle, while cyberwar refers more to the heavy information warfare type.

Cyberconflicts can act as a 'barometer' of real-life conflicts and can reveal the natures and the conflicts of the participating groups. The protagonists in sociopolitical cyberconflicts fight for participation, power and democracy. Evident in the anti-globalization and the anti-capitalist movement is an alternative programme for the reform of society, asking for democracy and more participation from the 'underdogs', be they in the West or in the developing world. In the anti-war movement, which is a single-issue movement, the demand is for a change in power relations in favour of those who believe the war to be unjustified. In new social movements, networking through the Internet links diverse communities such as labour, feminist, ecological, peace and anti-capitalist groups, with the aim of challenging public opinion and battling for media access and coverage. Groups are being brought together like a parallelogram of forces, following a swarm logic, indicating a web of horizontal solidarities to which power might be devolved or even dissolved. The Internet encourages a version of the commons that is ungoverned and ungovernable, either by corporate interests or by leaders and parties (for a theorization of electronic civil disobedience see Chapter 12, this volume; for conflicts in netarchical capitalism see Chapter 14, this volume).

Mobilization structures, for instance, are greatly affected by the Internet, since the peace groups used the Internet to organize demonstrations and events, to mobilize in loose coalitions of small groups that organize very quickly, and to preserve the particularity of distinct groups in network forms of organization. Moreover, the framing process was also affected, since email lists and websites are used to mobilize, changing the framing of the message to suit the new medium (see for instance Kavada's analysis of the organizing processes of the European Social Forum, Chapter 13, this volume). The political opportunity structure in this particular case refers to alternative media, but also to an opening of political space, or an opening of global politics to people who, previously, would not or could not get as involved (for instance see Ganeshpanchan's examination of web activism against gender violence, Chapter 11, this volume).

Dissidents against governments are able to use a variety of Internet-based techniques (email lists, email spamming, BBS, peer-to-peer and e-magazines) to spread alternative frames for events and a possible alternative online democratic public sphere. An example of dissidents' use of the Internet is spamming e-magazines to an unprecedented number of people within China, a method which provides recipients with 'plausible deniability'. Also, proxy servers, file-trading networks like Kazaa and Gnutella can help dissidents communicate, since they have no central source and are hard to turn off.

Ethnoreligious cyberconflicts primarily include hacking enemy sites and creating sites for propaganda and mobilizational purposes. In ethnoreligious cyberconflicts, despite the fact that patriotic hackers can network, there is a greater reliance on traditional ideas, such as protecting the nation or fatherland and attacking for nationalist reasons. The 'Other' is portrayed as the enemy, through very closed, old and primordialist ideas of belonging to an imagined community (for the impact on the Sri Lankan conflict see Chapter 10, this volume).

The Israeli–Palestinian cyberconflict saw the use of national symbols (like the Israeli flag, Hebrew text and even a recording of the Israeli national anthem) when hacking the Hezbollah homepage. This explicitly draws attention to issues of national identity, nationalism and ethnicity. Also, the language used by hackers relies on an 'us' and 'them' mentality, where Israelis and their American supporters, or else Palestinians and Muslims, are portrayed as barbaric, reflecting discourses of inclusion and exclusion. The Internet in this cyberconflict became a battleground and was used as a weapon by both sides, and full-scale action by thousands of Israeli and Palestinian youngsters involved both racist emails and circulating of instructions on how to crush the enemy's websites. Similarly, in the Indian–Pakistani cyberconflict, the Indian army's website was set up as a propaganda tool, and hacked pictures of alleged tortures of Kashmiris by Indians were placed on the site, in a similar propaganda tactic. Also, the Internet was used as a weapon, when the worm Yaha was released by Indian hackers. In particular discourses, religion is mentioned (religious affiliation), the word 'brothers' (collective identity and solidarity), and 'our country', a promised land (Karatzogianni 2006; see also here Rawnsley's analysis of the Taiwan Strait cyberconflict, Chapter 2, this volume).

The more recent Estonian cyberconflict is by no means then the first cyberconflict. We have been witnessing conflict in computer-mediated environments as early as 1994. The reason the Estonian case has been coined the 'first cyberconflict or cyberwar' is because a nation's infrastructure was targeted in its entirety, in an orchestrated, unprecedented and sustained manner. The attackers used a giant network of bots, as many as one million computers, in places as far away as the United States, Peru, China and Vietnam to amplify the impact of their assault. As a sign of their financial resources, there is evidence that they rented time on other so-called botnets.

The scale of the Estonian cyberconflict points to the deficiency of the international community to regulate cyberconflict, to create mechanisms for defining and then reacting to cyberattacks on a state, especially one linked to NATO and the EU, in a sensitive geopolitical area (for regulation issues see Chapter 7, this volume). Despite the magnitude of a monthly assault on a country nicknamed e-Stonia, due to its reliance on online services, and the home of Internet pioneers, NATO sends experts to learn from it, refraining from directly addressing the allegations made by the Estonian government or challenging Russia's standpoint.

Keeping the socioeconomic implications in mind, the real impact of the Estonian cyberconflict operates on multiple political levels. First, whether the attacks were by the Russian government, Russian diasporic communities, or more likely Ethnic Russians in Estonia, the fact remains that NATO does not yet define electronic attacks as military action even if the guilty party is identified. Second, information communication technologies are a very convenient and cost-effective tool for protest, but the real spark are the uncertainty about the enemy within and the anxiety about the always incomplete project of national purity so that 'these geographies are the spatial outcome of complex interactions between faraway events and proximate fears, between old histories and new provocations, between rewritten borders and unwritten orders', as Appadurai (2006) puts it. This cultural struggle, which integrates war and politics at the borders with vigilance and purification at the centres, is exacerbated by the media in general and by new communication technologies in particular. The fight to win the global war of messages, propaganda and ideas has often produced unpredictable results, especially in cyberspace. In essence, they are then defending the purity of their national space, and they do so by skilfully using online media technologies. To put it simply, globalization and its technologies can expose pathologies in the sacred ideologies of nationhood (for a discussion on small, virtual states and minorities online representations see, Chapter 9, this volume).

As today's ethnic groups number in the hundreds and thousands, their mixtures, cultural style and media representations 'create profound doubts about who exactly are among the "we" and who are among the "they" in the context of rapid migration or refugee movements, how many of "them are now among us"' (Appadurai 2006). The statue and its removal in Estonia, and the cyberconflict that ensued is a reflection of the instability of the EU enlargement project, especially in relation to Russia's hegemonic aspirations, energy disputes and legacy in the region, pointing to an emerging second Cold asymmetric War by Russia, such as the recent missiles dispute with the US and Russia's relentless involvement in the region as a whole (supporting secessionist states, intervening in coloured revolutions, embargoing products, etc.).

In the final analysis, the true bigger picture must include a recognition that Russia is an oligopoly (some even goes as far as to say a dictatorship cracking down on civil liberties), not to say that the US is the paragon of democracy, holding together through the illusion of still providing a countervoice to US imperialism. As the US has a lot currently on its plate, any future action in defence of NATO countries in the former Soviet sphere of influence will destabilize consensus on the war on terror. Ultimately, regulation and prevention of cyberconflict and its future implications might indeed require a bigger electronic Pearl Harbor than that of the Estonian cyberconflict.

It seems that the accusations against the Chinese attempting cyber-espionage might be a turning point of how seriously governments take cyberconflicts and their regulation. The Chinese government has denied that the Chinese military is to blame for the cyberattacks involving systematic network penetrations against the US, Britain, Germany, France and New Zealand, also pointing out that such accusations are irresponsible and have ulterior motives. They are arguing that they have long opposed cybercrime and have explicit law and regulations against it and that China 'does not do such despicable things'. The German chancellor, Angela Merkel, after her own office and several government ministries were found to be infected with spyware, brought up the issue directly during her visit in China, warning that the two countries should observe 'a set of game rules'. The response by the Chinese government was to distance themselves from the accusation while promising to cooperate with international efforts to combat cybercrime.

Although the Chinese government is rounded and blamed by most experts in the field for these attacks, the countries attacked in most cases avoid directly accusing the Chinese, and mostly 'raise the issue' with them or stress that they are not implying that they did it, like the French, hoping that the Chinese will control their military or their rogue citizens more effectively in the future or that they will not succeed in getting classified information next time.

Nevertheless, the reality of the situation is much more complex – interestingly a word used by President Bush to describe the American relationship with China – as it points to problems in reporting instances of cyberconflict without hyberbole; combating with formal international regulations cybercrime, cyberterrorism, information warfare and industrial espionage; putting more strain to bilateral relations with China on a global level; pointing to serious doubts over the Chinese government's control of their own military; and threatening the country's image in the community of states just before the Beijing 2008 Olympics.

The cyberattacks can also be in the future an extra problem for diplomatic relations with China, side by side with intellectual property rights, freedom of expression, aggressive industrial growth and monetary policy, environmental concerns etc. China is currently feared by these powers. The reason is not plans for cyberattacks against navies. There were plenty of those lurking on the Internet, published years ago by military futurologists in China, where the information warfare field has produced all sorts of scenarios on par with the US. The Chinese information warfare theorists have been discussing this a long time now from a technologically inferior position, arguing that information warfare can provide them with an asymmetrical advantage.

China is feared because it is growing at great speeds and is hungry for information, as is currently every other country in the world. Understandably, competition on commercial, military technology and cutting-edge industrial secrets is fierce. China is by no means the only country at it. Even if the compromised system is unclassified, combined information can produce good intelligence perhaps compromising industrial, military secrets and so on. For China to sustain its economic success, she must become a centre of innovation and technology, and she looks particularly keen to, which is why she is the main suspect.

When attacks happen, they normally either never become public or do become public years down the line. Governments refrain to tell the world that their systems are vulnerable. The US has suffered attacks that have been traced to provinces in China since 2003 with Titan Rain, when systems at NASA and other networks (agencies in Arizona, Virginia, San Diego, Alabama) were attacked, retrieving information on aviation specifications and flight-planning software. This became public only in 2005. Therefore, it is especially curious that the attacks in June 2007 came out as quickly as they did. Reactions of the countries under attack will vary, as there is no regulation over information warfare on an international level. There is not even international cooperation on the issue of ICANN and Internet governance, despite efforts at a world summit, let alone against cyberterrorism. For example, as pointed out by American officials, tracing hackers who use Chinese networks is complicated by the lack of cyber investigation agreements between China and the United States.

Generally, response varies from counter-attacks, for example such as the one reported by *The Times* during Titan Rain when US security expert Shawn Carpenter counter-hacked the intruders to the restrained recent reaction of the of New Zealand prime minister, Helen Clark, who says she knows which countries tried to hack into her government's computers but is refusing to name names commenting that 'that's not the way intelligence matters are handled'. Interestingly, she also said that it is something every country is experiencing.

The reaction of the US president, George W. Bush, was that he was aware that 'a lot of our systems are vulnerable to cyber attack from a variety of places' and that he might bring the issue up with the Chinese, which he never did, apparently confirming the role of his administration as a cheerleader to the 85 per cent of networks controlled by private business in his country. The UK's reaction is also interesting since alarm bells have been ringing for a long time by the country's experts, as the National Infrastructure Coordination Centre had warned of the attacks in 2005 and the scale as 'industrial'. Andrew MacKinlay, a Labour member of the Commons Foreign Affairs Committee, went on record as saying that the attacks came from China and accused the government of covering up the scale of the problem and appeasing the Chinese.

Unfortunately, not every country has cyberlaws, and there is no law that deems cyberattacks as military attacks against a nation, so it seems that everyone is doing it now that there is no international regulation, and now they can get away with it. In the case of China, even if their military was involved and the Chinese government was turning a blind eye or was buying the data from independent hackers (although one has to be sceptical as the Internet is controlled fiercely in China), who can be sure that other state or non-state actors did not disguise their attacks to come from China, since China was blamed anyway? British official Roger Cummings of the National Infrastructure Security Coordination Centre (NISCC) talks of 'countries' probing attacks against his country, while New Zealand talks of 'countries', and the US mentions attacks by state and non-state actors. The whole reaction of these countries feels like there is more to this than China.

Finally, there might be more to this than China and hackers, as it seems a particularly clumsy attempt to be orchestrated by senior state or military officials. Also, in China, as in everywhere else, the field is scattered, information warfare specialists and hackers are not under a centralized command, and it might not be easy to control their plans, scenarios and attacks. What is for sure though, is that this revelation and the circus that followed it, has come just before the 17th Party Congress expected to be held in October in China, and just when the Chinese needed to look more friendly towards the West. Also, all this 'China-but-other-countries-we-cannot-name and non-state actors too' is confusing, and rounding up only China when she is doing so 'well' is somewhat suspicious.

Whatever the developments and transformations in the sphere of global politics, the new media technologies and the political opportunities they present are unsettling the world system, they are rendering it chaotic and they are having a deeper systemic effect than the more powerful actors care to admit. It remains to be seen whether information age ideologies, new modes of capitalism, conflict, activism, terrorism and war in cyberspace will ever transfer to the 'real world' reversing the opposite trend, and causing everyday effects on a bigger scale than we are witnessing today. Even so, we are undoubtedly living in interesting times and systemic uncertainty has always produced the most beautiful and monstrous changes in global affairs.

This volume explores, through theorization of contemporary empirical examples, some of these changes and cyberconflicts situated in the global political environment. Part I is dedicated to identifying, theorizing and exploring the general problems and research questions emerging from the complex interaction of new media, ICTs, the Internet, social networking, v/blogging, global conflict and its coverage. Part II discusses the challenges ICTs pose for global security, in regard to theorizing, regulating information warfare and explaining the use of technology by radical Islamist groups or groups in ethnic cyberconflicts. Part III explores empirical examples of new conflict zones emerging, such as militant jihadism online, and the effects of vast virtual communications on gender violence, virtual states and small states' online representations, anxieties and cyber-cultural environments. Part IV explores the symbolic power, organization and communication of sociopolitical groups and the socioeconomic conflicts linked to global capitalist practices, netarchical or otherwise.

Part I

Transforming media and global conflict

2 War and the media paradox

Hall Gardner

> The dangers of war are heightened by intolerance, national chauvinism, and a
> failure to understand varying points of view. This should never be forgotten by
> those who have responsibilities in the media. Above all national and political
> interests, there is the supreme interest of all humanity in peace.
>
> (International Commission for the Study of Communications Problems,
> UNESCO: Paris, 1980)

Introduction

Media and the information technology (IT) revolution are radically altering the
way societies interact – as well as the way that states (and anti-state partisans)
fight wars. In military-technological terms, it is clear that the continuing fusion
of the computer, satellite communications and media revolutions has radically
'improved' warfighting capabilities, even if the IT revolution has not
fundamentally altered the geostrategic and political-economic rationale for war
itself (Gardner 2005, 2007a).

While computers, satellites and rapid access to 'real time' information have
helped to make the 'revolution in military affairs' possible, and have proven
their effectiveness with regard to the very rapid interventions in Afghanistan in
2001 and Iraq in 2003 in particular – taking updated blitzkrieg concepts to their
fullest extent possible through 'network-centric warfare' at least in the opening
phases of each intervention – these IT innovations in general have had several
unexpected consequences for American policy-makers and military strategists.

The first largely unexpected consequence is that global access to the Internet
has made the battle for the 'hearts and minds', as the Pentagon puts it, all the
more difficult. This is due to the ease in which propaganda, involving valid
information, mixed with dis-information, mis-information and excessive
information (coupled with mis- or dis-interpretation of that information) can be
disseminated and utilized globally on the Internet Tower of Babel.

Even if not all societies possess equal access to computers, the mobile phone
and the Internet, elites in differing communities do possess such access and can
disseminate their desired messages accordingly. (Ironically, as to be explained,
Bin Laden himself does not use high-tech systems, as does his organization and

often self-proclaimed affiliates.) In essence, while innovations in computers and communication have assisted tremendously the speed and accuracy of contemporary military capabilities, they have concurrently facilitated both criminal and 'terrorist' activities.

The second issue of concern is that the new IT technologies appear to possess the 'seeds of their own destruction' due to the very nature of their interconnected networks. IT systems can be countered, or at least disrupted, by both states and anti-state partisan groups (as well as by pranksters and criminal hackers) through various techniques of cyber-sabotage, which in effect, seek to disrupt, if not destroy, the most vulnerable 'nodes' of various systems of information and its distribution, through planting Trojan horses, hacking, denial of service attacks, exploiting errors in software, etc. Storage of classified information, bank accounts and computer operations of different kinds, have all been targets of cyber-sabotage. Finding and knocking out the 'Achilles heel' of one communication system can, in turn, disrupt all other systems connected with that system. The first 'cyberwar' took place between Russian and Estonian computer hackers in April 2007 (Ifrah 2007).

A third issue of concern is the socioeconomic effects of the new IT innovations. On the social side, the mass media (since Marshall McLuhan's 'global village') has had a stunning psychological and social impact. The homogenizing effects of the globalizing media have tended to alienate groups and leaderships who subconsciously (and consciously) absorb the images, values and conceptions presented by the new media. On the one hand, new systems of communication diffuse new ideas and images that can possibly assist reforms, if not peaceful and 'progressive' revolutions. On the other hand, they can also work to alienate elites and large segments of the population, possibly causing a violent backlash. What differs now, particularly since the advent of the personal computer, mobile phone and Internet, is that the new IT revolution provides greater opportunities for alienated activists to intercommunicate, interact and intervene together.

On the economic side, the glorified commercial benefits of the new computer revolution have largely been overplayed. In effect, the new innovations in IT have not yet brought about a recovery (as compared to previous technological revolutions in history) as many had forecast, particularly because the IT sector touches only about 12 per cent of the economy. Moreover, the new IT economy already appears to be suffering from diminishing returns since the 1990s and is regarded as helping to widen gaps in income both within and among states. In addition to the difficulties of managing macroeconomic policy, in which global sales, currency flows and exchange rates have been significantly impacted by IT technologies, the major problem is the length of the 'lag time' in which new innovations begin to directly impact the world economy on a greater scale. The longer the 'lag time' without recovery the greater the difficulty in managing macroeconomic policies, and the greater the chance for geopolitical and socio-economic conflict to erupt.

Related to this concern is the fact that increasing job insecurity makes it more difficult and risky for journalists (and academics) to 'speak truth' to those in power – and even more so during wartime. IT transformations provide governments as well as large multimedia conglomerates – which are increasingly interlinking print, online services and television together – a significant advantage in disseminating 'information' and 'analysis' though their differing media outlets. Big Brother appears to be on the rise again in that the new information technologies, fused with other innovations, not only allow for greater surveillance by corporations and individuals, but also permit far greater governmental coordination of public surveillance. Using IT, governments can now link together financial and banking information, travel documentation, video surveillance and personal profiles – with new panoptic and pan-sensual surveillance innovations on the horizon (Hawksley 2007).

While the prospects of instant communication had been hailed as a means to prevent conflict and to help negotiate an end to disputes and wars, and although the new media possesses tremendous potential in expanding advertising and markets globally and can still be used for very positive purposes, such as the publication of the world's classics in multiple languages, one of the major paradoxes is that a number of media innovations are actually helping to cause, if not perpetuate, social and political conflict in general. The danger is that despite the new IT revolution's potentially positive role in fostering peace, economic development, technological advancement, and in providing worldwide distribution of knowledge through instant communication, the greatest actual impact of IT innovations may be in further refining instruments of violence and public surveillance.

Media and the war paradox

Writing in the late 1960s, in his book *War and Peace in the Global Village*, Marshall McLuhan argued that the new media technology represents an extension of human senses, affecting the nature of our perceptions, if not our very process of conceptualization. The new, ever-globalizing, and all pervasive, media influences our personal psychology, social behaviour, attitudes and concepts – in that the 'mess/mass-age' of the 'global village' (to rephrase McLuhan's famous catchphrase, 'the medium in the message')[1] permeates our subconsciousness whether we attempt to ignore it or not (McLuhan and Fiore 1967).

In McLuhan's views, the globalizing media, rather than leading people to look to the future, can lead alienated groups and societies to look to an ostensibly more secure and glorified past (much as Al-Qaeda glorifies the Islamic Ummah prior to the collapse of the Ottoman empire). In effect, new media innovations subconsciously disturb the self-image of individuals and their societies, so much so 'that fear and anxiety ensue and a new quest for identity has to begin' (McLuhan and Fiore 1968). By increasingly exposing different societies, ethnic groups and social classes throughout the 'global village' to the ways of the materially and technologically advanced societies in particular, the media subconsciously contributes to a significant degree of psychological and social imbalance – or alienation.

The new media can thus lead alienated groups to demand the same advantages as those of the wealthier classes and societies, among other sociopolitical concerns, for example. In this sense, the ultimate subliminal message projected by globalizing media can be deeper than mere political propaganda, and can affect the core values, norms and ideologies of a given society and its culture in very different and often conflicting ways. This process can potentially shatter traditional conceptions of the self and society, and possibly create a nostalgic longing for past ways – what McLuhan called an 'orgy of rear-view mirrorism' (McLuhan and Fiore 1968: 126).

Innovations in the global media can accordingly send out both positive and negative signals depending upon one's judgement of the status quo. Media images can radiate hope for a better, more positive world through both overt and subliminal messages, but such images can more disturbingly undermine traditional values of those societies that have not been previously exposed to that media, often causing dissonance, possibly leading whole communities to engage in a fundamental re-assessment of their values, norms and beliefs. Such a forced re-assessment, coupled with efforts to safeguard that society from change, can in turn result in backlash and violence.

In terms of the causes of war, McLuhan thus argues that new media technologies endanger the identities of individuals and of whole communities and societies. As the new globalizing media, particularly given its homogenizing tendencies, can distort one's self-image and identity, there is a tendency to lash out in self-defence. On an even deeper level, McLuhan argues that all sensory change is 'levered' by new technological innovations, since 'the new technology inevitably creates new environments that act incessantly on the sensorium' (McLuhan and Fiore 1968: 136). In effect, new technologies represent 'self-amputations' that then replace former organs of perception, and permit new ways of looking at the world, and new changes in the social environment.

One can add to McLuhan's observations that the new IT revolution not only represents an appendage that extends human organs of perception through 'self-amputations', but it is also extending new prosthetic capabilities to the human body, replacing old extensions. The IT revolution not only changes the way we see the world, but also the ways that we can interact and intervene in the world. This fact makes for permanent change, and hence opens the potential for permanent dispute and conflict. New media and IT innovations have increasingly become prosthetic appendages that provide interactive and activist tools that can be manipulated or leveraged for interventions by differing actors and groups for either beneficial or nefarious purposes.

The IT revolution itself thus becomes the source (and object) of potential conflict in that it uproots traditional personal and sociopolitical identities by displaying alternative lifestyles and by spreading radical or differing ideas and images that subconsciously (or consciously through alternative information and propaganda) upset the perceived status quo. The mandate for war is then justified by the need to 'recover' the 'old image' at any cost in McLuhan's view. Or, from a differing perspective, it is also possible that individuals and groups might seek to obtain the 'image' that some other admired group is projecting, or else seek to project their own image. The latter is even more possible given the pros-thetic options available in today's technology as compared to that of McLuhan's era.

Whatever the case, the imaged symptom – at which alienated individuals and groups can lash out – is caused, in McLuhan's view, by 'something about which we know nothing. These hidden factors are the invisible environments created by technological innovation' (McLuhan and Fiore 1968: 97). In effect, the global media can disseminate messages that subliminally alter one's perceptions and interpretations of oneself, and can raise questions as to one's role and ulti-mate goal in society, and can work to change behaviour and attitudes toward one's political, social, technological and ecological environment. This can lead individuals to critically question their state and society, while states and political groups can, in reaction, seek to prevent individuals from gaining access to crit-ical information and concepts. In a word, from the perspective of state authori-ties, the prosthetic IT revolution is potentially more dangerous than media of the past in that IT can provide alienated individuals and groups with wider opportunities to communicate with like-minded individuals and to then poten-tially act in defence of strongly held values or beliefs, in pursuit of common goals. IT can also provide state leaderships with new tools to fight wars, adding a new dimension to the 'dialectics of insecurity and security' (Gardner 2007).

Truth, war and the question of media domination

What the global or 'mess/mass' media says is happening, and how that media appears to interpret sociopolitical activities, tends to become a point of a refer-ence in every day discussions and social life. Differing media may present a variety of perspectives that can be openly accepted, ignored or else criticized and rejected, if the individual has the opportunity or the willingness to listen to various viewpoints. Yet as the predominant global media has tended the reflect the values, norms and a narrow range of political ideologies that are 'acceptable' primarily to American and European societies, the 'mess/mass' media (particu-larly in its blandest forms of homogenization!) is likely to cause dissonance among those individuals and societies which do not accept or share those values or political ideologies.

In the mid-1970s and 1980s, American, British (and French) media predomi-nance (with four agencies controlling some 80 per cent of global news flow), coupled with Soviet media dominance in Soviet spheres of interest, led develop-ing states (particularly the non-aligned group) to call for a New World Informa-tion and Communication Order (NWICO). Also then at issue was the control of the radio spectrum (often for military usage) and of the control of orbiting space for satellites (which could be used for multiple use military and commercial pur-poses). The NWICO proposal represented one pretext for the US and UK to both withdraw from UNESCO – in ostensible opposition to the concern that 'third world dictators' who supported the NWICO would seek to control news dominated by US and UK multinational media conglomerates.

US and UK opposition to the NWICO occurred despite the fact that the report, *Many Voices One World* (1980) by the International Commission for the Study of Communications Problems, chaired by Sean MacBride, strongly supported a truly 'free flow' of information, but opposed an 'one way' flow. In seeking ways to enlarge both national and international influence, as well as the influence of non-governmental sources, over all information, the MacBride report strongly condemned all barriers to freedom of information and speech in accord with the Universal Declaration of Human Rights.

> In denouncing what it called 'retrogressive autocratic measures and increasing monopolistic trends,' the report strongly condemned authoritarian government efforts to block access to information and to threaten, harass, if not assassinate, journalists. But it also opposed monopolistic controls of media: When the public has only a single source of news, or where various sources have the same orientation, it is the monopolist who is in a position to decide what facts will or will not be presented, what opinions will or will not be conveyed.
>
> (MacBride 1980: 137–8)

Furthermore, the report argued that true democracy was not possible without radical reform in media:

> Without a two-way flow between participants in the process, without the existence of multiple information sources permitting wide selection, without more opportunities for each individual to reach decision based on broad awareness of divergent facts and viewpoints, without increased participation by readers, viewers and listeners in the decision-making and programming activities of the media, true democratisation will not become a reality.
>
> (MacBride 1980: 173–4)

From this perspective, *Many Voices One World* was very critical of the repression of freedom of information by totalitarian and illiberal regimes; yet it was also critical of the limitations put on information by monopolies in the advanced democracies. The report furthermore underscored the important role that journalists should play in attempting to prevent conflict and war.

In the contemporary situation, the efforts of states and private multimedia conglomerates to control the flow of information can, at least in theory, be countered by global access to the Internet. Yet critics and truth-seekers themselves need support (plus funding!) in order to survive in a situation in which powerful vested interests can still influence public opinion. This is particularly true as multimedia conglomerates are now more consciously interlinking and synchronizing press, online and TV information media. Moreover, as more and more free services available on the Internet become subscription services, a number of 'free voices' may be forced to close down if they cannot sustain their commercial viability. At the same time, however, the number of media options involving excessive doses of information, misinformation and disinformation that are available tend to create an Internet Tower of Babel in which truth tends to dissolve in virtual reality.

As technology has advanced, in order to break the monopoly over the control of information, individuals, organizations and developing countries, as well as advanced countries, have all sought to develop their own alternative news services and cultural media, as well as satellite reconnaissance capabilities, in part in response to the threat of war. The European Ariane space system was developed, at least in part, to launch European satellites as an alternative to American control over satellite imagery in the first Persian Gulf War in 1990–1. Interestingly, the first Ariane 5 space flight failed in 1996 because of a computer bug that led to a malfunction in its control software! In addition to the Europeans, China, India and Japan have all been developing significant space and satellite programmes so as to expand their national controls over information. Other countries are at various stages of their satellite and launcher programmes: Ukraine, Israel, South Korea, Brazil, Iran, Malaysia, Pakistan, Turkey and Taiwan (Casarini 2007). Japan launched its first reconnaissance satellite in 2003 after North Korea launched a ballistic missile that soared over Japanese airspace in 1998 (Embassy of Japan 2003). Both Japan and China are reaching for the moon, as is India.

Conflict and war affects major media in the developing world as well. India's Bollywood (the world's largest media industry in terms of output) reaches out to central and south Asia, as well as to the Middle East and Russia. Yet, despite high demand for Bollywood media products in Pakistan, the Pakistani government has continued to ban most Bollywood films since the 1965 Indo-Pakistani war, except for a few major classics that were permitted by Pakistani authorities to be shown in 2006 (Wilkinson 2006). Qatar's Al-Jazeera – which, in effect, has attempted to counter American control over information in the wars in Afghanistan and Iraq in particular and to counter American and European bias with regard to the Arab/Islamic worlds in general – has reached larger audiences as a state-subsidized company, broadcasting in both Arabic and English. Venezuela's Telesur and France's 24 (the latter broadcasting in French, English, Arabic and eventually Spanish) also hope to compete with CNN, CNBC and the BBC. (The BBC, however, which is sponsored by public taxation, is now suffering from a nearly four billion dollar debt crisis resulting in cost cuts and restructuring partly in response to the new demands and competition in the 'digital age' in which both media and audiences are 'transforming' (CBC News 2007).)

Historically, differing forms of media – leaflets, books, posters, newspapers, telegraph, radio, TV, film and the video cassette (shown in Mosques during the Iranian revolution as propaganda against the Shah, for example) – have always represented a psychological tool in helping to disseminate information and propaganda by states, as well as by anti-state movements. In part due to Roosevelt's fireside chats, Marshall McLuhan saw the Second World War as a radio war as much as an industrial war; film clips were also used to disseminate propaganda in the name of 'news' prior to movies shown in theatres primarily for entertainment.

Vietnam was the first TV war; as McLuhan points out, the introduction of new 'mess/mass' media technologies (TV and film) initially tended to cause havoc in undermining cultural habits and self-images in the 1960s. But even here, the US government attempted to channel public opinion in a pro-Vietnam War direction even if the media could not be totally controlled or 'regulated'. Propaganda in support of the Gulf of Tonkin resolution, for example, appeared to mimic earlier propaganda at the time of the Spanish American War in 1901 in which the 'Yellow Press' of William Randolph Hearst and Joseph Pulitzer vehemently supported the Spanish American War (a fact regretted by Pulitzer).

After the Vietnam War, the Pentagon attempted to control journalists' access to the battlefield during the US interventions in Grenada and Panama and in the first Gulf War in 1991 at least until the second Gulf War in 2003. The Pentagon acted, in part, in response to the critique of neo-conservative groups who attempted to blame the 'mess/mass' media for permitting the US to lose the Vietnam War. But the major reason that the US lost the war in Vietnam was Chinese support for the Vietnamese and the threat of Chinese intervention which limited US military actions, and kept the US from landing military forces in the north (Morgenthau 1970).

Concurrently, much as was the case for the Yellow Press before the Spanish American War, the global media of Rupert Murdoch (Fox News and the neo-conservative *Weekly Standard*, among many others), vehemently propagandized in support of US military intervention in Iraq in 2003. In 2007, the Murdoch multimedia news conglomerate then bought out the *Wall Street Journal* (whose editorial page had also vehemently supported intervention in Iraq in 2003), in order to expand Murdoch's already considerable media empire and to compete with the rival multimedia conglomerate, C-NBC. Purchasing the *Wall Street Journal* has been seen as 'the hub for the digital transformation of newspapers' that Murdoch already owns around the world and 'as an engine for a global financial information business with print, online and television components' (Siklos 2007).

While the Pentagon had hoped to keep restrictions on journalists and media in Afghanistan and Iraq, as previously pointed out, Al-Jazeera and other news services were able to enter both countries to provide alternative perspectives, often enraging the American, Afghan and Iraqi officials. (In 2004, the Iraqi government banned Al-Jazeera reporters.) In China, in April-May 1989 just prior to the Tiananmen Square repression in June 1989, it had been the portable transistor radio that provided alternative views to those of the government. Following the Tiananmen Square repression, Chinese authorities have developed the most sophisticated Internet filtering system in the world, as compared with Iran, Saudi Arabia, Vietnam and Burma, among others (Berkman Center 2002). In the Afghan and Iraq wars, it is now the Internet, the mobile cell phone and digital camera that have worked to influence public opinion as well as the more traditional news media. Mobile phones, for example, took pictures of American torture abuse at Baghdad's Abu Ghraib prison. The interactive and interventionary nature of today's media, as compared to movies, TVs, books and newspapers has consequently created an open minefield for the dissemination of competing ideologies and interpretations of information, misinformation and disinformation.

As it appears almost impossible to control IT innovations, the US and Iraqi governments have attempted to engage in a counter-propaganda offensive in an effort to outflank journalistic and academic critics; as in past conflicts there have also been attempts to question the patriotism of those who have dared to dissent. Here, only a few journalists dared to question the pretexts used by the Bush administration to engage in a so-called 'pre-emptive' (really preclusive, if not predatory) intervention in Iraq in 2003. Former CBS anchorman, Walter Cronkite, warned that cost-cutting efforts and consolidation on the part of multimedia news conglomerates not only threaten the jobs of journalists, but also put 'American democracy' and 'freedom' at risk (Associated Press 2007). The problem of telling 'truth to power' is not that of journalists alone, but that of intellectuals and academics in general, who need free access to all dimensions of information and who need to be able to interpret that information as freely as possible, but who also need job security and relative independence to testify (Morgenthau 1970). Apparently increasing trends toward non-permanent non-tenured positions in academia and job cuts in journalism, coupled with increasing restrictions by governments on obtaining access to public records, threaten the right to free speech and to freedom itself.

Subverting the global economy

Economists have split over the socioeconomic effects of the communications revolutions after the 'dot.com crash' of 2000–1 and the 9/11 attacks on the World Trade Center and Pentagon. Optimists believe the IT revolution will make profound positive changes in the world economy, as have previous innovations in history. Pessimists, however, argue that the new revolution is not as 'epoch making' as believed. By contrast with Schumpeter's theory of 'creative destruction', the new IT revolution appears more destructive than creative – at least after its initial boom in the 1990s. If anything, the most important impact of IT innovations after the declaration of the 'global war on terrorism' might well be that of enhancing military technologies and public surveillance capabilities.

Writing before the 9/11 attacks, the economist Robert J. Gordon argued that the greatest benefits of computers had already taken place in the 1990s. Unlike previous innovations, Gordon argued that the productivity gains from the new IT revolution represent a far smaller increment in the standard of living as compared with previous technological revolutions. These epoch making innovations included: the introduction of electric light, the factory efficiency achieved by the electric motor, the automobile, air travel, the chemical industry, the telephone, radio and the TV, and perhaps least appreciated, the improvements in life expectancy and health achieved by urban planning and indoor plumbing (Gordon 2000). There is consequently a major problem of diminishing returns in that the new IT economy in general, and the Internet in particular, have failed to boost multifactor productivity growth. This appears true because as much as 88 per cent of the economy lies outside of the durable manufacturing sector, which includes the manufacturing of computers and semiconductors and other goods.

Much, as has been pointed out by Janet L. Yellen, IT innovations, improved communications and new financial technologies, have facilitated a vast expansion in global trade and increase in global capital mobility. The new IT economy has generally permitted firms to become much more efficient; companies have been able to alter relationships between suppliers and customers though changing production methods, re-engineering jobs, and organizations. At the same time, however, firms have also 'vastly increased outsourcing both at home and abroad' (Yellen 2001). American firms (unlike European ones) have not been prohibited from shedding workers and thus reorganizing the work force. IT innovations have furthermore tended to raise wage inequality – not just among countries but also within them, largely by favouring skilled workers. Increased global trade, assisted in part by Internet marketing, however, has raised a significant dilemma related to trade linkages and job outsourcing that could increase spillovers across borders. This makes the GDP of differing countries much more sensitive to foreign shocks while it likewise makes national business cycles 'more synchronous' (Yellen 2001). Greater capital mobility then creates a dilemma whereby countries are forced to either let their currencies adjust freely or else to link them directly to a strong currency (the dollar or, increasingly, the euro), thereby putting to an end relative banking and financial independence. Global operations of hedge funds and venture capital funds, enhanced by IT, can furthermore exacerbate financial volatility. In the case of the US itself, this new reality can work to limit the leverage of the Federal Reserve over the US economy (Yellen 2001). Such increased trade and financial inter-vulnerability on a global scale raises the need for more concerted fiscal and monetary policy coordination – if political economic disputes and rivalry among both liberal and illiberal states are not to intensify.

Even those who are somewhat more positive about the new IT economy have argued that significant macroeconomic risks and adjustments lie ahead in the not-so-distant future. Here, the period of rapid productivity growth in the 1990s, combined with the greatest degree of structural change, can be best compared and contrasted with the roaring 1920s – followed by the catastrophic 1930s, which resulted in global war. While there is absolutely no necessity for history to repeat itself in quite the same way, 'the largest short-run impact of the 'new economy' may be that it increases the stakes at risk in macroeconomic management' (Delong and Summers 2001). On the one hand, the IT revolution exacerbates problems related to macroeconomic management; on the other hand, it is not clear how long the 'lag time' between innovation and leading growth sectors – or the gap between the time when innovations are introduced and then actually begin to impact the larger economy – will last (Delong and Summers 2001: 21; Rivlin 2001).

How long the IT 'lag time' will prove to be thus remains to be seen. A very long 'lag time' without significant economic recovery looks increasingly likely given the significant rise of world oil prices since the essentially unilateral US intervention in Iraq in 2003 and the continuing possibility of war with Iran, coupled with the failure to develop viable alternative energy sources, and energy-saving technologies, as forewarned since the 1970s. These interrelated geostrategic, political economic and technological factors themselves forewarn of major social and geopolitical conflict ahead – if more concerted geopolitical and political economic policies, in which alternative energy and IT technology could play a major role, cannot soon be adopted.

New military and surveillance technologies

From this perspective, particularly given the global crisis following the 9/11 attacks, the major factors pushing for IT innovation thus far tend to be non-productive and non-economically related – but security or military-oriented. In addition to employer concerns with office surveillance, the risks of cyber-sabotage to both the public sector and to corporations will necessitate higher security and thus investment in even more sophisticated technology (and thus more redundancy) to protect information services. Similarly, military spending in Afghanistan and Iraq should result in significant governmental purchases of the most advanced IT services. But once again, these latter innovations are largely non-productive although they might begin to 'trickle down' to the greater aggregate economy but at a much later date.

Ironically, new innovations do not tend to arise from the request of the military itself, but can still possess military applications, if oriented in that direction (DARPA 2007). Here, the 'global war on terrorism', efforts to control illegal immigration (through the introduction of biometric methods of identification), coupled efforts to sustain a high degree of military readiness against both actual and potential threats, involving increasing public surveillance, should work to sustain high US and European governmental and corporate spending on advanced information technology.

In the US case, the Defence Advanced Research Projects Agency (DARPA), for example, seeks to create a whole range of new technologies related to fighting the 'global war on terror' that might or might not possess commercial applications. DARPA had helped develop Internet technologies in the 1960s and 1970s with the ARPANet and its associated TCP/IP network protocol architecture; in the 1990s, DARPA also helped to invent satellite navigation, now used in cars, and it likewise assisted in the development of stealth systems (DARPA 2007).

In addition to seeking advances in space technology (such as nano-satellites), DARPA has envisioned: new advances in network-centric warfare; a chip-scale atomic clock designed for more accurate time in order to assure network communications; technologies to identify and defeat terrorist activities, such as the manufacture and deployment of improvised explosive devices; rapid unmanned air vehicles that can hover for long periods; supercomputers for a variety of military operations, including weather forecasting, cryptography and the design of new weapons systems; real-time high quality machine language translation of text and speech; the development of prosthetics that can be controlled and perceived by the brain; the examination of quantum phenomena in the fields of computing, cryptography and communications; plus alternative technologies and energy sources to help reduce the military's massive reliance on petroleum, among many others (DARPA 2007). (The development of alternative technologies and energy sources, among other innovations, could possess significant commercial applications.)

DARPA is additionally developing panoptic computer systems so that a facial image on a surveillance camera can be matched to a person's gait, height, weight and other elements and then be identified. In addition, new pan-sensual surveillance technologies are being developed that can detect radio signals emitted by humans, and can pick up breathing and heart rates through walls. New devices that can give indications of what people are thinking are forecast to be feasible within ten years (Hawksley 2007).

Media and asymmetrical warfare

Writing in the 1960s, Marshall McLuhan noted how the Algerian resistance was quickly able to utilize the new media technologies to channel its supporters, and combat the French enemy. Citing Frantz Fanon, McLuhan noted how the radio went from being an alien European instrument or 'enemy object' – that was regarded as undermining traditional Algerian society – to the 'primary means of resisting the increasingly overwhelming psychological and military pressures of the occupant' (McLuhan and Fiore 1968). The Algerian resistance was consequently able to use the radio in Arabic, Kabyle and French to unify the Algerian resistance.

The same paradox is true today for various anti-state partisans, such as Al-Qaeda, who have attempted to resuscitate medieval traditions of Islam (if not pre-Islam) while, at the same time, manipulating both common and advanced technologies against their enemies in radically new tactical forms. In the US, for example, there are at least 100 Internet sites used to disseminate pan-Islamist propaganda (Moss and Mekhennet 2007). Many sites use the latest up-to-date media technology and cultural forms, such as rap music, to get their 'mess/massage' across. Here, however, some propaganda may be more effective than other forms. Al-Qaeda, among other spontaneous groups of similar pan-Islamist Weltanshauung, have backed efforts to resuscitate Malcolm X's ideology. One can speculate that reviving Malcolm X, for example, could possibly appeal to some militant black Muslims in the United States much more than would the Iranian 'Review of the Holocaust: Global Vision' in December 2006 which was officially sponsored by Iranian President Ahmadinejad, and which most likely offended many black Americans (a large percentage of whom are Muslim). This is due to Hitler's absolute racism and because of the official invitation of David Duke, the Imperial Wizard of the Ku Klux Klan, to Tehran, among other holocaust sceptics. On the other hand, Iranian propaganda might better appeal to right-wing white extremists.

Concurrently, as other Internet bloggers have criticized the treatment of black Africans by Arab states, it is not absolutely clear what kind of individual will listen to which kind of extremist message. A problem to be studied is whether the excess of material on the web will lead to endless surfing, or else the opposite, complete anomie? Or does the problem of excess information on the Internet Tower of Babel lead many individuals to identify with websites that already support their own preconceived notions?

Much as McLuhan predicted with regard to a possible negative reaction to the globalizing media, Al-Qaeda is engaging in a orgy of violence, watching backwards in the rearview mirror, while still moving forward. In other words, Al-Qaeda and related ideologies see the US and European media as disseminating values of materialism, individualism and hedonism. From this standpoint, the shallow argument that pan-Islamist terrorists criticize the 'West' from a medieval perspective, but then use 'Western' technology, forget that technology is not a 'Western' but a universal asset, and in which its origins may not necessarily be derived from the 'West'. (Here, for example, gunpowder was first invented in imperial China, but was largely refined as a more effective tool of warfare by the Europeans.)

The larger issue raised here is that a number anti-state extremist organizations (and not just pan-Islamist groups) not only use high-tech communications for their propaganda purposes, but they can also do much more damage through new prosthetic IT technologies. The Internet permits anti-state partisan extremists to bypass traditional media (television, radio or print media) and engage in fundraising, propaganda and recruitment; it can display libraries of speeches, training manuals and multimedia resources (Qin 2007). Internet sites explain in Arabic, Urdu and Pashto, among other languages, how to mix ricin poison, how to make a bomb from commercially available chemicals, how to sneak through Syria into Iraq, how to shoot at American soldiers. Partisan groups can secretly communicate with email, online dead drops, satellite phones, cell phones, encryption and steganography; they can also use 'spread-spectrum' radios that randomly switch their broadcasting and receiving signals – thus camouflaging their messages. With access to satellite photos on the Internet, they can locate potential targets. In sum, partisan groups can post their plans on the web, or send information by encrypted Internet, where it will get 'lost in the billions of messages that are out there' (Coll and Glasser 2005). Mobile phones, for example, were used to detonate sophisticated bombs in Madrid in 2004.

Here, however, it should noted that Bin Laden himself uses more traditional foot couriers who can then disseminate information using high-tech techniques. This is due to the fact that Bin Laden was aware of the fact that the US National Security Agency (NSA) could eavesdrop on his conversations. It is also because of the experience of the Chechen leader Dzokhar Dudayev who was killed in the spring of 1996 after NSA spy satellites located the position of his satellite phone signal, and forwarded the coordinates to Moscow. A Russian Sukhoi Su-25 fighter jet then killed him with two laser-guided air-to-surface missiles. Ironically, Dzokhar Dudayev had spoken too long on his cell phone, lured by the prospects of peace talks with Moscow (Gaudin 2001a).

In Iraq, differing Islamist groups have been producing instructional videos and electronic newsletters on the Internet that outline techniques from encryption to booby-trapped bombs to surface-to-air missiles (Moss and Mekhennet 2007). Those cyber-manuals have largely replaced the 1967 *Anarchist Cookbook*, which appeared on the web in different variants, such as the Anarchist Cookbook Version II, III (Mieszkowski 2000). US and European law has been working to penalize those who place such information on the web. But then again, the Bush administration itself has been responsible for disseminating information related to nuclear weaponry: in the effort to prove that Saddam Hussein did possess a nuclear weapons programme, highly technical documentation taken from Iraqi archives that could help make nuclear weaponry was inadvertently placed on the US government website (Broad 2006).

One of the major concerns is that both government and private business could come under attack. Anti-state extremists and hackers can use advanced technologies to undermine networks of businesses, computer information, highways, fibre optics, railways and defence arrangements that are interconnected. The more complex and deeper these systems are interlinked (and the less protected through redundancy), the greater the potential for rupture (Gaudin 2001b). As illustrated in the first cyberwar between Russian and Estonian hackers, denial-of-service attacks (DOS), which involve saturating the victim's server with numerous external communications requests sent simultaneously through 'root-kits', 'spams' and 'storms' can be so powerful that they can destabilize a country's economy or interrupt nuclear power plant controls, stock exchanges, financial institutions and insurance companies (Ifrah 2007).

One additional problem raised here from the corporate perspective is that of the right to privacy: in order to better protect against cyber-threats, the US government hopes that corporations will share proprietary information about networks they have built or manage between the federal government and private sector and within the private sector itself (Homer-Dixon 2002). The fact that roughly 85 per cent of critical infrastructure is, however, in private hands creates a tension between government and business because of the government's proposed intrusion in private affairs (Buxbaum 2007). The issue furthermore raises questions as to the possibilities of inter-corporate cooperation because of the very nature of competitive private enterprise and the desire to keep secrets away from one's rivals.

Information systems as a tool of state warfare

Once the global media has helped to stimulate conflict (by means of political propaganda or by more subconsciously challenging social values and identities or 'images' in McLuhan's view), advanced technologies connected with that same media can become a tool in fighting that war. Historically the media has been used in disseminating information and propaganda, but in contemporary circumstances, with the revolution in information technologies, the new media technologies and computers provide instant 'real time' communications for states to fight wars.

In many ways, the IT revolution was first stimulated by the Soviet launch of the Sputnik-1 satellite in October 1957. This IT revolution has continued to influence the commercial uses of information technology as well as those of the military, particularly following the formation of the Defense Advanced Research Projects Agency (DARPA) in 1958. To be most effective, contemporary warfare needs to integrate actions in the air, land, sea and outer space with rapid information and speed of execution. Satellites, for example, are needed to conduct military reconnaissance, to pinpoint nuclear tests and to direct guided missiles and other 'smart' weaponry. The Pentagon is consequently evolving new missions related to space control (to defend US satellite constellations), not to overlook national and theatre missile defence, global psychological operations and global information operations.

In the 1991 Gulf War, only 8 per cent of all bombs were laser-guided; by the 2001–2 intervention in Afghanistan, some 60 per cent of all bombs were either laser-guided or guided by commercial Global Positioning Satellites. Moreover, during the 1991 Gulf War, the total bandwidth required for information exchange was 100 megabits per second (Mbps); the 2001–2 war in Afghanistan required more than double that amount, or 250 Mbps. Ironically, it was primarily commercial geosynchronous satellites orbiting 23,000 miles above the earth that provided the Pentagon with nearly all of this bandwidth. The military's need for satellite communication systems can be seen in the following example: just one Global Hawk Unmanned Aerial Vehicle (which provides the Air Force and joint battlefield commanders with near-real-time, high-resolution, intelligence, surveillance and reconnaissance imagery) utilizes 50 Mbps (Hastings 2003).

Yet the American dependency upon satellites is not limited to guiding missiles. The American military is highly dependent upon satellites for all of its major war operations – from the foxhole to the Pentagon – by virtue of its reliance on computers and information. In effect, satellites represent 'flying computers' in the words of Dr Daniel Hastings and thus represent the ultimate in advanced multiple-use IT systems that can engage in commercial transactions of various forms as well as military actions (Hastings 2003). The fact that space assets can also be information assets – as they gather, process and pass on information – makes space warfare and information warfare interconnected.

Here, for example, GPS (Global Positioning Satellites) are positioned in outer space for multiple-use commercial and military purposes, while GMTI (Ground Moving Target Indication) can be used for traffic monitoring and control in cities and for military purposes. Less detectable, and more sophisticated, nano-satellites (miniature satellites) are beginning to replace the functions of larger satellites. The fact that launching costs are getting lower and that satellites are getting smaller means that both commercial firms and less wealthy states can send up satellite systems. (This was not the case when the UNESCO report, *Many Voices One World*, was published in 1980 as previously discussed). Concurrently, commercial satellite imagery is catching up with the resolution of secret reconnaissance satellites of the US and former Soviet Union during the Cold War, making it possible for any kind of state or extremist group to access visual information. Satellite maps available on Google.com have already been raising security concerns.

The security issue arises in that commercial systems are less expensive but they also mean that the Pentagon loses control over them. Concurrently, private owners expect military protection. This generates a continuing tension between military security and private interests that have, in turn, begun to generate demands to expand military capabilities into outer space in part for protection of private satellites. Dr Daniel Hastings described the military situation in outer space in the following terms due to the mix of defence and commercial satellites: 'Space warfare will be surrounded by non-combatants: Like fighting guerrillas in an urban setting' (Hastings 2003).

These facts make the US military highly dependent upon space-based assets; but the fact that satellites represent 'flying computers' makes them potentially vulnerable, as they can be struck by cyber-attack. The development of nano-satellites that can attach themselves like parasites to larger satellites raises new security concerns, in that they could later explode or disrupt communications. Other threats include the possibility of a high altitude nuclear burst; this threat would require multiple redundant satellites so as to safeguard communications. Military users themselves will thus need to protect their own information by means of 'massive diversity' or else attempt to 'harden' communications and satellite systems (DARPA 2007). While American military officials have proposed an Unconventional Warfare Command to fight against cyber-sabotage and other extremist activities, the US Senate has considered new legislation (such as the Critical Infrastructure Information Security Act) to address the protection of both government and private computer and information systems (Boot 2006).

In addition to the importance of satellite communications for multiple-use military and commercial purposes, the global sales produced, at least in part, by Internet marketing have begun to rationalize an expanded role for the US Navy. Here the argument that 'terrorist' groups, pirates or states might seek to disrupt global trade and attack undersea fibre optic cables, for example, has become a major issue in the need to secure the globalizing economy. It is thus argued that products sold over the Internet generally travel by sea and consequently need naval protection:

> Ultimately, the open ocean is still the prime medium and symbol of globalisation – for the thoughts transmitted along the Internet must be translated into products, which must in turn be transported to far markets. Even the financial flows that might travel along the wires and fibre-optic cables of today's information network have the eventual purpose of producing goods

that are sold and consumed. If these goods are to be sold and consumed in somewhere other than a localized, domestic market, they are likely to be transported by sea.

(Bowdish 2002)

The concern raised here, however, is that US plans to forward deploy naval capacities to protect burgeoning global IT-inspired trade from terrorism and piracy and to prevent weapons proliferation, drug trafficking, and other illicit activities (Cooperative Strategy 2007), could come into conflict with expanding navies of Russia, India and China – if Washington cannot establish more concerted relations with these states.

The first Internet 'war' has already taken place in April 2007 between Russian and Estonian hackers; the initiation of the conflict was blamed on the Russian government, but it is not absolutely clear who was actually behind it (Ifrah 2007). In 2005, there were about 1,300 successful intrusions into Pentagon computers out of more than 79,000 attempts; in September 2007, China's People's Liberation Army (PLA) was accused of hacking into Pentagon, UK and German computers (charges denied by Beijing). China's military goals purportedly seek to achieve 'electronic dominance' over the US, Britain, Russia and South Korea by 2050 (Reid 2007). In January 2007, Beijing tested a missile capable of destroying satellites in orbit. Assuming a treaty effectively banning further tests or use of anti-satellite weapons (ASAT) cannot be implemented soon, China's anti-satellite test could spark a renewed weapons build-up in both outer space and on the ground, coupled with new forms of IT rivalry (Kahn 2006).

The high dependence of the Pentagon on communication links and information operations make these areas 'Achilles heels' for potential jamming, disruption or attack. In addition to the real threat of cyber-sabotage against key communications systems, satellites, as 'flying computers', would represent one of the first targets in a major power war, as both China and Russia have begun to threaten – in part to counter the deployment of US ballistic missile defences which depend upon satellite communications (Gardner 2007).

Conclusions

As a 'multiple use' technology, the IT revolution has possessed global military-technological, political-economic, as well as sociocultural ramifications. While heralded as a means to resolve conflict through 'instant communications', the new media may not or may not help resolve disputes or conflict. On the contrary, the new media and IT revolution itself can represent a potential cause of conflict through the dissemination of propaganda. But even if the new media itself is not the actual cause of disputes, then it can perpetuate conflict in the sense that it tends to uproot traditional socio-political-personal identities, causing backlash.

At the same time, however, the new media does not necessarily offer a substitute for those lost or altered identities. Marshall McLuhan's famous statement that the 'medium is the "mess/mass-age"' (as re-phrased) is misleading. This is true in the sense that the media is not a religion or ideology in itself and can only transmit 'images' and 'messages' related to those religions or ideologies; but in transmitting various ideologies it also alters those 'images' and 'messages'. Not only that, media is no longer merely a means to disseminate propaganda (as a brain-washing 'massage'), but can become an active agent used in warfare by both states and anti-state partisan groups in that it has become a prosthetic appendage for active intervention in the 'mess'- of the 'mass-age' created by the globalizing media that has, in part, been fostered by with the assistance of 'flying computers' and by the Internet Tower of Babel. Sources of communication thus become potential objects for attack.

The need for satellite communications has helped to expand military technological and geo-economic rivalries into outer space while underwater fibre optic cables and globally expanding trade assisted by Internet marketing have helped to expand such rivalries both under and over the sea. Moreover, rather than working to foster economic growth, the new computer and communications innovations have actually helped to cause socioeconomic insecurities, largely through exacerbating gaps in income among skilled and non-skilled workers, and by raising profound questions for the stability of the international political economy in terms of a very long 'lag time' – in which it is not certain when the new IT innovations will begin to directly impact the world economy on a greater scale.

In addition to the rise of authoritarian and illiberal states determined to 'filter' Internet access, increasing international political economic instability, coupled with the rise of multimedia conglomerates determined to fuse and synchronize 'information' for profit in print, on TV and on the Internet, not to overlook American and European state efforts to enhance public surveillance in the 'global war on terrorism', all raise profound questions for the ability of critical individuals, academics and journalists to tell 'truth to power'. And finally, the new media and IT revolution presents an existential paradox in that it offers tremendous opportunities of instant communication and infinitely expands capabilities for knowledge and activity, but provides no certainty as to the prospects for successful negotiations to put an end to conflicts or to the actual impact that these significant technical advances will ultimately possess on humanity as a whole.

Note

1 Marshall McLuhan's famous slogan, 'the medium is the message', was accidentally transformed by a printer's typo in his book's title, to *The Medium is the Massage*. McLuhan left the altered title, so that the medium could imply four signifiers: as a form of message, as a form of brain-washing 'massage' or else as the 'Mess-Age', or 'Mass-Age'. The mistake also illustrated the role of accident in the process of creation. The idea of a 'mess/mass-age' almost worked, but it was not quite poetry!

3   The Internet as a weapon of war?

Radicalisation, publics and legitimacy

Andrew Hoskins and Ben O'Loughlin

Introduction[1]

This chapter sets out the theoretical and methodological underpinnings of a new investigation entitled *Legitimising the Discourses of Radicalisation: Political Violence in the New Media Ecology*.[2] From late 2007, researchers at universities in the UK and elsewhere will identify and analyse the circulation of Jihadist discourses through Web 2.0 and mainstream media, and the role of these discourses in legitimating Jihadist actors, acts and ideologies. The context for this research is a new 'media ecology' (Cottle 2006) in which the availability and interactivity of a range of news sources contributes to a proliferation of (online) public–private spheres or 'sphericules' (Gitlin 1989) with loose and problematic engagements with mainstream public institutions and debates. The emergent and amorphous character of these communication networks demands innovative, dynamic research methods and conceptual frameworks, particularly in an investigation of their shaping of a new language of radicalisation. This includes the mediated contestation of the divergent meanings of this term and thus divergent responses to the nature of the 'threat' it describes. Through a 'nexus analysis' of radicalising discourses and language and a dynamic iteration of Web 2.0 spaces, mainstream media and news audiences, the project will generate a model of 'cascading network activation' to map and explain the relationship between critical security events, radicalising discourses and the legitimation of political violence. This chapter sets out the conceptual and methodological underpinnings of the project.

'Radicalisation' is a highly contested and salient concept in public debate. The term occurs regularly in news and political discourse, often with a lack of explanation or context. In the UK, some commentators presume that when young Muslims become involved in certain groups, they board a 'conveyor belt' to radicalisation, yet these processes are complex and may be marked by deradicalisation and eventual disillusionment (Birt 2007). To take another simplification in public debate, just as violent films and computer games have been connected to teenage violence, and junk food commercials connected to childhood obesity, so Jihadist media have been implicated in radicalisation processes. Yet such claims appear to assume a 'hypodermic' model of the media, as a syringe injecting messages into gullible young Muslims. There is confusion about how and whether radicalisation occurs online or in tangible locations such as prisons, hospitals and religious schools. Nor is there a necessary link between radicalisation and Islam; radicalised individuals and groups are a recurrent feature of all political movements. Additionally, radicalisation does not necessarily lead to violence. Explanations of radicalisation identify psychological and sociological influences, often focusing upon socioeconomic circumstances, demographic shifts, and religious and ethnic identity politics as determinants of radicalisation and potentially violence. In a UK context, between 2004–7 an earlier project[3] identified a growing 'securitisation of everyday life' in Britain whereby the ritualised interactions of policymakers, journalists and citizen audiences constitute the 'media-security nexus' as a 'battlespace' of mutual disrespect and suspicion. This contributes to the marginalisation of British Muslims and is one of the many antecedents to potential radicalisation (Awan 2007a). These developments suggest that policymakers face a range of new and difficult challenges, at the heart of which is the legitimation of security policy to hostile and sceptical national and diasporic media, many of whom question key policy assumptions. An analysis of radicalisation must address this intersection of media, security and identity.

Following Awan (2007b), we propose Web 2.0 to be the emergent forum of choice for terrorists and for those intent on radicalising and recruiting individuals, groups and organisations to their cause, precisely because it does not fit into conventional models of media *and* warfare. Web 2.0 is an overarching term used to describe a wide range of second generation services available on the web to which users can contribute as easily as they can consume (O'Reilly 2005). It is the collaborative and participatory potential of these web tools and environments that make them rich attractors of support, combined with their ease of creation, access and mobility (to other web spaces and at other times). Thus, Web 2.0 facilitates asymmetrical warfare, particularly with regard to a 'war of ideas', by allowing relatively insignificant non-state actors to compete with (and often supersede) state entities, whilst cloaking the personal or organisational security of those non-state voices.

The *Legitimising the Discourses of Radicalisation* project is timely, given that the traditional concepts (and their related theories and methodological approaches) of mass media form, content and influence have imploded. Indeed, the diffused prolificacy of the Internet appears in a perpetually '*pre*paradigmatic' state insofar as there is no stable object around which a research paradigm could cohere (Hine 2005: 240, emphasis added). Although we have moved beyond the stage of the treatment of the mass media as separate and separable from the 'negatively globalized' (Bauman 2006) setting in which contemporary terrorism operates, government and academia appear to be increasingly ill-equipped to address the pace and the seeming perpetuity of the technological transformations that have ensured the 'weaponization' of media (Hoskins and O'Loughlin 2007: 16–21). The project introduced here seeks to contribute to an understanding of the connectivities and relationships that make up the new media ecology, especially those that appear to transcend the local and the global, accelerate the dissemination of radicalising discourses, and amplify media/public fears of political violence.

Our starting point is the theorisation of legitimacy undertaken through the *Shifting Securities* project (Hoskins and O'Loughlin 2007, 2008; Awan 2007a; also Gillespie 2006b; Gow 2007). Legitimacy matters because it helps explain the behaviour of agents in power relationships in particular societies: who will obey whom, what does obedience entail, and how is this obligation generated, disputed and altered? Following Beetham (1991) we approach legitimacy as afforded through: a power-holder's acquisition and exercising of power through rules, their supply of consent, and their meeting of the normative expectations of publics. Hence legitimacy is not possessed or not, but a matter of the extent to which these processes are fulfilled (Beetham 1991). It is intimately bound to the concepts 'authority' and 'credibility'. While analyses of legitimacy usually focus on nation-states, other actors and institutions such as clerics, scholars or news sources who may not be seeking to rule can possess credibility to certain publics in making political and/or religious claims, and consequently contest processes of legitimacy. Our *Shifting Securities* project data indicated the plurality of such credible sources; that their authority cut across territorial boundaries; hence processes of legitimacy and acts of consent entail complex, near-instant feedback loops between national, translocal/diasporic and global public opinion. Moreover, both the salience and the epistemological or evidentiary base for these claims and their evaluation by publics was plural and contested, making it apparently impossible to convince all possible publics of the 'rightfulness' of certain problem-definitions and courses of action. Individuals' media consumption and discussions around media, with friends, family and colleagues, are critical to processes of legitimation. Hence, legitimation is further complicated by the ongoing fragmentation of media audiences and individuals' supply and usage of a greater range of news sources. If 'public' refers to shared matters of concern as well as a shared space (Couldry *et al.*, 2007: 7–10), then it must be more accurate to speak of overlapping publics. Overall, this pluralisation of possible constituencies, sources of claims, and evidentiary basis of claims, has led to a more complex and volatile environment. If processes of legitimation are to hold, more consideration is required for the mode, content and basis of political claims, and more investigation into what makes counter-claims credible. The latter is our focus.

The context for this study, then, is a new media ecology in which people, events and news media have become increasingly connected and interpenetrated through the technological compression of time–space. This media ecology must be situated within a larger 'information ecology' (Thrift 2004) in which computing becomes increasingly embedded in spaces, surfaces, objects and indeed people, through the ubiquity of wireless, bluetooth, smart tags and so forth. The consequence is a new set of backgrounds for social life, rendering life more calculable and mapped in some respects (Thrift 2007), but more chaotic in others (McNair 2006). Saturation, connectivity and immediacy characterise many aspects of everyday life, enabling new forms of interaction, collaboration and enactment, notably through Web 2.0 spaces. Social dynamics become both more controlled and more open-ended or emergent; for instance, in place of Giddens' reflexive individual we move towards an everyday subjectivity based on 'roving empiricism' (Thrift 2004: 223) characterised by a tolerance of not being fully in control or being presented with clear goals. The Web 2.0 'user' does not just rove, as would a flaneur wandering through 1930s Parisian arcades (Beer and Burrows 2007); or merely become lost (in indifference) in the *Soft City* of Raban's early 1970s streets of London (Raban 1974). Rather, they can create and contribute to the 'inhabitable map' they occupy (Thrift 2007: 23). This forms the context in which news consumers, policymakers, and indeed researchers find themselves in today.

This context transforms the opportunities and problems not just for Western policymakers, but also for Jihadist leaders. To the extent that contemporary Jihadist ideologies offer continuity to pre-Internet radical strands of Islam, it would appear that Jihadist leaders have lost their monopoly over the ideas reaching constituencies in different parts of the world too. An individual in the Middle East with access to Jihadist media also has access to alternative Islamic media, to Western media, and so on. Consequently, Jihadist media must work harder for credibility and legitimacy too. This may help explain the complex combinations of styles in Jihadist media content, blending derivations of Western professional media templates with their own particular discursive and iconographic styles.

There are three strands to the radicalisation project. The first identifies, maps and evaluates the discursive legitimation of the culture and ideology of Jihadism in Web 2.0 and related emergent Internet spaces, and which is our focus here. The second strand investigates how these Jihadist discourses are represented in mainstream media by identifying, mapping and evaluating mainstream media representations of political violence and the uses of the term 'radicalisation' and its associated terms, contexts and discourses. The third strand addresses public perceptions of these discourses of radicalisation. Through audience ethnography we are identifying, mapping and evaluating mainstream news public understandings and interpretations of political violence and the term 'radicalisation' and its associated terms, contexts and discourses. These three strands work iteratively, with ongoing findings in each strand contributing to the foci of others. For instance, if a documentary or drama on mainstream television addresses issues of radicalisation, we will examine responses in Jihadist forums and through audience research. Consequently, researchers will operate in a dynamic, responsive mode as events salient to radicalisation, Jihadist discourses and legitimation proceed in the coming years. This integrated research develops and extends the methodology of collaborative ethnography integrated with media text analysis and processes of legitimation pioneered by Gillespie (2006a, 2007).

This chapter presents a series of considerations about how we can research and understand these processes, and focuses in particular on the key concepts 'public', 'counterpublic' and 'legitimacy'. We bring together literatures from political theory and media and communication studies to derive a set of propositions about what publics and counterpublics are, and how legitimacy operates, which can then be deployed and tested through empirical research. At a time of great attention and no little sensationalism around the area of 'cyberterrorism' and 'cyberconflict', we suggest that the urgency for research in this field must not necessitate the abandoning of conceptual and methodological clarity. This chapter is written with this aim in mind.

Conceptualising publics and counterpublics

Before introducing the framework for our analysis of Jihadist discourses and what it means for those discourses to be legitimated, we must lay out the conceptual and empirical difficulties surrounding the category 'public' and relations between publics and counterpublics.

In the *Shifting Securities* project, we found that in the period following the 2003 Iraq war and particularly after the 7/7 London bombings, certain groups and individuals felt excluded from the UK national public sphere. Some Muslims felt that it would be dangerous to express their political views in public spaces – at work, on the street, in cafes – even if these views, such as opposition to the 2003 Iraq War, were presumed to be held by a large section of the British population as a whole. They self-censored to a remarkable extent, yet within private spaces with friends or family, political discussion was lively and often diverse. The distance between these public 'sphericules' (Gitlin 1989) and mainstream public life was reinforced by the availability and use of alternative media. For instance, Arabic and Muslim audiences felt the presence of Al-Jazeera and other Arabic news channels problematised the credibility of mainstream news (e.g. BBC News), even if they did not actually watch Al-Jazeera themselves. The project identified complex dynamics that seemed to indicate the presence of publics and counterpublics' uneasy sharing of geographical spaces (on unease and discomfort, see also Noble 2005). For instance, in one city, white working-class Christian and secular women and working-class Muslim women shared the same streets, buses and schools, and expressed a mixture of curiosity and suspicion about the other's dress, habits and views. Some white Christian/secular women joked about Muslim women's dress concealing bombs, while some Muslim women appeared to be second-guessing how they were perceived, and modifying their behaviour to avoid contact and potential conflict. The resources each drew upon to imagine the other's motives were often media stories rather than first-hand experience of the other. How the dominant public (including media) represent a counterpublic *and its relation to* that counterpublic was an implicit focus of much deliberation. The fault lines of publics and counterpublics can generate tensions that may lead to radicalisation and even to violence.

What can 'public' mean? What is the relation between the noun *the* or *a* public, the verb *make* public, and the adjective denoting public-*ness*, e.g. public scandal, public outrage? To answer these questions we draw upon theorists such as Michael Warner (2002) and Clive Barnett (2003) who conceive publics as transnational, loose and fluid – so, theorists that emphasise communication and circulation in their constitution. Warner identifies seven features of a 'public'. *First*, the existence of a public depends on a chicken-and-egg moment: a public exists 'by virtue of being addressed' and yet it cannot be addressed unless it exists to be addressed (Warner 2002: 50). It is elusive insofar as the address that conjures the public must presume the public it is addressing and conjuring. This is a performative process, if we accept Barnett's definition that: 'A performative is an act that produces the identity or state of affairs it appears merely to represent' (2003: 21). Democratic representation seems performative because it *enacts* a public which it purports only to represent. It is only through opinion polling and elections that we can speak of 'public opinion' and the 'public's decision'. By representing a public, opinion polls and electoral counts bring that public into existence, even while suggesting that such a public pre-existed these acts of representation. This is not to say a public does not exist, only that it cannot exist 'without a certain medium' (Derrida 1992, in Barnett 2003: 24).

Whether it is the Queen's Christmas speech in the UK, the State of the Union address in the US, or a call to prayer at a major metropolitan mosque, the addressor can never be sure exactly who is listening, or when they are listening (they might record the speech and watch the next day), and there may be a spectrum of counterpublics within those receiving the address. Modern publics cannot be created by a state or other authority; to an irreducible extent, publics are self-organising and sovereign. This can make it hard for some to have confidence in a public. If you are a political leader or policymaker, or in a minority position in a society, it can be disconcerting to confront the existence of a public that is once real yet elusive, felt yet ultimately unidentifiable. The best solutions to date, such as opinion polls, cannot resolve this circularity or specify a public with any exactness. A little misrecognition is inescapable, but even a little misrepresentation can appear antagonistic to those feeling powerless or victimised.

It follows, *second*, that a public is composed of strangers. Due to the circularity identified above, a public is necessarily made up of people who do not know each other and probably will never come to know each other. The members of a group, nation, a club or other collective may be identified by particular independent criteria, but not for a public. Stranger-hood is not a barrier to united action, but the very condition. Why? Partly because, *third*, a public address is addressed not to an ideal citizen but both to an undefined mass of strangers and to us, personally. In this way, public addresses connect us as individuals to public life and society, since we recognise that a speech addressed to everyone is also relevant to us. It would make sense, by these propositions, to say that Al-Qaeda is a public: its constituent members are indefinite in number and location, they are often strangers to each other, but they feel part of a larger grouping because addresses from Osama bin Laden or Aymen Al-Zahawiri seem both personal to them and impersonal insofar as the messages are to those other followers or cells presumed to be out there.

Fourth, it matters less how much attention individuals give to a public address, merely that they do give some attention. Attention is the criterion of membership of a public. If nobody is paying attention to an address, it lacks a public. But *fifth*, this attention must be sustained. There can be no public of a single address or text; a public is generated through a chain of texts, such as newspapers, television news broadcasts, or regular addresses by leaders. Publics assume there are texts that preceded and that will follow. What links this past, present and future is interaction: public speech addresses not just specific listeners, as per a dialogical model of a public sphere, but an indefinite audience, and one cannot know in advance who will listen and respond. Warner writes of a public address, 'the principal act is that of projecting the field of argument itself' (2002: 63). It imagines and projects the field of communication:

> The interactive relation postulated in public discourse … goes far beyond the scale of conversation or discussion, to encompass a multigeneric life-world organized not just be a relational axis of utterance and response, but by potentially infinite axes of citation and characterization.
>
> (Warner 2002: 63)

This can be clarified by a case of what is *not* public. Nina Eliasoph's (1998) study of the political talk of country-and-western club goers and volunteer and activist groups in a US community is postulated by the author as a study of the US public sphere. But Eliasoph's analysis is principally focused on face-to-face interactions in halls, clubs and homes, with identifiable addressors and addressees. The *public* quality of these interactions is questionable, for there is an absence of risk, of projecting an address into an unknowable field of potential listeners and readers. We will present some examples of this public circulation below when we examine communications triggered by the Daniel Pearl execution video of 2002 and by the open letter sent by President Ahmedinejad to President Bush in 2006.

Box 1 Warner's seven features of a public

1   A public is self-organising, through a chicken-and-egg process.
2   A public is a relation between strangers.
3   The address of public speech is both personal and impersonal.
4   A public is constituted through mere attention.
5   A public is the social space created by the reflexive circulation of discourse.
6   Publics act historically according to the temporality of their circulation.
7   A public is poesis world-making: it has particular styles, genres, idioms and so forth.

Sixth, a public 'can only act within the temporality of the circulation that gives it existence' (Warner 2002: 68). When the circulation is predictable and on punctuated cycles, it would seem publics are more able to act in politics. The punctuation allows decisions to crystallise, as with elections. The agency of publics is tied to their awareness of these cycles and possibilities. It allows members to understand themselves as belonging to a historically situated sociopolitical entity; to be comfortable with, and oriented to, a common-sensical temporality of decision, evaluation and reconsideration.

Radicalised publics and terrorists may operate according to particular temporalities. In Palestinian Hamas communities, for instance, 'living martyrs' dress in white robes and attend funerals as they wait to be called to action (Arena and Arrigo 2006: 149). The individual's role affirms broader social meanings and expectations, as this notion of 'waiting' constructs a link between past, present and presumed future. But radicalised and violent groups also form relations to the temporalities of democratic societies. Famously, Al-Qaeda have fitted their messages to align with, and intervene in, election cycles in the US, UK and other Western polities. Hence the communicative webs between Western and Al-Qaeda leaders must be mapped on both temporal and spatial axes.

Finally, *seventh*, an address does not simply try to define a public by specifying the field of communication, of expected listeners, but also by specifying an expected *style* of communication for that public. Warner posits an 'ideology of language': public discourse is characterised by assumptions that certain types of utterance will have sense for audiences, that audiences will form opinions by interpreting utterances in predictable ways. 'Strangers are less strange if you can trust them to read as you read, or if the sense of what they say can be fully abstracted from the way they say it' (Warner 2002: 83). If only confusion about the sense of utterances could be dissolved, and the essential contestability of political concepts rendered transparent, so conflict and political disagreement might evaporate! Or at least, all micro- or counter-publics could participate in a valid and intelligible manner within a general public sphere if they held to the prevailing modes of communication and sense-making.

However, the consistently marginalised and structurally disadvantaged – Nancy Fraser's 'subaltern counterpublics' (1992: 123) – may find more strategic advantage in forming a conflictual relation to any general public sphere that produces their sustained disadvantage. But as Warner points out, a subaltern group's *counter*public-ness would rest not in finding a separate space within which they can formulate their needs, interests and opportunities, for that could simply replicate the rational, Habermasian mode of politics, only in a separate space. Once such a group would attempt to influence the mainstream public sphere, their terms may get appropriated and their strategies co-opted, as has happened in cases to feminist and environmental movements.

We might ask, then, what makes a counterpublic a public that is counter to another public? Warner writes:

Dominant publics are by definition those that can take their discourse prag-matics and their lifeworlds for granted, misrecognizing the indefinite scope of their expansive address as universality or normalcy. Counterpublics are spaces of circulation in which it is hoped that the poesis of scene making will be transformative, not replicative merely.

(Warner 2002: 88)

By increasing the circulation of particular idioms, genres and other modes of com-munication, a counterpublic advances a different 'language ideology', the reading model described above in which all members of a public assume a mode of reading and sense-making that rest not just on a sovereign reader, who can read, interpret, then speak; but also on a transposition of the sovereign reader to sover-eign public, for do we not speak of a public that will listen/read/watch, deliberate, and speak 'public opinion'? By advancing different poesis, a counterpublic seeks to reconstitute the public sphere, and in that way agency is attributed to counter-publics. They act in the public realm, but more importantly they act on it:

Counterpublics are 'counter' to the extent that they try to supply different ways of imagining stranger-sociability and its reflexivity; as publics, they remain oriented to stranger-circulation in a way that is not just strategic, but also constitutive of membership and its effects.

(Warner 2002: 87–8)

In our *Legitimising the Discourses of Radicalisation* project we consider the extent to which Jihadist discourses advance a different poesis, a different stranger-sociability and different forms of reflexivity to that of the mainstream Western/liberal public. Thus, an important task is to identify different forms of knowing, speaking and sensing that contribute to, and constitute, Jihadist net-works as counterpublics.

However, relations between publics and counterpublics are not necessarily antagonistic. Iris Marian Young (2002) suggests we should value plural speaking styles (dramatic or playful, speech or gesture) as well as plural perspectives because such different styles are a resource, not an obstacle to a general will. Pro-vided groups express their interests as claims for justice, and others can recognise the claims and feel able to respond, then there is universality: a recognition and willingness to talk. This could allow change within a public sphere or a gradual, agonistic transformation of a public sphere (see also Butsch 2007: 1–14). Yet in the 'war on terror', and for the politics of terrorism historically, there have been claims for justice deemed unfit for recognition or response by mainstream publics. In Britain, for instance, Mohammed Siddique Khan's video testimony explaining his motives to explode himself in London on 7 July 2005 contained claims for justice, the various forms of speech and gesture, but this was deemed unacceptable by some, for instance Prime Minister Tony Blair (Blair, 7 July 2005).

In studying radicalisation and violence, we are analysing politics at and beyond the limits of agonism (Mouffe 2005), unlike much research of the

Internet and political communications (e.g. debates on whether the Internet brings pluralistic deliberation or fragmented, self-reinforcing 'communities of interest'. For an overview see Dahlberg 2007). Groups and individuals position themselves, and are positioned, in antagonistic relations, often at war. Our conception of publics and counterpublics must account for this. Next in this chapter we will describe how publics and counterpublics, as the circulation of their communications, can be mapped and analysed.

Theorising political communication: cascading network activation

So far, the critical measure of publics and publicity is attention to circulating communications. But even since the publication of Warner and Barnett's conceptualisations of mediated publics and counterpublics, information and communications technologies (ICTs) have developed rapidly. In the context of expanding access to ICTs and more interactive modes of engagement facilitated by Web 2.0, the circulations Warner identifies can be characterised as 'vectors' (Wark 1994) generated on spatio-temporal coordinates that are quicker, wider, and interacting in ways harder to predict. As a result, our analytical framework

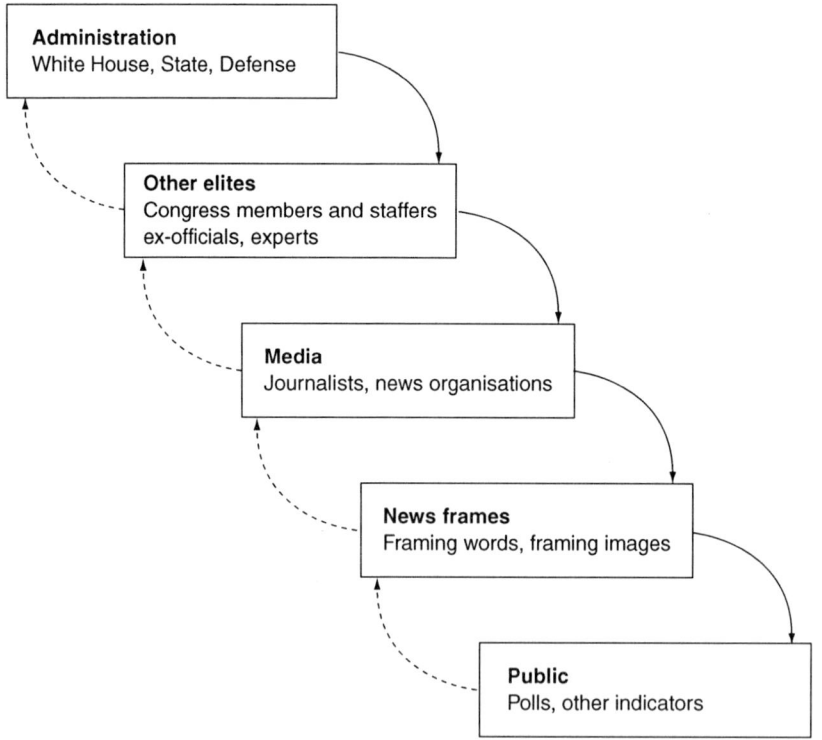

Figure 1 Cascading network activation.

for mapping Jihadist discourses is more complex than traditional models of political communication. How can we move, as McNair proposes (2006), from a *control* to a *chaos* paradigm? As a *control* approach, Robert Entman's (2003, 2004) Cascading Network Activation model has been highly influential in recent political communication research (Cherribi 2006). The model identifies overlapping stages of information dissemination and response:

However, as Justus and Hess (2006) note, a single message will now be received by multiple national and cultural audiences, and leaders cannot control these multiple interpretations. Here they represent *three* sets of media, frames and publics, which responded to the release of photos by US military press officers depicting the dead Abu Musab al-Zarqawi in June 2006:

Representing global public response as just three significant sets of media, frames and publics is an oversimplification, as audience studies show individuals may shift between perspectives and positions (Aksoy 2006; Hoskins and O'Loughlin 2007) and that audiences of Jihadist media may converge with audiences of other non-mainstream media (Awan 2007b). Nevertheless this stylised analysis offers a starting point for a more nuanced, temporal mapping and analysis of the competing claims, frames and perspectives of Web 2.0 users.

Our work synthesises a new model of cascading network activation for the communications surrounding critical security events in Web 2.0 spaces. Next we give two brief examples that suggest the global networks 'activated' by momentous communications, one a video, another a letter. Following these examples, we set out what legitimacy is and how it might be analysed.

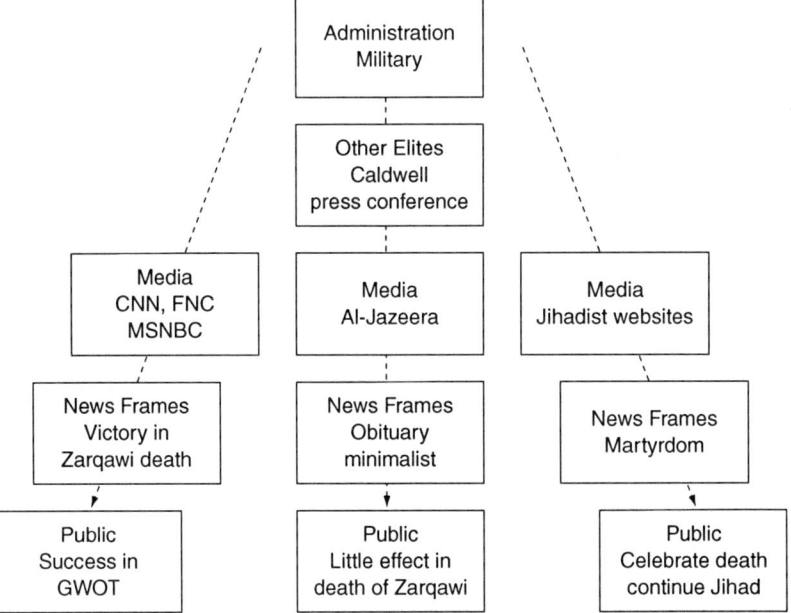

Figure 2 Global cascading activation networks model (based on Justus and Hess 2006: 8).

Cascading network activation: example 1: Daniel Pearl's body

On 23 January 2002 the *Wall Street Journal* reporter Daniel Pearl was kidnapped in Karachi, Pakistan, by the National Movement for the Restoration of Pakistani Sovereignty (NMRPS). Pearl had been investigating the connection between Richard Reid, the 'shoe bomber', and Islamic organisations. A month later the US consulate in Karachi received a videotape of Pearl making a confession and then being executed. The video became the focus of political and media statements around the world, and it soon appeared on the Internet for mass consumption (Weimann 2004), despite FBI requests for the images not to be posted (McCullagh, 28 May 2002; Talbot 2005; *USA Today*, 28 May 2002). In particular, Pearl's body itself became the object around which different actors made claims and counter-claims (Grindstaff and DeLuca 2004; see also Scarry 1985). Beginning with Pearl's 'confession', through torture the kidnappers were able to make Pearl say what they wanted. The confession itself signifies the power of the torturer, who is able to appropriate Pearl's voice through harm to his body. Pearl's voice is used to speak words that would validate the kidnappers' ideology. For instance, he speaks of being a Jewish American, whose great-grandfather was a founder of the Israeli state. His voice has an American-English accent. The video switches between shots of Pearl, and shots of Muslim, Arab and/or Palestinian bodies, in particular of children's bodies, thereby connecting Pearl to policies of the US and Israel that have apparently caused this suffering. Pearl's body is used both to stand for the US and Israel, and validate the kidnappers' ideology.

The video became a matter of public debate in Pakistan and the US. As Grindstaff and DeLuca (2004) document, the Pakistani press was divided between those that condemned the killing but remained opposed to US policy, and those who simply used the event as the platform to express grievances against the US. Pearl's body was also the focal point of Pakistani politics. The President, General Musharraf, supported the prosecution of the executors so as to signal to domestic and international audiences his government's opposition to Islamic extremists. Meanwhile in the US, political debate centred upon the role of Pearl as a heroic agent in the 'war on terror', as a servant of the American nation, but also Pearl's body became used as a justification for retaliation against not only the group responsible but against 'terrorists' generally. The media response was mixed. As mentioned, only a few websites published footage of the video, as well as CBS News and the *Boston Phoenix*. Dan Rather of CBS News argued in the broadcast, on 14 May 2002, that it was the responsibility of media to show such footage so audiences could be aware of the kind of propaganda terrorists were producing.[4] Others, including Pearl's family, asserted the need for a blanket ban on the video, on the grounds that seeing it did not make audiences any more aware of the issue, and because making the contents of the video public was what the video's producers would want – CBS News was providing the 'oxygen of publicity'.[5]

What received less publicity were some events triggered by the video of Pearl's execution. Grindstaff and DeLuca note,

In the same week as Pearl's murder, a 10-year old Pakistani named Abdullah was shot and killed by an 11-year-old American boy because Abdullah was Pakistani. Instead of an international outcry, there was deafening silence across the globe.

(2004: 316)

There was an outcry in Pakistani media about the lack of outcry elsewhere compared to the attention devoted by politicians and journalists to the death of Daniel Pearl. The very invisibility of the story elsewhere could only have added to anti-US sentiment in Pakistan and the success of Islamist, anti-Musharraf political parties. Hence, through an exchange of dead bodies, one intensely mediated, the other gaining insufficient media coverage for some, we see unfold a complex web of political communication.

Cascading network activation: example 2: Ahmadinejad's open letter to Bush

On 8 May 2006, President Ahmadinejad of Iran sent a letter to President Bush of the US. This eighteen-page letter was delivered by Swiss go-betweens, and it was also published online. President Bush did not reply to the letter. Annabelle Sreberny (2008) has likened the situation to Edgar Allen Poe's story, 'The Purloined Letter'. In the story, a Queen receives a letter and, while being visited in her boudoir by the King, to her evident embarrassment an attempt to hide the letter is seen by her Minister, who contrives to replace the letter with a substitute, to the knowledge of the Queen who can do nothing for fear of attracting the King's attention. After eighteen months of frustrated police attempts to find the letter, a detective, Dupin arrives at the Minister's office, only to discover the letter is in the most obvious place, hanging in front of the mantelpiece, whereupon he substitutes it for another letter unknown to the Minister. However, Dupin's letter has a message in his own handwriting that will make his act known to the Minister, if and when he opens the letter.

As Sreberny suggests, the story leads us to ask who sees what, about who has power over whom, about interpersonal politics and the deceits that are performed. With Ahmedinejad's letter to Bush, it is unclear who the letter was intended for. In a sense, everybody received the letter, and many people responded; not just commentators, journalists, experts and politicians, but also postings made from around the world to Internet chatrooms. The world became a 'hall of mirrors', Sreberny argues. As people responded and reacted to each other, a global public sphere could be said to exist – around an object, a letter. The only person who did not respond to the letter was Bush himself. One satirist wrote, 'At the white house, aides said that writing a letter of such length to President Bush, who is known for his extreme distaste for reading, was the most provocative act Mr Ahmedinejad could have committed' (Borowitz 2006).

For Sreberny the episode exemplifies features of the new media ecology: how a global response can be triggered; that everything may be seen, by anyone, by everyone, instantly, relayed, directly, translated – but witnessed; that even in such a debate, little attention was paid to the content of the letter; and that no political or media agent can control the response of any act or word. This is not to say this transparency applies to all processes. Israel managed to conceal the nature of its air strikes in Syria in September 2006 from the world's media for a month. Nevertheless, the likelihood of images and information 'escaping' is greater in the new media ecology.

This section has introduced some examples of patterns of 'cascading network activation' in the new media ecology we are analysing in the *Legitimising the Discourses of Radicalisation* project.[6] Next we turn to the critical phenomena within those networks, legitimacy.

Analysing legitimacy

Having defined publics and counterpublics, and seen how the political communication – the circulations constituting publics – have been transformed in the new media ecology, we now turn to the problem of legitimacy. Legitimacy is inseparable from questions of power. Power necessarily affects others, whether conceived as 'power over', power to set public agendas, or more nuanced neo-Marxist or Foucauldian conceptions. Since it affects others, power will require justification. In social science, the problem is to explain what makes power legitimate in particular societies. Following David Beetham (1991), we contend that the question is not 'do people *believe* power to be legitimate?' If legitimacy was simply what people believed, then a regime with very effective public relations operations would count as a legitimate regime, since it had convinced its peoples to believe in its legitimacy. It would imply, for instance, that 'the reason for the collapse of the communist regimes in Eastern Europe in 1989 lay in a deficiency in public relations, rather than anything actually wrong with the system of rule itself' (Beetham 1991: 9). Beetham repeats the point: 'A given power relationship is not legitimate because people believe in its legitimacy, but because it can be *justified in terms of* their beliefs' (Beetham: 1991: 11). Our interest is in the extent to which there is a *correspondence* between people's beliefs about what is a defensible political regime or leadership and the regime or leadership they actually have. If a regime, say, conforms to people's normative expectations about what a political regime should be like, then it is legitimate. If a regime begins to depart from those normative expectations, for instance if low electoral turnout in a democratic regime led to governments without a popular mandate, then the regime lacks legitimacy. If citizens notice, they might believe the regime lacks legitimacy. But the legitimacy eroded *prior* to them noticing, when the potential of the system to depart from expectations began to be realised.

A social science analysis of legitimacy does not simply report on a group's beliefs then. Analysis of the legitimacy of power entails evaluating the extent to which the regime meets particular criteria: first, did the regime gain and exercise power within the law; second, has consent been offered freely by those obeying the regime; third, is the regime justifiable in terms of the society's beliefs and values? Unlike political philosophers who seek an objective or universal standard of legitimacy, or legal scholars who analyse a regime's legal validity, the task for social scientists, Beetham argues (1991: 14), is to give an account of 'legitimacy-in-context'. In particular societies, to what extent are these three criteria fulfilled? What is the gap between expectation and actuality?

How does this apply to Jihadist discourses and networks? The category 'legitimacy' is, like 'class' for Marx, a general concept that can be applied to various historical societies (Beetham 1991). The content of each of the three criteria will vary: the particular laws and legal system might vary, the content of a society's beliefs and values might vary, and the form through which consent is conferred might vary. By evaluating the fulfilment of these criteria we could conduct comparisons of the different forms of legitimacy in Jihadist discourses compared to liberal democrat discourses or other strands of Islam. Our principle and initial focus, however, will be Jihadist discourses. Any illumination of the legitimacy of certain key Jihadist figures (and their texts and policies) may help explain the behaviour of members of those discourse networks.

Such an analysis might focus on:

- **Principles of differentiation**. How is the dominance of power-holders justified? Is it through birthright or through demonstrating merit in some field (science, diplomacy, religious knowledge)?
- **The demonstration of a common interest**. Inequality of power has historically been deemed necessary in many societies as a means to realise the common interest or some larger common purpose. How are principles of differentiation reconciled with this notion of a common interest?
- **Evidence of consent**. To give consent, those qualified must evidently have freedom and independence from the power-holders, otherwise there is no consent. How is free acceptance of subordination organised and communicated?
- **Relational legitimacy**. How is the perceived legitimacy of other regimes used in appeals for legitimacy in Jihadist discourse? Does it have the capacity to form a system that generates its own legitimation, or is that capacity dependent on the actions of other political discourses and systems?
- **Tests of legitimacy**. To substantiate correspondence between a society's beliefs and values and whether a political regime or system reflects those beliefs and values, 'tests' occur (Boltanski and Thévenot 2006: 40). For instance, critical debates or responses to events may re-establish the principles underlying power relationships.
- **Justifications of violence**. How does the relation of domination–subordination that accompanies any legitimation of power produce justifications for violent acts by those in that relationship towards others? How are political/religious philosophical systems that contain justifications of violence applied by particular agents to historical and contemporary social situations? Such an analysis entails bridging political philosophy and the

critical evaluation of key texts justifying violence (e.g. Frazer and Hutchings 2007) with sociological analysis of situated actions and 'lay' theories in everyday communications (for an instance of such a bridging study, see Boltanski and Thévenot 2006). Identifying justifications in a stable text is one thing; identifying justifications in Web 2.0 forums, where texts are ephemeral, changing, and often without an identifiable author, presents a range of methodological problems.

This project is an integrated empirical study of new media forms and content. Our approach draws on a recent development in the field of discourse and new media, namely, *nexus analysis* – 'the study of the semiotic cycles of people, objects, and discourses in and through moments of socio-cultural importance' (Scollon and Scollon 2004: x). Thus, we are investigating radicalising discourses as dynamically configured through synchronic and diachronic mediated spaces and narratives. In this way our research responds both to the emergent aspects of radicalising discourses, evident in and immediately after events represented and/or experienced as 'nodal' and as 'crisis', and also to the now established and perhaps enduring narratives and templates (Hoskins 2004) that frame media, public and political interpretations in the post 9/11 context, but also those established much earlier. So, a key aspect of nexus analysis is *circumferencing*: The identification of the past origins of action; its future direction; its expanding circles of engagement with others near and far; the time-scales on which the action depends and the layers of geopolitical discourses in which it is embedded (Scollon and Scollon 2004). Through using this approach, not only will the temporal trajectories and trends of radicalising discourses be identified, but also their spatial connectivities, local and global influences.

Hence, it is not that legitimacy is a 'problem' to which there are 'solutions', but rather that we can offer a way to analyse legitimacy (Barnett 2003) which at least renders its various dimensions and constitutive processes more transparent and intelligible. For instance, the criterion of consent is problematic because as our discussion of 'publics' demonstrated, a people, or a public, cannot be known. It is only through technologies and staged events that the 'public opinion' and its meaning are established (ibid.: 21–2). Analysis of legitimacy in the new media ecology must be based upon de-centred notions of 'media', 'public' and indeed 'counterpublic' (ibid.: 78); de-centred as in neither media or public are identifiable or measurable agents or subjects, but exist as dispersed and fluid relations. Nexus analyses of communications around critical events and crises allow for the mapping and tentative discernment of the 'media', 'publics' and 'counterpublics' at work.

Finally, analysis of Web 2.0 and other media content will employ a multimodal framework. This entails investigating the social actors (as presented), processes and patterns of textual, visual and sonic use involved, as well as interpreting these discursive constructions in terms of the competing systems of knowledge/power about the world that they bring about. Multimodal analysis allows for the study of the interrelationship between different communicative modalities in the texts being examined. This is essential to the interactive media of Web 2.0, which relies variously on visual and auditory as well as verbal modalities. Multimodal analysis has been deployed productively to political communication (e.g. Kress and van Leeuwen 2001; LeVine and Scollon 2004; Chouliaraki 2006; Hoskins and O'Loughlin 2007).

Conclusion

This chapter has introduced a series of initial conceptual discussions that underpin our ongoing research project. By reconsidering the key concepts 'public', 'counterpublic' and 'legitimacy' for the context of a new media ecology, we are able to develop a model of cascading network activation that can be applied to the study of Jihadist discourses in Web 2.0 spaces, particularly as critical security events and controversies unfold. By making use of the tools of nexus analysis, multimodal analysis, and examinations of legitimacy and justification in political theory, we have a framework to explore the correspondence between Jihadist acts of violence and the discourses that surround them, as well as to address how Jihadist discourses and notion of 'radicalisation' circulate in mainstream media discourses and in public/audience understandings.

Notes

1 An earlier draft of this paper was presented at the Conflict Research Society Conference, 'Future Conflict', Mary Ward House Conference Centre, London, 4 September 2007.
2 This is a two-year project funded by the ESRC New Security Challenges Programme (Award no. RES-181–25–0041) led by Andrew Hoskins, Ben O'Loughlin and Akil Awan.
3 'Shifting Securities: News Cultures Before and Beyond the Iraq War 2003' funded by the ESRC New Security Challenges Programme (Award no. RES 223–25–0063) see www.mediatingsecurity.com.
4 It was also defended online by CBS News National Security Correspondent David Martin (15 May 2002) the next day.
5 See the discussion page on the Daniel Pearl entry on wikipedia.org.
6 We are aware of the possibility that a study such as this may itself form part of the new media ecology under scrutiny, for instance by contributing findings to public debate. We are also aware of the difficulty of using concepts in our analysis that are used by participants, and that our study is in no way external to the world studied.

4 Transparency and accountability in the age of cyberpolitics

The role of blogs in framing conflict

Maria Touri

Introduction

For more than a decade, the democratic potential of new media has been discussed extensively in relation to their capacity to empower citizens. They have been credited with enabling an information explosion and the creation of a more transparent political environment, the importance of which is heightened during conflict and war, as theories of International Relations have also underscored.

The impact of transparency and publicity on human behaviour is hardly new with Kant being amongst the first to argue that the principles of human action could be ethical only if they were public (Kant 1963 in Brown 2005: 58). In the case of conflict and war and based on Kant's observation that even if state leaders do not suffer personally, they suffer through the loss of office (Schultz 1999), an open political environment facilitates the unseating of a government that undertakes costly strategies (de Mesquita and Lalman 1992). According to Fearon (1994) and Schultz (2001) domestic political institutions in democratic states enable the disclosure of information about governmental incentives and preferences in a given crisis; and as governments become less likely to engage in bluffing behaviour, bargaining processes are more likely to result in peaceful solutions.

In light of the notion of political transparency, this chapter seeks to offer insight into the role of new media in situations of conflict, examining the dissemination of news through the blogosphere and drawing upon the unique quality of blogs to enable citizens 'to emerge from the spectating audience as a player and maker of meanings' (Coleman 2005: 274). More specifically, this chapter demonstrates how the contribution of the news *framing* theory can provide a conceptual tool to unpick the subtle and unseen process through which blogs can form a more open political environment and create a news media system capable of facilitating conflict prevention

A brief description of blogs

The emergence of blogs (short for 'weblog') has marked the arrival of a 'new form of mainstream communication' (Rosenbloom 2004: 31), one that allows millions of people to publish and exchange knowledge and information. The phrase 'weblog' is said to have been introduced in 1997 by Jorn Barger in reference to his own site, *robotwisdom*, which comprised a list (or log) of the web pages he found interesting (Du and Wagner 2006). Since then, a number of definitions have been formed to describe this recent phenomenon. Drezner and Farrell define blogs as web pages 'with minimal to no external editing, providing on-line commentary, periodically updated and presented in reverse chronological order, with hyperlinks to other online sources' (Drezner and Farrell 2004a: 5) while Allan describes them as 'diaries or journals written by individuals seeking to establish an online presence' (2006: 44). Along similar lines, Herring *et al.* see blogs as 'frequently modified web pages containing dated entries listed in reverse chronological sequence' (Herring *et al.* 2007: 3). The effort to define blogs has led to some consensus with regard to their distinctive quality as a citizen-based form of journalism, which enables the audience of mainstream media to become actively engaged in the dissemination and interpretation of news, setting blogs apart from traditional media. The connectivity they allow through the provision and posting of links is one of the key components of their function. Links can be provided by a blogger to inform readers of an item they consider interesting, they can connect blogs with one another as a way to respond to a point another has made or they may direct readers to a story the blogger found useful. The network of blogs connected through links comprises the blogosphere (Tremayne 2007).

The so-called 'news blogs' that focus on politics and current affairs and whose profile was raised significantly after the 9/11 terrorist attacks, are perhaps the category of blogs fitting the concept of citizen-based journalism most. So far, studies of the quality of blogs as original news sources or platforms for citizen journalism have offered different and, at times, contradictory evidence of their position in the production and reporting of news. The present work does not intend to offer conclusive answers to these questions. Although the core argument lies in the power of blogs to offer greater transparency, which sprouts from the notion of citizen journalism, it is the implications of the blogging phenomenon in its deeper and broader sense that this chapter addresses. A somewhat narrow focus is taken in relation to blogs that offer information on politics and current affairs, which are thought to have the greatest impact on mainstream media (Tremayne 2007). Such blogs include those maintained by news organisations, by professional journalists outside news organisations and by individuals with an interest in politics and policy issues, often referred to as 'citizen journalist' blogs. A systematic way to evaluate the role of blogs in creating a more transparent news media environment, that would place government decisions under greater public glare, is by locating the blogging phenomenon within the wider context of news construction. Theories of *framing* can be particularly informative in this case, addressing key underpinnings and unpicking certain aspects of the news construction process, through which greater political transparency can be achieved.

News framing and the challenge of blogs

In general terms, the concept of framing embodies the social construction of reality approach to the news media (Adoni and Mane 1984; Berger and Luckman 1966; Gamson 1992, in Wolfsfeld 1997). Often, it is associated with the principles of selection, salience and exclusion that 'enable journalists to process large amounts of information quickly and routinely [and to] package information for efficient relay to their audiences' (Gitlin 1980: 7). In what Carragee and Roefs (2004) describe as the most significant contribution to framing research, Gitlin (1980) and Tuchman (1978) linked the production of meaning through frames to structural and ideological processes that involve journalists, news organisations and their sources (Carragee and Roefs 2004: 216). Since news frames are not shaped in a vacuum but through the frames sponsored by multiple social actors, news stories become a platform for framing contests, where political actors compete by sponsoring their preferred meanings. In essence, as framing sponsorship is determined by the distribution of economic, political and cultural resources across the various actors, examining the media construction of reality through framing, necessitates that focus be placed on the role of power in the production of meaning (Carragee and Roefs 2004). The issue of power forms the basis on which the contribution of blogs is located, especially since they are seen by users as conduits to raw information, less corrupted by power than mainstream news media.

Given that journalists and opinion leaders consume blogs too, blogs offer an effective combination of expertise, real-time collective response to breaking news, and public-opinion barometer. Those few blogs that function as aggregators of information enable journalists to obtain meaningful analysis predictions of political developments, while they have also given shape to a hierarchical structure to the chaos of cyberspace (Drezner and Farrell 2004b). As Tremayne (2007) suggests, mainstream media can learn from bloggers how to take advantage of active citizen writers to generate better products. Blogs can give journalists and other bloggers free access to first-hand newsworthy information (Thompson 2003) from multiple areas, offering voice to a wider range of progressive groups and access to alternative interpretations. They can also challenge news media frame production through the extensive use of hyperlinks, which becomes an integral process of meaning construction. The dependence upon hyperlinks to various kinds of text, places stories in a broader cultural and political context (Pavlik 2001), offering information abundance and scope for diverse interpretations of events.

The distinctive content found in blogs that relates to, comments on, interrogates and analyses information already on mainstream media news (Kivikuru 2006; Thelwall and Stuart 2007) allows blog authors to re-access and re-frame current news material and produce frames that divert from the official meanings traditionally sponsored by political elites. This is especially the case for blogs maintained by professional journalists, who use the blogosphere as a conduit to a writing that is free from journalistic constrains. Robinson's (2006) study of

130 blogs published within mainstream news media outlets in the US showed that blogs could supply various interpretations of the day's news. Reporters were able to let loose in some creative and interrogating writing, and build stories using feedback and contribution from readers (Robinson 2006: 79).

The plethora of information sources, made available through blogs, allows for a greater number of actors to enter the framing contest and gradually dilute the issue of power over news frames. At the same time, given the space to use their knowledge and expertise to comment on and analyse current media coverage, bloggers could nudge journalists to provide more inclusive and evenly balanced framing of events, generating greater political transparency. The centrality of this development is most visible in the reporting of conflict where the power relations between political leaders and news organisations are the primary determinants of frames.

Reporting conflict: an unequal framing process

Dictated by issues of power, the framing of conflict situations favours the promotion of meanings that serve primarily the interests of authorities and of media organisations raising questions with regard to the democratic role of the news media as an agent that constrains politicians from waging war. In the study of frame production during conflict and war operations, the compelling work of Wolfsfeld (1997) and Entman (2004) can offer a solid basis for the evaluation of the influential power of blogs.

A central premise of Wolfsfeld's work is that political power offers important advantages in influencing the news media frames during conflict. He asserts that the inherent importance of those with political power, can lead to dignified frames, while progressive groups that divert from the official line can only compete with their more powerful adversaries if they produce frames that resonate with the media's culture (Wolfsfeld 1997: 42–5). Wolfsfeld makes clear how the power of political actors to shape news framing is embodied in their ability to interpret events, in a way that resonates with the media's political and professional culture. To this, Entman has added the importance of promoting frames that resonate with the wider culture of a given political environment. In his cascading activation model, Entman (2004) introduces the concept of cultural congruence as the ease with which a news frame will fit the schemas habitually used by most members of a society and will be more likely to induce similar responses among the majority of these members. Consequently, a great deal of an actor's power to ensure their preferred interpretations are successfully adapted by the media and public alike, lies in their ability to promote frames that are congruent with the schemas that dominate the respective political culture. Culturally congruent frames tend to stimulate similar reactions by elites and the public, minimising the possibility for domestic opposition and rendering news framing easier for governments to control. They can prove professionally useful for the news media too, enabling journalists to process large amounts of information and fit it in a culturally familiar narrative. Wolfsfeld cites the example of the conflict between the Catholics in Northern Ireland and the British government and its coverage by the American press. He explains how the frame of *terrorism* was established as culturally congruent and professionally useful, making it virtually impossible to find alternative explanations such as the struggles by an oppressed people against British occupation (Wolfsfeld 1997: 34).

According to Entman, the more culturally ambiguous a frame sponsored by a political leader is, the less sense it will make with the media and the public, paving the way for more alternative perspectives to enter the news framing process (Entman 2004). The implications of ambiguous frames lie in rendering the anticipated reactions of the public less predictable, reinforcing the media's role in representation (ibid.: 21) and, consequently, in holding governments accountable. Especially in situations of instability and conflict, when control over news tends to heighten, the production of less congruent news frames and more alternative justifications might eventually signify a more transparent media environment. A representative example can be traced in the Iraq War 2003. Mainstream media coverage in the US may not have been very efficient in elevating sources outside official Washington power circles and posing a serious challenge to the administration stories. However, as Bennett *et al.* (2007) and Entman (2004) explain, the frame promoted by the Bush administration – to build a case for the US invasion of Iraq – remained ambiguous enough to create some space for a few opposition voices and enable a framing of the war that, overall, was less tightly controlled than in past operations. It is beyond doubt that, to say categorically whether and to what extent blogs could have influenced the news framing of the Iraq War 2003, an in-depth and systematic empirical investigation is required. Nevertheless, existing theoretical and empirical evidence of the performance of the blogosphere during situations of conflict and tension can serve as an indicator of the future potential role that blogs in the reporting and framing of conflict.

Framing conflict on the blogosphere

The popularity of blogs in reporting conflict was boosted during the recent Iraq war, with the blogosphere functioning not just as a news source, but also as a means for soldiers to remain connected to their families (Palser 2002; Seipp 2002; Smolkin 2004). Not content with the one-sided news reporting of the conflict offered mainly by the US media, significant numbers of the public turned to the Internet for information. As Allan (2006) remarks, from the moment news of the first attacks was reported on 19 March 2003, Internet traffic increased dramatically. The demand for more comprehensive coverage of the war led audiences to the search of information through news websites and blogs.

Although, according to Pew Research, only 4 per cent of the Internet users would turn to blogs during the Iraq War, Johnson and Kaye (2007) underline the fact that their influential power exceeds their readership. Their increased popularity during the war was due to featuring writers with varied political perspectives that offered insights different from those of the American traditional media

(Hamilton 2003; Hastings 2003; Reynolds 2004). They also provided links to other sites and allowed readers to respond to the postings, enabling a healthy debate about the war (Hastings 2003). Their influential power becomes even more apparent when one considers the efforts of the military to censor or shut down several blogs posted by soldiers in Iraq for fear they would contradict the Pentagon's official version of events (Schulman 2005, in Johnson and Kaye 2007: 165).

The Iraq War is not the only example where mainstream media and blogs offered contradicting coverage. As Murilo (2006) points out, with reference to the East Timor crisis, the Anglophone media would report a different story from Portuguese language blogs. The latter expanded awareness of the many sides of the conflict, bringing the gaps in interpretation within the different language spheres into high visibility. Considering the reported dependency of journalists on blogs for news and analysis they did not see elsewhere (Reynolds 2004), blogs cannot but reinforce the anticipated impact of their challenging voices and views on the framing of the war by mainstream media.

Based on current theoretical and empirical evidence from the blogosphere, the following paragraphs attempt to build a theoretical case of the *why* and *how* blogs can enable the diffusion of control over news frames during conflict and create scope for a more transparent and democratic political environment. The core argument lies in the ability of blogs to make a wide range of sources accessible to mainstream media, representing voices that are distanced from political power and able to provide intelligent commentary without sponsorship of a corporate news company. This does not only enhance their credibility (Kaye and Johnson 2004; Wall 2004: 165), but also gives them the potential to erode the barrier of political power that blocks alternative voices from entering the framing contests. Considering that political power translates into one's ability to sponsor news frames that resonate with the wider political context and the media's professional culture, challenging the issue of power could consequently enable a frame diversity that is central to the creation of a transparent media and political environment.

The contest over procedural framing: alternative voices, alternative frames

Empirical evidence of the multiplication of the sources cited and quoted in blogs during the Iraq War in 2003 offers some first indication of the diversity of frames that could decentre the process of news media coverage. In a content analysis of newspapers and blogs covering the operation, Vaina (2007) examined five major newspapers and six popular political blogs and counted the number of sources they cited over seven days in late March 2007. Overall, he found that blogs included a higher number of total sources and a slightly wider range of sources. Even if the gap between newspapers and blogs was considerably narrower when evaluating the types of sources, Vaina underlines the fact that blogs were still more diverse in their sourcing. Hyperlinks offered another route for voices and perspectives to proliferate and dispute the trustworthiness of mainstream media during the Iraq War. Matheson's (2004) investigation of the *Guardian* blog demonstrates how linking to other newspapers and sources from the Middle East, indicated the end of the monopoly of the media's professional logic (Matheson 2004: 459).

Among the most prominent sources that offered independent investigation and in-depth commentary and analysis, were those knowledgeable and passionate professional and citizen journalists that participated actively in the coverage of the Iraq war. Allan (2006) remarks on the number of front line bloggers, that were not even associated with a news organisation, but worked as 'solo journalists', writing their own copy for online print and broadcast media during the war. Being always on the move and equipped with mobile technologies, these bloggers became popular among blog users due to their ability to divert from official lines and the mainstream media's editing scrutiny and pursue stories that mattered most to them (Allan 2006: 109).

The case of the so-called 'solo journalists' resembles the self-styled 'unilaterals' in the Gulf War 1991: a number of journalists that decided to break away from the pool systems organised by the military and get stories that were at variance with the official line, offering alternative perspectives originally unavailable in the coverage of mainstream news organisations. Taylor (1998) underlines the contradictory views offered by the unilaterist version of events in comparison to the unanimity of the official line; but at the same time, he questions the effectiveness of this activity and its contribution to a wider public understanding of the war. In fact, unilateral journalists were only a small minority and their interpretations created more confusion than the clarity they had intended. With this in mind, the reporting of bloggers emerges as a unique opportunity for independent sources to provide more clarity to a conflict operation by multiplying the already existing alternative voices in its reporting and challenging mainstream media frames in a more forceful manner.

The anticipated influence of this amplification of voices is embodied in the 'procedural' framing of an operation such as a conflict, once these voices get noticed by mainstream media. Procedural framing is described as the framing that focuses on the process and politics of decision-making, in which case, some aspects of a given process are selected and highlighted to promote the desired interpretation. This could include mentions of the president's leadership, attributions regarding consultations with other leaders and comments concerning the manner that policy was formulated and carried out and it could also relate to the likelihood of military success or failure (Althaus 2003; Entman 2004). Procedural framing is distinguished from 'substantive' framing. The latter addresses policy decisions, such as unilateral military action, conducting weapons inspections, opposing the option of war and other proposals, and the logic used to support and justify them (Althaus 2003; Entman and Page 1994; Herman and Chomsky 1988; Mermin 1999).

The so-called 'milblogs' – blogs posted by soldiers in Iraq – represent a useful example of a potential source of procedural framing of events. Schulman

(2005) describes the case of a milblog written by an Army infantryman named Colby Buzzell, who posted his account of a vicious firefight with insurgents on his blog, *My War*, describing the horror of the battle. Interestingly, the Pentagon ensured the operation received scant media coverage by playing down the extent to which Buzzell's brigade had been involved in the fighting. When a report in the Tacoma, Washington, *News Tribune* noted the discrepancy between Buzzell's version and the Pentagon's, Buzzell's officers ensured his and other blogs were either censored or ordered to shut down. The specific incident draws attention to the potential silencing of such blogs by officials fearing the exposure of information that would contradict the government's line. But at the same time it illustrates the power of the alternative versions of the unfolding events, featured in blogs, to attract the attention of mainstream media and disrupt their procedural framing line.

Cooper (2006) cites another example of a blogger offering a dissenting interpretation that could have potentially influenced later media coverage. He describes the framing of an Iraqi insurgent attack on an American military convoy, with twenty-four Iraqi insurgents left dead, by the *New York Times* in March 2005; and how it was disputed by communication professor Cori Dauber on her blog, *Rantingprofs*. Cooper explains that Dauber's critique was triggered by the way the, otherwise factually accurate story, misled the audience by framing the Iraqi assault as an unusually large and bold battle and glossing how they were eventually routed badly by the Americans (Cooper 2006: 106). Another misleading aspect of the story, according to Dauber, was the way the *New York Times* reporter stated that morale was deteriorating among the Iraqi civilian population as a result of insurgent attacks. As Dauber noted in her blog, the story explicitly concealed the optimism that prevailed among Iraqi people as well as the existing polling data confirming this optimism (Cooper 2006: 107).

Dauber's disputing of the *New York Times* frame offers a clear example of the different procedural framing and interpretation that individual sources can provide, especially when they are not limited by professional standards and/or nationalistic incentives. Constructing a news story necessarily involves a choice of which facts to highlight and which to play down. Since the frame is a central idea that organises the salient facts in the story, disputing the story frame may take the form of highlighting different facts that provide an alternative perspective of a key event. If critiques like Dauber's create enough 'buzz' to attract the attention of the mainstream media, they can prompt more comprehensive and transparent media coverage of the actual procedures and outcomes in a conflict. This will be a crucial step towards hindering government efforts to control the substantive news framing and public justification of the legitimacy of the conflict in question.

The contest over substantive framing: justifying policies

Through the multiplication of sources, blogs can give access to those dissenting voices that divert from the culturally resonant beliefs and, using their expertise and knowledge, are able to recognise the existence of alternative justifications of the government decisions made during an operation. Dissenting voices could entail a more subtle criticism and disputing of mainstream media frames, challenging the production of substantive framing. Such challenge could comprise the promotion of culturally incongruent interpretations and justifications, and frames that do not fit the media's professional standards. Especially in situations of conflict and war, where national interest could be under risk, the blogosphere can provide citizens with a platform where they can publicly question the government's justifications of a decision that might jeopardise the country's interest and dispute the framing of a conflict by mainstream media.

Drezner and Farrell (2004b) cite the example of Juan Cole, a Professor of History at the University of Michigan, who channelled his expertise on the Muslim world and the war in Iraq into his blog *Informed Comment*. Cole's scepticism about the US invasion and occupation of Iraq diverted from the optimistic mainstream media coverage. In the summer of 2003, he wrote,

> The Sunni Arabs north, east and west of Baghdad from all accounts hate the U.S. and hate U.S. troops being there. This hatred is the key recruiting tool for the resistance, and it is not lessened by U.S. troops storming towns. I wish [the counterinsurgency operation] well; maybe it will work, militarily. Politically, I don't think it addresses the real problems, of winning hearts and minds.
>
> (cited in Drezner and Farrell 2004b)

His comments and analysis attracted wide attention from bloggers and journalists and Cole began appearing on media outlets such as National Public Radio (NPR) and CNN to provide expert commentary. As Drezner and Farrell remark,

> Cole's transformation into a public intellectual embodies many of the dynamics that have heightened the impact of the blogosphere. He wanted to publicize his expertise, and he did so by attracting attention from elite members of the blogosphere. As Cole made waves within the virtual world, others in the real world began to take notice.
>
> (Drezner and Farrell 2004b)

Cole's example is noteworthy, as the attention he received by bloggers and news media was the resultant of his expertise, an implicit challenge of the official interpretations of the decision to wage the war in Iraq, and of the cultural congruence of mainstream news framing.

The case of Jeff Jarvis, director of the new-media programme of the Graduate School of Journalism at the City University of New York, offers another similar illustration (Cooper 2006). Jarvis attempted a substantial reframing in response to a *New York Times* story on the suicide bombers in the 7/7 London attack. Although the story concerned a crisis event, rather than a conflict, the framing included elements, such as a problem definition and cause identification, which are typical of the coverage and framing of conflict. Jarvis's critique of the *New York Times* story addressed the explanation advanced by the newspaper for the specific terrorist activity, which presented the atrocity as the resultant of the despair of angry young men in Arab nations who have no hope of economic prosperity and freedom. Jarvis's objection to the frame stemmed from observing that the London bombers did not fit that explanation. In contrast, they were young men living in a land of freedom and opportunity, which in reality made them just murderers. Cooper cites the following text from Jarvis's blog:

> The problem with the analysis is that though it does not justify their actions – it tries to understand them – it gives a tacit logic, even a justification to the horribly illogical, unjustifiable, uncivilised crime. What they did is a crime. That's all it is, nothing more. A crime.
>
> (Cooper 2006: 112)

To support his reframing, Jarvis offered several cases of criminal acts and made a distinction between understanding criminal motives and disregarding criminal behaviours. These cases included manslaughter under the influence of alcohol, if alcoholism is treated as a disease and corporate fraud, with the excuse that the perpetrator was raised in a culture of competition (Cooper 2006: 113). The example demonstrates how different media can offer conflicting frames of the same incident including different justifications of a given problem and the causes of this problem. In the case of blogs, this could entail applying a form of implicit pressure on journalists to re-consider their own interpretations. By questioning the frame of the 'angry young man', Jarvis draws attention to what is perhaps the strongest asset of blogs: the capacity to engage in a more thorough evaluation of the causes of problems, such as terrorism, that could shed light on the deeper failures of a given political culture and attribute responsibility to those who are accountable. In situations of conflict, this capacity could eventually place the political realm under greater public scrutiny, facilitating peaceful resolutions.

Conclusion

In the era of cyber politics, the diffusion of communications technologies and the availability of multiple sources of information have generated a certain degree of openness and publicity, reducing the ability of political leaders to have complete control over the definition and framing of events in conflict and war. However, these developments have not succeeded to cease the propensity of traditional news media to defer to the best-packaged official political story and to frame conflict situations in accordance to a given political and professional culture. The endurance of a media environment, which is not conceptually distinct from governance, leaves little scope for the media to provide the degree of transparency that can hold governments accountable and help the prevention of conflict. As other areas of research have also demonstrated, the news media can even provide opportunities for political leaders to obtain benefits from war (Van Belle 1997: 406).

Within this context, the pervasiveness of blogs could prove pivotal. As this chapter has argued and as current theoretical and empirical evidence from the blogosphere indicates, the blogging phenomenon has not only amplified the sources of public information creating a more open communications landscape. It has also signified an extension of media freedom that is paramount for peaceful alternatives to conflict. To put it in Coleman's terms, 'blogs provide a channel for authentic expression that is free from the repressive controls of traditional media' and have become a source of information and analysis for people who no longer trust the spin and narrow agenda of the usual sources (Coleman 2005: 276). Added to this, is the impressive volume of knowledge and expertise available through blogs contesting official frames and interpretations.

It is beyond doubt that more in-depth and systematic research is needed to obtain robust evidence of this dimension of news coverage in cyberspace and its actual power to change the conventional media framing of conflict. Moreover, concerns about news blogs, especially those integrated in the structure of established news organisations, representing another attempt to strengthen the hegemony of market-orientated journalism and the existing power relations, should not be overlooked. Nevertheless, while blogs are beginning to shift the power over framing away from the usual sources in conflict and war, the media system is growing into a greater constraining factor for governments than even before.

Part II

Global security and information warfare

5 Web activism as an element of global security[*]

Michael Dartnell

While the World Wide Web and information technologies (IT) that emerged over the past decade have a transformative impact on global security, neither they nor the expectations that they arouse are unique to our time. In 'The Radio as an Apparatus of Communication', Bertolt Brecht argued that

> the radio would be the finest possible communication apparatus in public life [...] if it knew how to receive as well as transmit, how to let the listener speak as well as hear, how to bring him into a relationship instead of isolating him.
>
> (Brecht 1977: 52)

Brecht recognized that two-way and multiple-user IT would significantly improve human communication. This view is corroborated by the fact that IT creates enormous opportunities for non-state actors and enhances the global profile of previously marginalized or ignored issues and movements. IT is a highly visible embodiment of the complexity of contemporary global politics. It is present in many settings: facilitating the overwhelming dominance of conventional US military forces; integrating pre-existing technologies, such as computers and photography on a single platform; globalizing values, ideas and interests; privatizing information about world events for a significant minority of the global population; and, introducing a range of non-state actors who have transnational communication abilities into the global scene. As Brecht foresaw in radio, advanced communication devices have fostered a range of human relations.

IT practices and security of perceptions

Given that the Web is a political tool that facilitates new political relationships relevant to global security, the issue is how to qualify it and describe those relations. This discussion focuses on the influence of IT through examining two types of Web activism. It shows how Web activism is a vehicle through which perceptions and identities have become part of a complex global scene. IT embodies a transformation that is significant and needs qualification since it not seismic in the sense that it shakes basic realities. This discussion focuses on website and multimedia activism in the cases of the Peruvian Tupac Amaru (MRTA), the Revolutionary Association of the Women of Afghanistan (RAWA), and the Irish Republican Socialist Movement (IRSM) as well as an Islamic extremist multimedia file located on the Web, the *du'a* (prayer) of Sheikh Mohammed al Mohaisany.[1] These examples illustrate the variety of groups and technological practices linked to IT. The discussion outlines the issues and theoretical challenge of IT for the study of global security through referring to the websites and multimedia files, the types of messages transmitted, target publics (national, global, political elites, media and others), the results, and various transmission formats (especially multimedia and photographs). The examples discussed show how contemporary IT functions as *a messenger that shapes perceptions* by introducing values, ideas and identities that transform the notions of self and safety that are at the heart of security. In the case of the *du'a*, the transformation is especially dramatic and aims to revise the framework for understanding security.

The Web is not a threat to sovereignty-bound actors in the sense that it completely circumvents or overturns political and/or regulatory control. It is, instead, a device that facilitates political relations. As James Katz and Ronald Rice suggest, 'although the Internet has not led to any political revolutions, it has supported and encouraged them (as have – and do – the phone and fax)' (Katz and Rice 2002: 352). An important form that support and encouragement take on the Web is media, which has been transformed from a nationally regulated industry into a multifaceted global practice closely tied to the so-called information revolution. The transformation is both discrete and far-reaching. Since, as Susan Sontag notes, 'media are essentially contentless' (Sontag 2001: 149), global civil society and its many fractures, layers and divisions provide a transformative content for IT. The cases discussed here show how IT supports and encourages political relations in different ways: global witnessing (in the case of RAWA); networking (the IRSM); media relay (the MRTA); and, more straightforward propaganda (the *du'a*). In each case, support and encouragement means that identities that transgress the limits of state-based security are articulated and validated.

As anticipated in Brecht's comments on radio, the key impacts of today's IT are to spread of previously inaccessible information, and transform political communication by allowing non-state actors to directly address target publics. Since global telecommunication (telegraphy, telephones, radio, television, etc.) was regulated by states after the creation of the International Telegraph Union in 1865, the transformation has far-reaching impacts on the contents, issues and movements that enter the parameters of global security. The specific focus here is media activism by non-state actors, which reshapes perceptions in a global security landscape that was once regulated and controlled by states. The transformation became familiar through the electronic relays for the campaign to ban anti-personnel landmines, the anti-globalization movement, and, more recently, the mobilization of global public opinion against US intervention in Iraq. In these examples, IT transmits transnational movements into national contexts. In addition, IT also allows nationally focused groups to transmit local and national viewpoints onto the global scene. The latter type of Web activism is discussed here. The mix of national and transnational groups means that identity in any single global context might very well contain influences from another non-physically contiguous setting.

IT is a contributing factor in a complex global landscape that encompasses a range of technological, economic, social and cultural practices. In this context,

> many persons on the globe live in … imagined worlds (and not just imag-ined communities) and thus are able to contest and sometimes even subvert the imagined worlds of the official mind and of the entrepreneurial mental-ity that surround them.
>
> (Appadurai 2003: 41)

While IT does not determine behaviour, the influence of global communications devices is significant in a context marked by 'a vast decentralization of authority in which global governance becomes less state-centric and more the sum of crazy-quilt patterns between unalike, dispersed, overlapping, and contradictory collectivities seeking to maintain their coherence and advance their goals' (Rosenau 2003: 272). The consequences of the post-Cold War fragmentation of political identities and behaviours are still not completely understood. However, IT does contribute to the interplay, dissection and competition over the bound-aries of state, group and individual identities to an extent and at an intensity that was not possible in the bipolar Cold War system. The identarian impact of IT has received relatively less analysis in IR given that much attention has been diverted to those who deface or interfere with websites.[2] Yet the lack of attention cannot detract from what could very well be the most far-reaching impact of IT: support and encouragement in a wide-ranging struggle over boundaries and per-ceptions. Considered as such, the Web is the field for a vast, ongoing and para-doxical process of boundary redefinition that has enormous consequences for international relations and global security. *The redefinition bears on basic per-ceptions of self and the links between self and society that are the bases for global, national, and private security: 'who I am', 'who I want to be', and 'what I need to feel secure'.*

Web activism

Three distinct areas of IT practice parallel contemporary security trends. Con-sidered together, these areas point to a multi-centric world of global, local and private tensions in which non-state actors are players, but not dominant. The first area of practice is military, which is largely based in states since the latter still control coercive force on a planetary scale. The many applications of IT to mili-tary ends include satellite images, use of cell phones by the US military to contact Iraqi commanders during the 2003 war, airborne drones, night vision and sensor devices. The second context in which IT is relevant to global security is cybersecurity. These practices are associated with public anxieties over new technology in general even though the impact of cybersecurity threats is over-stated. An example of a cybersecurity threat to global security was the distrib-uted denial of service (D DOS) attack that flooded the website of the Qatari-based Al-Jazeera cable network with up to 300 megabits (Mbps) of data per second during the Iraq War. At the time, Al-Jazeera coverage of the Iraq War was highly critical of the US.[3] The third area in which IT relates to global security, Web activism, features an electronic battle that transgresses conven-tional state and identity boundaries. Web activism is distinct from cybersecurity issues since it centres on *struggle over perceptions* and reshapes the boundaries of global security. Although states once had determinant powers of regulation and control, Web activism makes it possible for non-state actors to provide information that recasts the forms and contents of identities.

Web activism is a form of electronic direct action in which previous one-way media are superseded by global communications devices. It is a practice through which individuals and groups use the Web to shape identity and perceptions and transform the relations that underlie global politics. Graham Meikle's *Future Active* points to a wide variety of groups that use the Web to extend offline polit-ical struggles into online environments. As Meikle notes, 'Internet activism is largely about raising awareness of the issues concerned, and this means getting more coverage than the purely online' (Meikle 2002: 26). Meikle examines anti-globalization activists, the Serb opposition radio station B-92, the Electronic Disturbance Theater, hacktivism,[4] and alternative and independent media. The groups examined here, the MRTA, RAWA and IRSM,[5] each reflect particular circumstances, produce distinct results, and use text and images to represent a particular political vision. The *du'a* is arguably unique, significantly different from the websites in that it is a standalone document with no claim of author-ship. The political results of all these cases of Web activism are not revolution-ary if such is understood in conventional political terms. Instead, they substantiate the model of a multilayered and fragmented global scene in which boundaries and identities are shifting and in which globalizing and privatizing tensions are widespread and intense.

Website activism

In 1996–7, the first group I examined, the Peruvian MRTA, engineered a dra-matic four-month hostage incident at the Japanese embassy in Lima when all guests at a reception held in honour of the emperor were captured.[6] As the hostage crisis dragged on for months, MRTA supporters simultaneously waged a Web campaign that seriously compromised the government of ex-president Alberto Fujimori. The MRTA network conducted a Web-based media barrage that highlighted the poor social justice and human rights record as well as the incompetence of the Fujimori government. The guerrillas who actually seized the embassy did not themselves conduct the Web campaign, which was managed by supporters and sympathizers in San Diego, California and Toronto, Canada. After four months, the Peruvian army stormed the compound and physically liquidated the guerrillas who carried out the action. Paradoxically, the physical defeat of the MRTA was another factor that discredited Fujimori's régime both at home and abroad. While the MRTA was physically defeated by the Peruvian state, its Web activism exposed the latter's unjust and authoritarian character to global civil society. MRTA Web activism transgressed the state by eluding its control, which highlighted its vulnerability. In this way, MRTA Web activism shifted the parameters of debate by directly communicating to mainstream media outlets around the world.

The IRSM website is paradoxical due to the nature of the group and its Web activism.[7] The IRSM is a notorious Irish republican fringe organization primarily known for a mix of strident Marxist–Leninism and gangster-style shoot-outs and rivalries. In spite of this, the IRSM website has a content of press releases, theoretical analyses and position papers as well as links to allied groups that contradicts the image of violent criminal militancy. Unlike the MRTA website, the IRSM website is not a direct media relay in a violent campaign or terrorist action in Northern Ireland. Instead, the website plays a role in the non-violent pursuit of political ends and suggests IT could direct political debate away from violence. The website also expresses a broader de-territorializing tradition in Irish politics that stems from connections to diaspora communities in the UK, North America and elsewhere. The tradition dates as far back as the massive immigration during the 1840s Irish famine. The website is a networking device, that is, a springboard, for the IRSM to gather a constituency of radical Irish Marxist–Leninist republicans scattered through Ireland and its diaspora. It illustrates how IT facilitates network forms of organization by easing communication for geographically dispersed movements. While the MRTA used Web media to influence global civil society, the IRSM uses it to enhance the cohesion of a long-standing network.

The RAWA website is distinct from those of the MRTA and IRSM and one of the most exciting and significant examples of Web activism.[8] The website provides a vast selection of audio, video and textual materials on the situation in Afghanistan, RAWA activities as well as political and human rights issues. It includes dramatic illustrations of human rights abuses by the former Taliban regime and the Northern Alliance that joined the post-2001 interim Afghan government. The Taliban responded to RAWA with a website of its own, which was repeatedly hacked and eventually shut down.[9] The RAWA website is distinct from those of the MRTA and IRSM in several ways. For one thing, it was not primarily aimed at Afghans in the period before the Taliban were overthrown, but rather explicitly tried to raise global awareness of the Afghan conflict and especially its impact on Afghan women. Ironically, the subject of the RAWA site, the Afghan people, are not online and still have little access to the Internet. By addressing global civil society about a context with extremely limited Web access, the RAWA website illustrates the potential and limits of IT in postcolonial settings. The website has tremendous potential for raising global awareness, but limited impact on concrete change in physical territory. Given these parameters, a key impact of the RAWA website is witnessing, that is, substantiating human rights abuses and providing a sense of events on the ground through electronic evidence. RAWA successfully used the Web to spread a message about Afghan women, which contrasts other contexts in which women's human rights have been gravely violated and global civil society has been unmoved. In the 1930s, for example, the Nazis obliterated well organized and broadly based Weimar feminist organizations and histories. Their physical liquidation and erasure from historical memory removed the Weimar feminist movement from West German political awareness until the 1970s. Extensive documentation on the RAWA website prevented a similar fate for Afghan feminists even if the concrete political, social and economic advances of women in that society since the fall of Taliban are modest.

Multimedia activism

A suggestive variety of IT practices and Web activism have appeared in the past few years. The examples point to the post-location, de-territorializing and post-realist impacts of IT-connected activism. An excellent case to illustrate the links of IT to contemporary global security is Al-Qaeda, which uses the Web to spread 'videos of terrorist attacks, proclamations by al-Qaeda's leaders and call to Muslims to take action against the West' (Ward, 12 December 2002). The Web carries many messages from groups that support Al-Qaeda's view that the West must be opposed by violence in order to prevent attacks on Islam. The formats of these messages show how IT is a highly adaptable tool for illegal non-state actors on the global scene at a time when websites that support radical groups are being shut down or limited. For example, several groups linked to the website 'BURN!' hosted on equipment at the University of California in San Diego (including the MRTA) were listed by the US State Department as terrorist organizations (Asarayala, 28 September 2002). This pressured UCSD to remove the groups from its server because the US Patriot Act makes it an offence to provide 'material support or resources' to foreign terrorist organizations. The Act effectively curtails the overt presence of some radical groups on the Web.[10] Islamic extremists circumvent restraints by using transferable files. The files are emailed between recipients or accessed by clicking on icons on webpages. They show how alternative IT practices are available to groups when they face state or even multilateral efforts to regulate Web content.

A striking example of multimedia Web activism is a ShockWave file[11] posted on the website of British-based firm, CityLink Computers[12] in July 2003. The file is an audio recording in Arabic of the *du'a* by Sheikh Muhammed al-Mohaisany delivered at the Masjid Al Haram (Grand Mosque) in Mecca during Ramadan in 2001.[13] It is accompanied by English subtitles and a powerful selection of digital photographs. The text says that the Saudi Arabian government arrested al-Mohaisany immediately after he delivered the prayer. The prayer asks for victory for the 'Mujahideen', complains of 'the injustice of the spiteful

Christians', calls on God to direct His 'forces against America', alleges that the US has 'killed Your slaves' and 'insulted Your religion', and invokes hurricanes as 'a constant for them' (i.e. Americans). The prayer further asks for release of 'our captured brothers' (i.e. prisoners in Guantanamo Bay), eradication of those who torture them (US soldiers), saving 'Al-Aqsa [mosque in Jerusalem] from the cruelty of the Jews', and protection for 'the hard-working scholars' (the passage is accompanied by a photo of Osama Bin Laden).

The impact of the *du'a* is based in a combination of audio recording, text and digital images. The latter include long shots of Mecca, Al-Aqsa Mosque, Osama Bin Laden, Chechen fighters, suicide bombers, the Palestinian Intifada, and destruction of the World Trade Center, Israeli and American soldiers, burning US flags, and a downed US helicopter. Other images depict dead Muslim children in Palestine and Afghanistan, US prisoners in the 2003 Iraq conflict, captured Islamic activists, Camp Delta in Guantanamo Bay, transport of Taliban prisoners in US aircraft, the destruction in Jenin, Israeli troops near Al-Aqsa, and political leaders such as Saudi King Fahd, Palestinian leader Yasser Arafat, Pakistani president Pervez Musharraf, US president George W. Bush, British PM Tony Blair, US Secretary of State Colin Powell, Egyptian president Hosni Mubarak, and former US president Bill Clinton. The images are standard wire service photos. The impact of the photos is derived from the accompanying words and captions, which transforms the relationship to viewers by providing an idiosyncratic interpretation of their meaning.

As a variety of Web activism, transfer of multimedia files has implications for global security since it occurs outside of state regulation and control. As such, Web activism embodies an ideological-cultural dimension of global security studies that is overshadowed by issues such as cybersecurity (a.k.a. hacking or 'website defacement') and transformation of the global financial and telecommunications sectors. The cultural dimension of IT is conventionally ignored by IR or sidelined as 'propaganda'. However, the rise of the Web means that the transformation of perceptions is a daily experience for a significant and influential minority of the global population. Since the Web is also linked to other communicative practices (including mainstream news services, print-outs of Web materials, and word-of-mouth), its potential impact extends far beyond this minority. Considered in this light, Web activism is important in terms of shaping the world in which we live, blurring conventional distinctions, and altering the parameters of state action and group and individual identities. It is a practice with both global and private characters and impacts. In the case of the *du'a*, the innovative dimension of IT is highlighted by Benjamin's suggestion that 'mute' photography needs to be supplemented by captions since this is exactly what the multimedia file does as a matter of course.[14] Use of multimedia influences the perceptions and boundaries that underlie contemporary global security, since it employs images with a strong emotional–moral impact alongside a text that shapes the contents of that impact.

The *du'a* of Sheikh al-Mohaisany is an example of how the Web poses a security challenge by conveying identities and reshaping perceptions. The file privately and individually delivers content that has global resonance. Trans-national ideological radicalism has of course previously existed, but messages were linked to states. The precedents for contemporary Islamic extremism were the global communist and fascist movements of the twentieth century. Those movements were transnational, ideological, and obviously not religious. They did not benefit from the extensity, intensity or velocity of modern IT or draw advantage from a global scene in which a variety of factors (from AIDS–SARS–Ebola to migration, stock markets, finance and technological exchange) mitigate the centrality of the state. The *du'a* appears in a context marked by IT, one in which nominal statehood but not substantive capacities for self-rule lead to a heterogeneity of global political forms, organizations and expressions. The context is one in which IT

> contribute to continuity in the areas of international security and in the world economy by enhancing the capabilities of states while at the same time they seem to be an element for change in these traditional areas by enhancing the capabilities of actors in the multicentric world.
>
> (Rosenau and Johnson 2002: 74)

In a post-realist setting, perceptions, values and intelligibility are no longer absolutely tied to hierarchical organization, territorial continuity and spatiality. The *du'a* takes advantage of the complexity and tensions of this context by drawing power from a multimedia presentation of photographs, audio text in Arabic, and English subtitles that directly aim at the viewer's perceptions. For an English-speaking viewer, the juxtaposition of photograph and caption[15] has a powerful impact because it plays on perceptions of power and allows a blurring of boundaries and identities in the absence of a prevailing meta-narrative. In this way, the file illustrates Benjamin and Sontag's view that photography's status as a mute, contentless image would be strongly enhanced by captions. The result is a performative artefact that idiosyncratically interprets Islam while transgressing the boundaries and identities of a state-based global security.

IT on the global scene: innovation, continuity and perception

Before the Internet, the IT–IR relationship was played out by telegraph, film, radio, video cassettes and television. The variety of contexts and practices that constitute this relationship suggest that media's impact is highly complex. The influence of television, for example, differs according to context and depends on many ingredients. A major consideration in evaluating global political impact of TV is its linkage to a constellation of factors, such as 'the type of policy in question' (Robinson 2002: 126). The influence of media is also conditioned by a complex global system in which various new players produce effects and broad transformations are underway (El-Nawawy and Iskandar 2002; Schechter 2003). The Internet platform is unique because it integrates existing technologies into a single medium in an accessible manner. Through platforms such as the Internet,

IT is an arena for '*imagined worlds*, that is, the multiple worlds that are constituted by the historically situated imaginations of persons and groups spread around the globe' (Appadurai 2003: 41). These imagined worlds are partly constituted by replacing *an audience that was inevitably passive and a recipient of messages* with a *potentially active-surfing public*. The transformation is highly relative since Internet access varies between global regions (e.g. next-to-no access in Africa versus high levels in North America, Japan and Western Europe). Even in US society, where the Internet is widely used, barriers to access and use persist, and provide an idea of the relative nature of the transformation. In the US, Katz and Rice

> identified three key barriers to Internet usage – cost, access, and complexity. Two of these – cost and access – were more strongly felt by nonusers, perhaps reflecting their lower incomes (ability to pay for the Internet) and educational achievements (ability to navigate the Internet). Most significantly, both users and nonusers were equally concerned about Internet complexity. Without improvements here, frustration levels will remain high, and potential user benefits will in many cases go unrealized.
>
> (2002: 322–3)

Outside the US, access differences are even more striking. In 2001, an OECD document noted that

> In 1997, more than 30 African countries had less than one telephone line per 100 people, according to OECD figures. It is not simply that the 'haves' are at an advantage, but that the 'have-nots' are at increasing risk of social and economic exclusion. Countries which lack a firm ICT infrastructure become marginalised as electronic commerce grows in importance. They are incapable of sharing in the new route to prosperity which e-commerce affords, and remain dependent on the export of basic commodities, for which the world price is often in decline. Africa's share of world trade has fallen from about 4% in 1980 to less than 2% today, according to IMF figures.
>
> (James, 14 January 2001)

These differences illustrate how today's IT practices reflect elites that have emerged as a result of the investments, skills, knowledge and infrastructures clustered around new communications platforms.

The Internet as an assembly of technological practices

Since technologies that support and encourage communication were key props in the processes of identity, state and imperial formation in the nineteenth and twentieth centuries, the extent and intensity of the penetration of contemporary IT suggest qualitative uniqueness. The Internet's impacts that might include enhanced participation and better government services to information overload and precipitous decision-making. Given that the Internet platform integrates a wide array of separate technological practices (radio, TV, databases, computers, email, chats, photography and so forth) and has only recently emerged, its paradoxical impacts on the global scene are still incompletely apprehended. Attitudes toward the varying 'truth-values' conveyed by IT can also be expected to change as societies grow accustomed to the latter's presence. Societies and individuals are still by-and-large in a process of experiential engagement with new IT and only beginning what will undoubtedly be an ongoing assessment of its impacts and limits. For this reason, this discussion draws on previous technologies that are integrated into the Internet. Photography, for example, is a widely used and highly visible component of the Web. It is also a controversial and ambiguous practice in which 'the press tends to play down the way it uses digital imaging techniques in photojournalism, since it recognizes that electronic retouching of imagery destroys the documentary value of witnessing' (Taylor 1998: 64). In this light, the claim that a new IT practice provides authentic and immediate representation of individual and social realities is better contextualized by remembering that communicative flexibility actually detracts from truth-value in the resulting artefacts.

Pre-Internet communication is also influential, especially since text-based IT elicits different responses from photographic images. The difference reflects a cultural mindset that values written expression of scientific, spiritual and intellectual experiences. It also expresses the status of text as a medium that is closely linked to quantifiable and rational discourse. The mindset devalues images and places words in a privileged position nearer a purported truth. It is activated, when email and website information are more readily viewed as authentic expression, that must be protected from interference by so-called hackers. In contrast, photos are seen as inherently *unstable indicators of value*. In fact, while website text defacement and interference with email transmission are episodically annoying, their impacts are usually contained and not system-threatening. Given this mindset, the impact of IT on IR obviously varies if image or text is the communicative focus. While a

> popular notion has it that as images became increasingly sophisticated, their power grew … the opposite may be the case. As images become more complex and multimediated, their truth-value is communicated in configurations that allow us to see less: in some cases it dissipates; in others it is reconfigured; in still others it completely disappears. Proclaimed vehicles by which we bear witness to events of the present and past, images in some cases become deceptively ambivalent, communicating contradictory messages about their ability to replicate slices of reality and their ability to aggressively reconstruct it, often to the point of fabrication.
>
> (Zelizer 1998: 215)

If contemporary IT is to fulfil the promise of immediate and authentic communication and enhance global security by lowering thresholds of conflict, producing more effective economic practices, and leading to the greater inter-state cooperation, such ambiguity needs to be overcome. As it stands, cultural ambivalence toward photographic practices suggests that today's integrated IT have less straightforward sets of impacts. As in the example of TV, the impact of today's IT might depend on a constellation of factors. On the other hand, if ambivalence is a long-term impact of IT, it could introduce a beneficial element of doubt into the certainties of statecraft, war and IR in general. Heated debate over proof for the existence of weapons of mass destruction before the Iraq War did not prevent conflict, but global dissemination of information regarding the issue cast serious doubt on simplistic notions of 'threat' and 'enemies' that underlie our concepts of security.

Complex practices and global complexity

Ambivalence, doubt, influence and truth-value combine to centre an assessment of the IT–IR relationship on complexity and a transformative global scene. Saskia Sassen argues 'the ascendance of an international human rights regime and of a large variety of nonstate actors in the international arena signals the expansion of an international civil society' (Sassen 1998: 99). James Rosenau concurs that 'an endless series of distant proximities in which the forces pressing for greater globalization and those inducing greater localization interactively play themselves out' (Rosenau 2003: 4). Arjun Appadurai refers to 'the complexity of the current global economy [that] has to do with certain fundamental disjunctures between economy, culture, and politics that we have only begun to theorize' (Appadurai 2003: 41). Each formulation suggests that IT-driven media, rather than relegated to the ghetto of culture–propaganda–superstructure, are a facilitator of global civil society, 'essential to the projection of influence and the mobilization of public opinion' (Hampson 2002: 74). The IT–media–global civil society relationship highlights complexity, extensity and theoretical challenges.

The globally dominant Western or Westphalian tradition of politics set terms of reference for Louis XIV and his military architect Sébastien le Prestre de Vauban. They resolved France's lack of defensible and coherent boundaries by building a series of fortifications that traced (with some subsequent alterations) the contours of what we know as the French nation-state.[16] The creation of France exemplifies how the principle of territoriality, or exclusive control of a set physical space by one governance apparatus, was implemented. The Westphalian model dominates IR research insofar as the basis for political power is always a defined physical space in which control or pretence of control (that is, 'sovereignty') is exercised. Political groups in this model always focus on criticism of, competition for, and control of the administration of states. This model, its export to the rest of the world via imperialism, and the intended and unintended consequences mark IR and global security since the seventeenth century.[17] However, contemporary IT exists in a global scene in which politics as a matter of territorial location is challenged. Since 1989, the global community has moved from a bipolar world order into a system of fragmented multi-centric concentrations in which state power co-exists with non-state actors such as international organizations, NGOs, media, multinational corporations, the nascent governments of Palestine, northern Iraq and Kosovo, and the failed states of Pakistan, Somalia and Indonesia. The variety of political forms in the system has profound consequences for nation-states, nationalism, and the global system because they effectively transgress and blur territorial boundaries (Kearny 1997).

Westphalian IR is based in a conceptually clear demarcation of boundaries for individual and state activities. These boundaries are both identarian and physical territories in which sovereignty is exercised. The identity component of Westphalian security encompasses both groups and individuals. Group identities derive cohesiveness, organization and language from their relationship to the state. Individual identities embody the lived reality of a political society and are the contents of politics insofar as individuals live, love, work and play in a secure and safe daily understanding of themselves and their environment. IT affects Westphalian identities because it carries information that can inform, disinform, alarm, soothe, motivate, agitate and impel. IT shapes identities through the Internet platforms that are 'a part of syntopia, a together place that allows people to pursue their interests but that is also a continuity of other parts of their lives, including their technology of communication, such as the mobile phone' (Katz and Rice 2002: 352). As such, Web-based media influences IR precisely through enabling individuals and groups to pursue interests, 'live lives', and validate perceptions. The influence extends far since IT does 'not impact existing actors and issues but, as an increasing body of knowledge notes, networked interaction itself constitutes actors and issues in global politics' (Singh 2002: 12). The effect is a dramatic and discrete alteration of the state and identarian bases of the Westphalian model.

Although the Internet suggests that cultural novelty and technological innovation are at the heart of the IT–IR relationship, we know that communication has a history. The telegraph, for example, was an innovation that facilitated European imperialism and helped consolidate global dominance. Seen as such, contemporary IT is part of a bundle of the globalizing practices of imperialism that also include military organization and legal codification. These practices are now embedded in the structure of global civil society along with all their contradictory implications (primarily seen as 'underdevelopment' of certain world regions and 'advanced' status for others). The specific impact of IT is paradoxical in an age in which overwhelming economic, technological and military assets do not lead to conflict resolution and fail to definitively structure perceptions. The Web's role in this context is both communicative and representational. Its value in relation to power is undercutting a view of politics as an ability to be physically present, occupy space, and define a place. As an electronic means of communication, the Web seems a priori facultative since it is 'flat', that is, it does not encompass the depth of human relations, only their breadth (in Katz and Rice's terms, it 'supports and encourages'). To explore the impact of IT thus entails reconsidering the notion of power at the base of this assessment.

A messenger that shapes perceptions: IT practices and global security

The power of non-state actors on the global scene evinces complexity outside of any discussion of IT. Non-state actors range from terrorist organizations such as Al-Qaeda to movements that focus on human rights, anti-globalization, the environment, AIDS, and many other issues. One non-state actor, the Raëlian movement, even claims to have cloned human beings, which usurps another area from state control: management of procreation. The presence of so many tendencies on the global scene means that it is now accurate to speak of a *post-realist global scene* in which *global politics are no longer a state prerogative in spite of the fact that, paradoxically, states remain the single most important agents of international power*. Even the conditions for US global action have changed.[18] The US, of course, retains enormous capacities for decisive surgical action, but appears increasingly unable to definitively control the course of global events in directions that meet its goals. In spite of enormous technological, economic, and military advance over all other players, the US is not clearly a hegemonic power that directs the internal affairs of other states, controls the international pattern of alliances, and dictates international economic arrangements. The limits on the single most powerful global actor underline how all states' abilities to act and influence events are now uneven.

The *constraining binds of post-realism* can be seen in the Afghan and the Palestinian–Israeli conflicts. In both settings, powerful states have surgically displaced and marginalized opponents, but not ended chronic violence nor satisfactorily addressed underlying social grievances. In addition, 9/11 marked the global scene by attesting to the transnational reach of organized violence by non-state actors. The shift affected conflict, security, and the centrality of the state in world affairs in a key manner linked to the coercive monopoly of the Westphalian-Leviathan form of state,

> The contours of these 'new wars' are distinctive in many respects because the range of social and political groups involved no longer fit the pattern of a classical interstate war; the type of violence deployed by the terrorist aggressors is no longer carried out by the agents of a state (although states, or parts of states, may have a supporting role); violence is dispersed, fragmented and directed against citizens; and political aims are combined with the deliberate commission of atrocities which are a massive violation of human rights.
>
> (Held, 5 November 2001)

Before being turned on New York City and Washington, DC, sustained global organized violence by non-state actors was already manifest in attacks on the USS *Cole* and US Embassy in Kenya. It continued in attacks in Bali, Indonesia and Mombassa, Kenya in late 2002. The violence has eclipsed the management approach and rhetoric of the 1990s with apocalyptic visions and language: US president George Bush refers to 'evildoers' and the 'axis of evil'; Israelis speak of the survival of a Jewish state; Palestinians and Chechens tolerate strategies of suicide bombings; and, Al-Qaeda continues a methodical and murderous programme designed to discredit the West. As the *du'a* shows, states have diminished control over the contents of IT that conveys apocalyptic messages and shapes perceptions.

Identity and representation in global security

Global communication devices have a political potential that is like eBay by comparison to the vendor–kiosk–location model based in the state. *IT suggests that actual power is relatively less defined by physical location and that territorial contiguity might be less able to actually influence the shapes of future human relations.* The potential has been hailed as the triumph of value, interests and beliefs over physical location. However, in light of the myriad military, financial, political, and other contexts in which it appears, IT more likely expresses a hybrid form of politics in which physical location is one factor among a selection of many influences on the outcome of events. The reported links between 9/11, websites, cell phones, and satellite communication moreover suggest that the values, interests and beliefs carried by IT will not usher in a digitopia. The latter vision presumes that human beings take up IT bereft of a history that is smeared by hatred and violence as much as reason and love. Evidence for this more sober assessment is readily seen in the hate, racism and misogyny on the Web.

File transfers and websites exemplify how unregulated Web communication by non-state actors in the post-realist world alters the boundaries of political society and identities. Web activism is based in image and text-based representation that communicates a post-territorial politics that transgresses identity, space, and the legitimation capacities of states like the US. It does so in two distinct manners: *while websites tend to inform, multimedia files lend themselves to a dramatic representation of events.* By combining text and images, websites offer allegedly immediate and authentic information from specific groups to global civil society. In contrast, multimedia more directly addresses the viewer's emotions and morality. When artefacts like the *du'a* express a sense of grievance and injustice rather than set out a programme, multimedia activism is strongly symbolic, image-driven and identarian rather than ideological. Artefacts such as the *du'a* are heavily representational, and draw their power from an ability to present a coherent view of reality that uses words to shape the perception of images.

The enhanced importance of representation and identity in Web activism expresses a shift across a range of political phenomena and raises the issue of how to characterize the change. Is the change in technologies of representation a deep (fundamental) or extensive (wide-ranging) transformation? Will the shift produce new elites and new rigidities? An examination of RAWA, the MRTA and IRSM Web activism as well as the *du'a* suggests that IT do indeed transform global politics, but in ways and to an extent that is more modest than initially apparent. The *du'a* shows how the shaping of perceptions and identities by multimedia activism has been privatized since it is a practice through which global issues are communicated on an individual basis. Web activists *do* have an impact, but do not overthrow states or necessarily even redirect public policies. The change might be tentatively characterized as wide-ranging rather than deep. Web activism occurs globally, but has not directly resulted in conventional political change (i.e. new governments or new constitutions) to date. Instead of a tool for revolutionary transformation, Web activism is a powerful new method for political organizations of all stripes in precise circumstances that favour their messages.

To characterize the transformation and its consequences, this discussion has moved beyond a description of networks to explore the impacts of technology and new media as a representational form. This analysis situates IT as not merely a messenger, but as *a messenger that shapes perceptions*. Shaping perceptions is done in distinct ways that depend on what IT is used. Since Web technology in fact integrates several previous communication practices, it is logical to integrate evaluations of those IT into an assessment of the new digital age. One such assessment are Sontag's writings on photography, which note that the photographic images are mute and have 'multiple meanings; indeed, to see something in the form of a photograph is to encounter a potential object of fascination' (Sontag 2001: 23). Another example is Paul Dourish, who argues that computers have a specific impact on how humans use them since their design 'favours performance over convenience, and places a premium on the computer's time rather than people's time' (Dourish 2001: 2). Sontag and Dourish point to the communicative limits of media and the technical limits of devices that contrast widespread unease over the allegedly limitless possibilities and boundless threats of technological innovation.

Conclusion: photographic practice and Web activism in global security

The Web activism of the MRTA, RAWA and IRSM as well as the multimedia *du'a* of Sheikh Mohammed al-Mohaisany exemplify the wide range of IT practices available to non-state actors on the global scene and point to a complex set of impacts. To analyse this rich diversity, the discussion adapted theoretical frameworks to specific IT, investigated groups that use specific IT practices, and assessed the impact in select cases. The discussion shows how IR must 'read', describe and interpret political content on the Web and in multimedia as it learned to read newspapers, listen to the radio and watch TV after the initial thrill of communicativeness passed.[19] The substantial complexity of post-realism is a context in which groups like the MRTA, RAWA and the IRSM and supporters of Al-Qaeda operate with varying degrees and measures of success. The Web activists discussed here struggle against very different opponents. They have little in common beyond using IT to send messages to global civil society and fail to produce conventional institutional-governmental results. Paradoxically, each case shows how IT profoundly impacts events by transgressing, re-articulating and re-shaping the boundaries of identities, power, and security. This impact is enhanced by a global scene marked by variable layers of authority, action and power, which Rosenau calls a 'bifurcation' between state-centric and multi-centric forms of international action (1990: 11). Web activism is a new area of IR that centres on *security of perceptions and intelligibility, form of security based in our ability to be persons: to project a sense of ourselves and our values into the world, to be who we are, and become who we want to be.*

The impact of photographic practices

This discussion of the relationship of IT to IR refers to Web activism to show how the Internet platform draws together existing technological practices (such as photography, television, data processing and others) in ways that transgress the identities and representations that are the bases of state-centric global security. The analysis 'unpacked' some features of specific types of IT in order to integrate insights regarding their impact. A path for continued analysis is examination of the component practices of the Internet platform, such as photography, television and computers as well as graphic design. Photography is instructive, since it is a technological practice that traditionally divides those who argue that photographers should intrude into the world and those who seek to efface their presence from images. The debate is based in the Western tradition of representation, a tradition in which a notion of self-effacement underlies the view that images can present 'authenticity' and 'accurate' views of reality.

Self-effacement in photo-magazines such as *Paris Match* and *Life* purportedly portrays 'daily life' in a specific period, presents a record of events, and provides photo-documentation. Photographs in magazine formats often become images that *mark* particular historical events or periods. Photo-narration has long had a role in fostering support for military campaigns.[20] In this context, self-effacement has served to enhance nationally based notions of power and security. On the Web, photographic and video images purportedly present an infinite range of values, ideas, causes, and situations. The context is a social formation called the information society, which reproduces existing practices on a massive scale on a 'global landscape'. Yet, as one observer notes in relation to satellite television is that 'while "global village"-inspired rhetoric touted the utopian promise of new satellite technology, it was complicit with Western discourses of development that worked to subjugate non-Western and postcolonial cultures and peoples' (Parks 2003: 89). The reproduction of discourses and practices means that while new IT explicitly refers to global values, its also risks favouring some groups or regions over others, both in how it operates and resulting perceptions of the world. Paradoxically, photography is also relatively uncoupled from states. The *du'a* shows how one group used the environment to reconfigure perceptions of photos through adding captions that transgress state-centric identities and representations.

Image, influence and identity

Globalization is a cultural, economic, technological, social, demographic and military process that produces new transformative combinations of human relations. It brings new groups, ideas, values, interests and forces into a global network of contact and conflict.[21] Web activism is one site where values are introduced, debated, and contested. While Brecht hoped that radio (and other media) would foster authentic human relations, our lived experience of politics is still very much marked by images, copies, representations and appearances. 'Reality' and 'image' are not neatly separated. Images still overtake reality. As the US stumbled into an Iraqi conflict with profound consequences in 2003, an obsessive focus on the image of terrorism contaminated the highest levels of defence and foreign policy thought and planning. The results are a focus on the so-called 'axis of evil', failure to capture Al-Qaeda mastermind Bin Laden and Taliban leader Mohammed Omar, continued Afghan chaos and insecurity, and explosive violence in the Middle East.

Global security is not enhanced if challenges are met in purely military terms at a time when conflict is multilayered, and ever more innovative, representational, perceptual and image-based. Web activism shows how contemporary conflict occurs far from a battlefield, in a media setting in which the US rapidly lost the moral-emotional advantage it had on 9/11 (The Pew Research Center, 4 December 2002). In this environment, the Web accelerates and intensifies transgression, reshapes and transforms the boundaries of identity and politics, especially since 'the instant we develop a new technology of communication – talking drums, papyrus scrolls, books, telegraph, radios, televisions, computers, mobile phones – we at least partially reconstruct the self and its world, creating new opportunities for reflection, perception, and social experience' (Burnett and Marshall 2003: 61). It is in the context of a battle over perceptions that the impact of IT on IR can be measured. The evaluation needs to be conducted in a variety of ways since the impacts are in fact a diverse body of content.

Notes

* An earlier version of this article has been published as 'Weapons of Mass Instruction: Web Activism and the Transformation of Global Security', *Millennium*, 2003, vol. 32, no. 3, pp. 477–99.
1 This specific multimedia file will be referred to as the '*du'a*' for the remainder of the discussion.
2 The lack of attention accorded to identity issues is not reflective of research on the implications of IT. See, for example, Turkle (1995).
3 Given that the perpetrator of these attacks was a US citizen, the incident simultaneously points to the globalizing and privatizing impacts of IT on security. See BBC News (13 June 2003).
4 Meikle defines hacktivism as electronic 'political resistance' rather than terrorism (p. 41).
5 Another group that I have examined, the Electronic Intifada, is presently active in the Middle East. I do not include this group in this analysis since the research is ongoing.
6 For a complete discussion, see Dartnell (1999).
7 For a complete discussion, see Dartnell (2001).
8 For a complete discussion, see Dartnell (2003).

9 The Taliban had a website, where a hacker posted porn, denounced Islamic fundament-
   alism, and left a Russian email address in August 2001 at http://www. taleban.com.
10 See USA Patriot Act HR 3162 (Uniting and Strengthening America by Providing
   Appropriate Tools Required to Intercept and Obstruct Terrorism (USA PATRIOT
   ACT) Act of 2001). In late February 2004, an English-language version of the
   'MRTA Solidarity Page' is no longer available on the Web. However, Japanese,
   Italian, Spanish and Serbo-Croat versions were readily available, further illustrating
   the difficulties in controlling information on the Web.
11 Shockwave   is   a   standard   software   technology   available   at   http://www.
   macromedia.com.
12 The URL for the website that posted the file is http://www.citylinkcomputers.com.
13 I would like to thank Mr Mohammed Zigby, a PhD candidate in Islamic Studies at
   McGill University, for his assistance in examining the multimedia file of the *du'a* and
   verifying the contents of the audio recording.
14 Benjamin stated that:

> photographs become the standard evidence for historical occurrences, and acquire
> a hidden political significance. They demand a specific kind of approach; free-
> floating contemplation is not appropriate to them. They stir the viewer; he feels
> challenged by them in a new way. At the same time picture magazines begin to
> put up signposts for him, right ones or wrong ones, no matters. For the first time,
> captions have become obligatory. And it is clear that they have an altogether dif-
> ferent character than the title of a painting.
>
> (Benjamin 1977: 228)

15 For a discussion of the interaction of caption/text and photograph, see (Sontag 2001:
   107–8).
16 These frontiers are seen, for example, in the fortresses built at Lille in the north and
   Bellegarde in Rousillon.
17 This discussion will refer to globalization as defined by Held *et al.* (1999: 16) as:

> a process (or set of processes) which embodies a transformation in the spatial
> organization of social relations and transaction – assessed in terms of their exten-
> sity, intensity, velocity and impact – generating transcontinental or interregional
> flows and networks of activity, interaction, and the exercise of power.

18 This new set of circumstances was widely commented on as the Clinton administration made some moves toward multilateralism (e.g. in Bosnia, Kosovo etc.). The
   advent of the Bush administration and the events of 9/11 seemed momentarily to shift
   the system back to realism, but the necessity of a recourse to the UN Security Council
   and the return of a UN monitoring presence to Iraq in late 2002 suggest that US
   action is no longer simply a matter of capacity, but of concertation.
19 For a discussion of the complex impacts of television and globalization, see Parks and
   Kumar (2003).
20 See, for example, Roger Fenton and James Robertson's photographs of the Crimean
   War, Felice Beato's images of the 1860 Anglo-French expeditionary force that
   invaded China, or the American Civil War photographs of Alexander Gardner, James
   Gibson, George Barnard, Andrew Russell, Timothy O'Sullivan, and Thomas Roche
   in Therese Mulligan and David Wooters (2002).
21 See, for example, Yuri the Yaba (2001: 56). Yabasta's vision is:

> post-ideological, and that's its innovative potential: it privileges strategies and
> specific actions, rather than affiliating with a historically burdened tradition.
> Yabasta practices direct action without sectarian divisions and does not try to
> decide what kind of change each community may want – they can organize and
> decide for themselves. It has no formal structure; we dress up to protect and
> support each other to become a critical mass.

6 The laws of the playground

Information warfare and propaganda across the Taiwan Strait[1]

Gary D. Rawnsley

> Ideas and myths can kill, and their manipulation by elite leaders for their own material benefits does not change the fact that in order to operate they first have to be implanted in the souls of men.
>
> (Prunier 1995: 40)

The Taiwan Strait[2] is, together with the Korean Demilitarised Zone (another left-over from the Cold War) one of the twenty-first century's most dangerous political and military hotspots. Taipei and Beijing are preparing for war against each other – Taiwan to maintain its democratic status and resist absorption into the People's Republic of China (PRC), Beijing to fulfil its manifest destiny of unifying China once and for all and to repel any moves towards *de jure* independence by the 'renegade province' Taiwan. China and Taiwan use annual military exercises to simulate the war that each is trying to avoid in the Strait; China has over 600 missiles in Fujian province pointed at the island, while the May 2007 Han Kuang 23 exercise revealed that Taiwan has developed its own offensive military capacity to attack targets on the Chinese mainland. Further, both sides are also compelled to consider the role of the United States that recognises but one China and calls for a peaceful settlement to the Taiwan issue, but also acknowledges Taiwan's right to defend itself in the event of attack by its neighbour. The Seventh Fleet, America's naval presence in the Pacific, has been used on more than one occasion to send a symbolic message to Beijing and Taipei that conflict will not be tolerated and that the US is prepared to intervene in the eventuality of war in the Taiwan Strait. So, given the apparent attention to conventional military hardware and strategies, what role does information warfare play?

Computer-based information warfare – 'cyberwar' – is judged in both Beijing and Taipei as an acceptable way of maintaining a state of hostility without having to launch a military attack. In my opinion cyberwar plays a role in the Taiwan Strait conflict that is comparable to the nuclear arsenals that defined the US–Soviet Cold War, namely acting as a deterrent but with the possibility that it may be deployed as part of an offensive or defensive strategy. Cyberwar offers the prospect of a fast and (relatively) painless victory should hot war break out, and this characteristic of information warfare is absolutely essential in a conflict that the Chinese government packages and sells to its people as a family feud. It is therefore not surprising that on both sides of the Taiwan Strait generous funding is invested in designing and creating new military structures, security architectures, training programmes and technology that promise to take advantage of each society's increasing dependence on vulnerable computer networks[3] and thus facilitate offensive and defensive information warfare (Finkelstein 1999; Office of the US Secretary of Defense, 26 February 1999; Wang 1995; Mulvenon 1999: 175–86; DPP Policy Committee 1999).

Assessments of China's information warfare capabilities vary. The first date given by Taiwan's Ministry of Defense for a possible Chinese cyberattack was 2010; that estimate was subsequently revised to 2005; and in 2000 General Lin Chi-cheng of Taiwan's Communications, Electronics and Information Bureau described how China was already far more prepared than Taiwan to launch an information offensive. How reliable are these estimates? The main argument presented here and elaborated in the following discussion is that while China has obvious reasons to inflate its own capacity to wage information warfare, Taiwan too may exaggerate the threat from China for its own strategic and political purposes. The discourse *about* information warfare *becomes part of* the information warfare strategy, and this chapter will propose that information warfare is both a valuable method and a prominent theme of propaganda. As yet there is no convincing evidence to indicate beyond reasonable doubt that either Taiwan or China does have the ability to launch a cyberattack against the other. Rather, all attempts have so far been limited to the relatively innocuous 'hacking' of Internet sites which can have profoundly psychological consequences. In short, there is no serious attempt to associate such violations of computer security to military scenarios, suggesting that the perceived threat from cyberattack is (perhaps deliberately) disproportionate to the levels of attention and investment devoted to it on both sides of the Taiwan Strait.

Theoretical framework

A state-centred approach offers a valuable means of understanding the integration of information warfare within a military and security architecture that is designed around the essentially realist principles of balances of power and the maximisation of state interests. As the politics of Asia continues to demonstrate, strategic competition between states for territory, resources and status continues to provide the core motivation for disagreement. Moreover, it is impossible to overlook the importance of the state when addressing issues of information warfare because the state controls the region's militaries and decides their investment and procurement strategies.

But a state-centred approach will only take us so far. It is not so helpful in understanding how information warfare broadens beyond the state the range of actors involved, or in appreciating how information warfare reveals a taxonomy of threats which includes, but extends beyond, the realist concept of 'national security'. Finally, this approach has difficulty grasping the diminishing relevance of spatial and temporal constraints on the behaviour of actors and regimes. For a more nuanced understanding of information warfare it is appropriate to embrace the so-called Critical Security approach to international relations and security which challenges the idea that military survival and national security are primary motivating interests, and contests the opinion that the unitary state is the only relevant actor. Critical Security provides for the 'extended security' which Alan Dupont (2001: 8) discussed and incorporates in its framework the 'non-state actors that challenge the state's traditional monopoly over taxation and organised violence'.

Moreover, the Critical Security approach is appropriate because it allows us to recognise how information warfare demolishes the boundaries between military and societal autonomy, and between peace and war (Johnson 1997). It offers the framework for understanding that a concerted cyberattack will cause massive disruption to any society that is dependent on computer networks, especially transport, energy supply and communications infrastructures (Dibb 1997). This conforms to Ole Waever's description of Critical Security as an approach that accommodates 'the ability of a society to persist in its essential character under changing conditions and possible or actual threats' (Waever *et al.* 1993: 23). Because it is largely invisible and targets a society's dependency on computer networks, information warfare does have the capacity to present a considerable threat to a society's 'essential character'. Thus the threat to Taiwan is clear: China could, if its claims are credible, launch a cyberattack against Taiwan that deliberately targets its economic, social and military infrastructures and therefore lays the foundations for a major national crisis. This may then (though not necessarily) expose Taiwan to attack by more conventional sources, such as the People's Liberation Army Navy (PLAN) or Airforce (PLAAF):[4] a 'unified information warfare campaign can be conducted alongside multiple concurrent or consecutive combat operations, can extend beyond the immediate battlefield, can cross the boundaries between peacetime, crisis, and combat' (Johnson 1997). Likewise the Kuang 23 military exercises demonstrated the assimilation of information warfare strategies by Taiwan's military into planning for an offensive operation against the Chinese mainland that would disrupt the PLA's invasion plans.

So to summarise: information warfare draws our attention to how national security is no longer synonymous with state security, and the Critical Security approach provides a framework in which a new catalogue of threats are presented against actors who can be both victims and aggressors. This approach also suggests that information is a political, military and social resource that can today affect the conduct of international relations as never before, for it has little regard for political or geographic boundaries. Moreover, information is increasingly outside the state's purview (Matthews 1997; Keohane and Nye 1989, 2000). In this way the association between security and such concepts as sovereignty and state autonomy diminishes.

Propaganda, psychological warfare and information warfare

Critical Security approaches to international relations rest on the premise that the perception of security is socially constructed, and in particular that it is inseparable from the creation of identity (of the self and the 'other') (Wendt 1999; Johnston 1995; Alagappa 1998). And this is fundamental to understanding the relationship between propaganda and information warfare, for most propaganda turns on creating a clear dichotomy between the self and the 'other'. It may also lean on specific interpretations of national history to strengthen claims that the 'other' is somewhat inferior or threatening to self-identity.

This has been especially important in modern Chinese history where the political discourse is rooted in the theme of historical 'victimhood', allowing the state and nation to construct a distinctly modernist reading of national identity:

> The territorial dismemberment of the country, the humiliation of a proud state by an avalanche of 'unequal treaties' and the dislocating tensions added to existing internal forces of disorder represent a powerful *leitmotif* of subordination, resentment and anger in nineteenth- and twentieth-century Chinese social commentary and political discourse.
>
> (Renwick and Cao 2003: 63)

The Opium Wars and the Unequal Treaties, the return of Hong Kong and Macao to the Chinese 'motherland', the Japanese occupation of China and the atrocities committed at that time, the anti-Japanese demonstrations of April 2005 and the continuing effort to integrate Taiwan into China all demonstrate the value of victimhood as a political discourse of popular mobilisation.

Taiwan too has designed specific themes to serve its anti-Chinese propaganda, packaged in the familiar rhetoric of the Cold War. Until 2000 the Republic of China on Taiwan maintained it was 'Free China', a simple juxtaposition with the 'unfree' PRC. The Chinese communists were routinely lambasted as 'gangsters', 'traitors', 'reds', and even 'the sons of Satan'[5], while even today Taiwan is still labelled in the Chinese media the 'renegade province', and the President is always referred to as either the 'so-called President' or 'President' to emphasise China's scorn for Taiwan's democratic system.

Such propaganda across the Taiwan Strait serves a symbolic and long-term political agenda, and since 1945 has acted as a dependable alternative to the outbreak of military conflict. Even the limited military activity that erupted in 1954 and 1958 had greater propaganda and political than strategic and military value: the fact that Taiwan and China fought over two outlying islands rather than Taiwan itself is noteworthy for it acknowledges the possibility of all-out war without actually committing the militaries to the ultimate prize. Moreover, until 1979 the shelling of these islands and the mainland in response occurred to a strict timetable and usually involved nothing more harmful than printed propaganda that was scattered on impact (Rawnsley 2000).

The continuing propaganda struggle across the Taiwan Strait is a form of information warfare that has enjoyed modest success beyond the recurrent exchange of political symbolism and rhetoric. However, it has helped to contain the conflict for the past fifty years; and we should not neglect how propaganda and psychological warfare, when carefully integrated into the political and military decision-making process, can be an indispensable instrument of warfare (Taylor 1996). Their problem, however, is their lack of precision, for propaganda has tended to pursue mass audiences through media of mass communications – radio, television, the movies etc. It is therefore by extension incredibly difficult to measure the impact of this propaganda: how do we know for certain that radio and television broadcasts can and do change the opinions or behaviour of the target audience?

Computer networks are therefore a significant new approach to information warfare because they can circumvent the problems associated with traditional propaganda and psychological warfare. Computer technology allows for:

- precise targeting of the message;
- measurement of the effects of the message;
- the possibility of causing social disruption;
- without violating the non-violent aspirations of propaganda (it is preferable to persuade your enemy to capitulate than force them to do so through violence).
- A greater degree of anonymity: anyone with access to a computer, a modem and the World Wide Web has the potential to be a cyberwarrior regardless of citizenship or residency.

Internet chatrooms, discussion groups and our growing dependence on email as our primary means of communication allow customised news and information to be delivered to our personal computers, laptops or mobile phones wherever we are in the world. This means that psychological operations can now target specific members of the desired audience via networked computers in a way that more traditional forms of propaganda could only imagine. At its most extreme, computer technology provides the capacity to launch 'semantic attacks' whereby an external actor is able to control a system that appears to insiders to be working correctly. This may, for example, involve distorting television images, delivering misleading signals and/or the spread of black propaganda (Freedman 1998: 56). Richard Szafranski ran with this idea and came up with the term 'neocortical warfare', meaning the ability to control the shape and behaviour of 'enemy organisms, but without destroying the organism' (Szafranski 1994: 41–55) – which brings us back to the idea of information warfare threatening Waever's 'essential character' of society. If the focus of neocortical warfare would be, Lawrence Freedman suggests, 'on enemy minds rather than capabilities' (Freedman 1998: 56) then computers are extremely valuable additions to the arsenal of propaganda and psychological warfare techniques.

This process is given sharper focus by the architecture of the information age, in which separate and previously autonomous units are integrated into a highly structured network that is connected by computer systems (Arquilla and Ronfeldt

1997; Harknett 1996: 93–107). This structure represents a new form of horizontal organisation that is less dependent on functional hierarchies and centralised decision-making; hence, what is known as 'strategic information warfare' (Molander *et al.* 1996) is designed to infect the network, and disrupt society's ability to remain connected and thus function efficiently (attacking its 'essential character'). This architecture makes it more rational to attack non-military targets in an effort to paralyse the nation-state system, especially its decision-making structure and process. Cyberattacks that assault the flows of information with the aim of confusing, delaying, manipulating, and/or paralysing the enemy's capacity to function will disrupt the quality of decision-making and thus the society's capacity to respond to the attack (Singh, 31 January 2006).

China's information warfare capacity

The 1991 war against Iraq and its invasion of Kuwait was a wake-up call for the Chinese military. Watching, along with the rest of the world, the first 'live' television war the Chinese could see the PLA's inferiority to American military technology, raising the spectre of 'asymmetric warfare' in any future conflict with the US. The Gulf War – described by the PLA as the 'epitome' of information warfare[6] – provoked the Chinese military to assess its implications and learn from its application, concluding that

> (a) modern war is high-tech war, and technology can not only fulfil tactical and combat missions but can also fulfil strategic objectives; (b) regional warfare can serve as a viable means for political resolution and render large-scale warfare unnecessary; (c) the existence of high-tech weapon systems holds out the possibility of 'quick resolution' by conducting long-distance, high power, and precision attacks; and (d) high-tech weapon systems have changed the needs of force composition and resulted in new types of combined operation.
>
> (Andrew *et al.* 1999: 49)[7]

These conclusions were apparently justified by the PLA's belief in information warfare having played a decisive role in the coalition's victory, even speculating that the US military had deployed computer viruses to disrupt Iraq's information systems (*Jiefangjun bao*, 25 June 1996: 6; Liu, 6 August 1993).

Greater attention within the PLA to information warfare led to the development of a new strategy: Local War Under High Technology Conditions [*gao jishu tiaojian xia jubu zhanzheng*].[8] Wang Pufeng, the PLA's leading information warfare expert, integrated information warfare with the new strategy. 'In the near future', he wrote in 1995,

> information warfare will control the form and future of war. We recognize this developmental trend of information warfare and see it as a driving force in the modernization of China's military and combat readiness. This trend will by highly critical to achieving victory in future wars.
>
> (Wang 1995)

In a future Taiwan Strait conflict the primary target of Chinese attack is likely to be the US military. The key to PLA success will be subduing Taiwan as quickly as possible and before US forces are deployed or preventing US involvement prior to the first strike. Hence information warfare might be crucial for the Chinese in launching a pre-emptive strike against US information targets to delay or disrupt the American response:

> For the PLA, using IW against US forces to Taiwan offers an attractive asymmetric strategy. American forces are highly information-dependent. ... If PLA information operators ... were able to hack or crash these systems, thereby delaying the arrival of a US carrier battle group to the theater, while simultaneously carrying out a coordinated campaign of short-range ballistic missile attacks, 'fifth column,' and IW attacks against Taiwanese critical infrastructure, then Taipei must be quickly brought to its knees and forced to capitulate to Beijing.
>
> (Mulvenon 1999)

It is not surprising, therefore, that the US Department of Defense claims to have evidence that China is creating computer viruses and is developing strategies to use them against the computer systems of potential adversaries (Office of the US Secretary of Defense, 26 February 1999). Intelligence about information warfare simulation centres, military exercises involving virus attacks (Beijing initiated the first cyber warfare military exercises in 2005) and hacking into computer systems (claims that in 1997 'Beijing conducted exercises in Nanjing and Beijing using computer viruses to interrupt broadcasting systems and military communications systems'. Asia Pacific Network Information Centre 1999), and the development of computer-based psychological warfare has prompted foreign militaries to take seriously China's growing capacity to wage information warfare (Thomas 2000; Wang and Zhang 2000). In 2000 the American Department of Defense noted: 'China has the capability to penetrate poorly protected US computer systems and potentially could use [computer networks] to attack specific civilian and military infrastructures' (Lemon 2007). Moreover, the Pentagon is described as 'concerned' because 'cyberspace is the one domain where the Chinese can challenge US dominance' (*Aviation and Aerospace* 2007).

Most recently we have evidence that China is using new communications technologies to gather intelligence on foreign governments. In August 2007 *Der Spiegel* reported that German security experts had discovered the Chinese military had planted spying software – disguised as Microsoft applications such as Word and PowerPoint – in the computer networks of German government departments including the Foreign Ministry, the Research and Development Ministry, the Economics Ministry and the Chancellor's office. Such intelligence operations, conducted without the problems associated with human intelligence gathering, will be a significant factor in any future conflict and will be an appreciable addition to the military's planning process. But are we seriously suggesting that only the Chinese do this, or are we really saying they are the only ones to get caught?

As I complete this chapter in September 2007 my Google Alert for 'Information Warfare' is working serious overtime. Every day, new stories about China pop into my email inbox, recounting tales of how the Chinese have hacked into not only the German Ministry of Foreign Affairs, but also Whitehall, the Pentagon and Australian and New Zealand government agencies:

> The Pentagon cyber attack was particularly disquieting, apparently, as it involved not just passive snooping, but disruption of networks as well. The [*Financial Times*] quoted a former official as saying that: 'The [People's Liberation Army, PLA, of China] has demonstrated the ability to conduct attacks that disable our system.
>
> (*Aviation Aerospace* 2007)

But as yet we do not have the evidence to verify once and for all that the Chinese were responsible for these attacks, or if it was the Chinese whether such hacking was at the instigation of the government/military. Much of the evidence cited is available from open sources in China – Sun Yiming and Yang Liping's *Tactical Datalinks in Information Warfare* (2005) for example. Again the security issues outweigh the benefits of public disclosure: the American and British intelligence communities refuse to confirm or deny Chinese involvement. Rather, we are faced with yet more speculation.

More instructive are reports that reveal the American military accepts the Chinese are investing resources into information warfare (though the Pentagon's 2007 assessment of the Chinese military did not specifically cyberwar) but does not believe that Chinese claims of information warfare capacity should be taken too seriously:

> Although the PRC has achieved certain results in information warfare tactics, their basic capability and technology in information science and technology is still at the elementary research and development stage. The major reason is that its domestic information industry is still mainly in re-processing manufacture and there is no real research and development capability to be mentioned.
>
> (Office of the US Secretary of Defense, 26 February 1999)

More bark than bite?

A crucial part of this psychological aspect of information warfare is the hype: China has redefined the Maoist strategy of People's War to incorporate the threat of thousands of Chinese armed with networked computers launching a serious and concerted cyberattack against an enemy (Thomas 2000; Ahrari 1999; Wang 1995). Given the exponential growth in computer use and Internet connectivity in China it is not surprising that People's War should now embrace new information technology. However, there is reason to suspect that this is more hype than reality. First, it is a dramatic leap from being an Internet user to being part of the operationalisation of such technology in combat conditions.

Second, the Chinese government's management of the Internet raises doubts that it would unleash such a large scale information war: could the Chinese people be trusted with their new capacity to launch a cyberattack? How would the government prevent such capabilities and the freedom they would require from being used against it in causes supported by domestic hackers and dissidents? (Chase and Mulvenon 2002; *New York Times*, 13 October 2002).

Hence my main argument that current estimates about Chinese information warfare and about such conflict across the Taiwan Strait conform to the laws of the playground which, in a classic example of psychological warfare and intimidation, oblige children to puff themselves up and appear stronger than they actually are. The ultimate deterrent in the playground is the familiar call of 'my father is bigger than your father'. Even the Pentagon expresses doubts about China's strength in information warfare, and the security studies community in the US has closely questioned the possibility that China might launch a cyberattack in the near future:

> Does the possible enemy have the capability to wage a large-scale cyber attack against the US? It is far from clear even in the intelligence community if strategic rivals like China or Russia already have the technology and, even more important, the knowledge and qualified personnel to hack into computers that control critical infrastructures. Traditional means of intelligence do not help very much ... because the capabilities for an attack largely consist of software, commercial off-the shelf hardware components, and an internet connection.
>
> (Bendrath 2001: 80–103)

Stories about information warfare feed upon the growing paranoia that societies are vulnerable to collapse because of their increasing dependence on computer networks and information technology. The daily obsession with 'identity fraud' is one example, but we are also warned against 'worms', viruses, 'Trojan horses' and 'logic bombs' that can penetrate our systems.[9] Connectivity, the heart of the information society, makes it incredibly easy to contaminate and infect networks, thus causing maximum disruption to functional capacity. But is the anxiety justified?

A report by Michael Sheridan in the *Sunday Times* (1 September 2000) is typical of such fears. Sheridan referred to 'a systematic campaign by the Chinese government to take on America and other powers on the 21st century battlefield of cyber warfare'. He alluded to a 'secretive department controlled by the Ministry of Information Industry' and a government-led initiative to 'break Internet encryptions and codes used by foreign firms and governments'. Sheridan's source, allegedly an employee of this secret department, was not shy in describing China's capabilities:

> If you knew how much we could learn from your computer you would never use the Internet in China. ... We can break almost any password and

get into your bank account. We can read your emails from your computer to your boss – in Chinese and in English

(Sheridan, 1 September 2002: 24).

Similarly, after the websites of Taiwan's National Security Bureau (NSB) and Vice-President Lien Chan were attacked in March 2000, the Director of the NSB Information Department commented: 'Although they were not from China and there has been no indication of any hacker attempts from China, *it does not mean China will not do it*' (*Taipei Times*, 7 March 2000, emphasis added). In other words, China – the convenient bogeyman for Taiwan – was not guilty *this* time, but in the future...

Another example: in 2003, the *Taipei Times* reported that China had launched a 'systematic information warfare campaign against Taiwan', using Trojan-horse programs to violate government databases:

National intelligence has indicated that an army of hackers based in China's Hubei and Fujian provinces has successfully spread 23 different Trojan horse programs [sic] to the networks 10 private high-tech companies here to use them as a springboard to break into at least 30 different government agencies and 50 private companies.

(Ko, 4 September 2003: 1)

To date, hacking remains the only way that both sides of the Taiwan Strait are able to operationalise their information warfare capacity, and anecdotal evidence is in abundance: In August 1999, hackers thought to reside in China were allegedly responsible for 70,000 separate attacks on Taiwan's computer networks. Targets included government agencies such as the Investigation Bureau, the Ministries of Economic Affairs and Justice, and the National Assembly. One example will illustrate how such infiltration worked: on 8 August 1999, an unidentified hacker from China's Hunan province infiltrated the websites of Taiwan's Control Yuan (a branch of the central government), the cabinet-level Construction and Planning Administration, and Pingtung County government. He infected these websites with a message in English and Chinese: 'Taiwan is an indivisible part of Chinese territory and always will be!' This sparked what the media in Taiwan referred to as a 'cyber alert', and prompted the immediate creation of a security department within the Institute for Information Industry to help government agencies protect themselves from future cyberattacks (followed in 2003 by the formation of a new unit within the Ministry of National Defense to protect the security of military and civilian computer networks). Only two days after the initial strike, Taiwanese hackers attacked China's railways ministry in revenge and planted a message that screamed: 'Only one Taiwan exists and only one Taiwan is needed.' The Shaanxi Science and Technology Information Network was infected with the call to 'Reconquer, Reconquer, Reconquer the mainland!' Beijing later admitted that nineteen government sites had been violated by pro-Taiwan hackers who planted programmes that made the websites play the Taiwan national anthem, display Taiwan's flag, and shout pro-Taiwan slogans at the viewer. Then after a Chinese F-8 fighter jet collided with an EP-3 American spy-plane over Hainan on 1 April 2001, Chinese hackers claimed to have defaced over 1,000 American websites in protest.

Taiwan is not innocent of such crimes, but is in fact a nursery for the development of new computer viruses: in 1990, Taiwanese hackers were responsible for the 'Bloody' or '6/4' virus protesting the Chinese government's violent crackdown against student demonstrations in Beijing's Tiananmen Square in 1989; the 'Michelangelo' virus was discovered in Taiwan in 1992; in 1997 the 'Con-Air' virus, designed to draw attention to social problems in Taiwan, was developed by opponents of the Kuomintang government; and in 1998 and 1999, Taiwanese were responsible for the CIH or Chernobyl virus that reportedly infected 360,000 Chinese computers (on 26 April 1999) causing an estimated RMB one billion in damages. Taiwan's military was optimistic that investment in the development of such highly infectious viruses gave it the edge over China: 'Should the People's Liberation Army launch an information war against Taiwan the military, armed with 1,000 computer viruses, would be able to fight back.'[10] This is important as Taiwan's military would have a very limited impact on the PLA, and China would be able to withstand far more punishment than Taiwan was capable of inflicting. Taiwan's 'fight back' with information warfare could be a vital addition to Taiwan's military capacity in the event of a war with a much bigger and stronger China.

More bark than bite? It is important to note from this admittedly anecdotal evidence that hackers in China and Taiwan have attacked *websites*, and not the mainframe computer networks that are responsible for maintaining the operational capacity of national political, economic or military infrastructures. There is reason to suspect that even if this was desirable, it would be extremely difficult to do. Speaking after the outbreak of cyberwar in 1999, Carl Nicolai, director of Transend (an independent Taipei service provider) admitted that 'The Taiwan military is completely shut-off from the Internet' (*Taipei Times*, 29 August 1999). A spokesman for Taiwan's Ministry of National Defense (MND) said in 1999 that

> the MND computer system can be separated from outside connections. He went on to say that the ability to separate was why the MND computer system was not affected during the July 29 islandwide power blackout nor by recent incidents of website invasion by computer hackers.
> (Asia Pacific Network Information Centre, 16 August 1999)

Besides, information systems are not particularly easy targets: thanks to anxiety about identity theft, users are now more aware than ever before of how vulnerable they are and they therefore recognise the need to maximise the security of the computers they access. Users are encouraged to install security mechanisms – virus protection, firewalls – and adopt security-conscious routines, such as changing passwords, 'backing-up' data, making sure that security software is up-to-date.

For China, repelling a cyberattack may be far easier than it would be for Taiwan simply because of the existence of the Great Firewall, or 'Golden Shield' which the Chinese government imposes on the Internet (Rawnsley 2007). Blocking inbound and outbound traffic means that the capacity to infiltrate the Internet in China is more difficult than in Taiwan where the autonomy of the Internet may be a vulnerability, and the freedom of information is considered a cornerstone of the democratic system.

Information warfare and propaganda

So if we accept that the current discourse about information warfare across the Taiwan Strait is more bark than bite, focused on the hacking of websites rather than the penetration of mainframe networks in the doomsday scenario, then is there any real threat? I suggest that we can only understand the information warfare between Taiwan and China if we appreciate how computer networks are used as tools of propaganda and psychological warfare within the framework offered by Critical Security. This is because of the possibility of disrupting a computer network to affect perception, knowledge, and ultimately the information needed for rational decision-making. John Arquilla and David Ronfeldt described this as 'netwar', that is: 'information-related conflict at a grand level between nations or societies. It means trying to disrupt, damage or modify what a target population knows or thinks about itself and the world around it' (Arquilla and Ronfeldt 1993: 144, 146–7). The possible consequences are chilling: 'To be able to put out a fake story about Microsoft merging with Apple, for example; just rumours about those kind of stories can send stocks skyrocketing' (*Yahoo! Asia-News*, 7 March 2000). Now imagine what these kind of rumours could do in a developing economy like China with an annual growth rate of almost 10 per cent; or in an economic powerhouse but fragile democracy like Taiwan. On 6 August 1999, a Chinese-language website registered in the US (but owned by a Chinese company) posted a false news report that a Taiwanese F-5E fighter had been shot down by the Chinese Air Force. Taiwan's stock market fell by 2 per cent in a single day. In May 1990, Taiwan's media reported that a Chinese submarine was engaged in manoeuvres off the island's southern coast. This was immediately followed by a record 510-point stock market crash. Beijing denied the story (*Shijie Ribao*, 11 May 1990: 32; *Shijie Riabo*, 17 May 1990: 1), but does it matter? Taiwan is psychologically weakened by the kind of rumours, stories and information that can be easily generated and circulated through computer networks. It is likely that the deliberate planting of rumours of imminent Chinese military attack would destabilise the island, provoke a massive exodus of capital, and increase the pressure on Taipei to capitulate to Beijing's terms. This strategy is the most useful for the PRC, for it conforms to China's ambition to force a political settlement on Taiwan with minimum violence: 'unification (with Taiwan) first and rule (the island) later.' After all, the military destruction of Taiwan would not bring China any benefit, but would only add to Beijing's military and political burden and create a less than compliant population in Taiwan. A military victory is not necessarily synonymous with a political victory.

In other words, I suggest that computer-based information warfare – like propaganda – may be a form of psychological pressure that minimises the need for military conflict, and this assessment is consistent with Chinese approaches to information warfare that emphasise its value in psychological, denial and deception operations (Farris 2001: 38). Taiwan's Ministry of National Defense claims that there are over 300 Chinese agencies disseminating false information in Taiwan to spread panic and destabilise the stock market. Is this yet another example of propaganda? In 2006 Taiwan's Ministry of National Defense and the American Institute in Taiwan (AIT) reported how both had been 'maliciously attacked by hackers *believed* to be operating from China' [emphasis added] (Minnick, 9 June 2006). This was part of an alleged 'misinformation campaign' which involved a fake press release about a bribery scandal among Taiwan's politicians, designed to 'manipulate the Taiwan media'. What was the evidence for suspecting China? 'Part of the attack used simplified Chinese characters that are only used in mainland China, while traditional characters are still used in Taiwan' (Minnick, 9 June 2006). On such tenuous facts the future of the region may depend. The geographical uncertainty and anonymity offered by modern communications technologies means it will become increasingly difficult to separating fact from fiction and speculation from confirmation, and will confound observers seeking easy redress of network violations.

Conclusions

The value of using information warfare is that it helps to realise political objectives without causing the quantity of fatal and non-fatal casualties associated with more conventional military strategies. However, this does not imply that information warfare is entirely clean and bloodless because of the inevitable 'collateral damage' caused by disruption to a society's infrastructure. The indirect costs are therefore potentially enormous: electricity grids, power stations, water treatment plants, hospitals, transport networks etc. could all be casualties of these 'non-lethal strategies'. Bombs and missiles may not be directly responsible for fatalities in modern or 'virtual' warfare, but the disease and poverty than may result from the disruption to vital social services are equally effective killers.

Moreover, the so-called 'war on terror' has forced us to turn to a new series of questions which governments, militaries and societies must address. A suicide bomber may walk into a crowded market place in Jerusalem, Baghdad or London and detonate explosives strapped around his or her body. It is increasingly possible that he or she received instructions via a coded email sent from a laptop computer in the mountains of Afghanistan. The military and intelligence communities no longer have exclusive control over flows of information: the proliferation of technology has empowered those with even minimal computer competence, as both the 'hacker' and 'blogger' cultures demonstrate. The collapse of space and time, the shift of attention from the state to civil society, and the increasing capacity for anonymity will allow computer-based information warfare to play a progressively more important role in facilitating conventional forms of warfare.

As methods of information warfare propaganda and psychological warfare have been integral to conflict since ancient times: the sword has always fought the mind. Control and management of information was a prominent theme in Sun Tzu's *Art of War*, a guide to warfare written in the sixth century BC that is still a major influence in Chinese military thinking. As the Chinese military were turning their attention to cyberwar after the 1991 Gulf War, they also took greater interest in the application of psychological warfare and how to integrate the media into military strategy (Thomas 2003: 2–11).

Computer-based information warfare allows for a more precise and therefore potentially more effective form of propaganda than print, radio and television, but it is also an instrument *of* propaganda. The laws of the playground determine that across the Taiwan Strait the threat of information warfare is both limited and exaggerated. This is not to discard claims that both sides are actively preparing offensive and defensive capabilities, but it is unlikely that either will deploy their information warfare arsenal without first deciding to launch a conventional military attack. The jury is still out on the probability, though not the possibility, of conflict across the Taiwan Strait. Rather, information warfare continues to play a pivotal role in cross-Strait propaganda, as demonstrated by the hacking of computer systems and in the rumours and stories planted on Internet sites and in the media that can have dramatic and detrimental effects on the psychology of the other side.

Moreover, the laws of the playground dictate that one must project an image of strength even in times of weakness and vulnerability. The People's Liberation Army has initiated a Revolution in Military Affairs that has prioritised high-tech and information-related development, but this is designed to consolidate the projection of strength to the regional and international community with little regard for actual capabilities (O'Hanlon 2000).

Both Taiwan and China are mistaken to believe that computer-based information warfare will provide the principal architecture for any future military confrontation. Beijing must calculate the American response to any intervention in Taiwan, and Taiwan certainly faces a formidable military machine across the Taiwan Strait:[11]

> Today, the PLA is more combat-capable, multilayered, and integrated. Its conventional forces are more streamlined, lethal, mobile, versatile, better co-ordinated, and have a greater operational reach.... [T]he downsized Chinese forces have retained their quantitative superiority.... Barring US intervention, the PLA could overwhelm Taiwan's modernizing army.
>
> (Lin 1995: 34)

Yet despite the conventional military forces ranged against Taiwan, Major-General Chen Wen-chien of Taiwan's Ministry of Defense communication electronics and information bureau described information security as the 'top priority task of the military' (*Taipei Times*, 3 January 2001). The daily reports in September 2007 of alleged Chinese hacking of foreign government websites add to the paranoia. Clearly China is winning the information war; propaganda about its capacity to inflict heavy damage on Taiwan through its application of information technology is sufficiently intimidating to push Taiwan towards a self-perception of inferiority. Reinforced by the reality of 600 missiles located in Fujian province and aimed at the island, this propaganda exerts substantial psychological pressure on Taiwan and its inhabitants.

The imponderables of information warfare are many. The discourse nurtures the propaganda strategies – and it is propaganda that has characterised the Taiwan Strait Cold War – but the promise of information warfare remains, as yet, unfulfilled. Risk estimates always move between paranoia and carelessness, without ever being precise. Terms like 'capability', 'possibility', 'could' and 'might' pervade the discussion. On both sides of the Taiwan Strait the militaries have yet to move beyond this level of discourse.

So There

> My dad is bigger than your dad.
> He's bigger and stronger
> and fights off the monsters,
> he can keep running for longer
> and go for days without food or water.
>
> He can leap tall buildings in a single bound,
> in fact
> he can tear them right out of the ground –
> right out of his way.
> But he doesn't need to, 'cos
> Because ... my dad can fly.
> Can your dad do that? Can he?
> No? Well your dad's crap.
>
> My dad's bigger and
> faster and fitter
> and tougher and quicker
> and he always buys sweets for me and my sister.
> He can withstand extreme conditions for hours,
> and he wears red underpants over blue trousers;
> he's got an 'S' on his chest because he's the best.
> So don't get me mad.
> 'Cos he's bigger than your dad.
> > (http://www.wyrdlittlesister.co.uk/poetry.htm,
> > November 2001, accessed 9 August 2007)

Notes

1 An earlier version of this chapter first appeared in *International Affairs* (London), volume 81, number 5, October 2005, pp. 1061–78, and is reproduced with permission.

2 In this chapter I use the names 'China' and 'PRC' interchangeably to refer to the People's Republic of China (capital city Beijing), and I use 'Taiwan' to refer to the Republic of China and the island of Taiwan (capital city Taipei). This is merely short-hand and should not be taken to indicate the author's position on the prevailing conflict over Taiwan's political identity.

3 On the vulnerability of such networks see Johnson 1997. Lawrence Freedman (1998: 52) has noted that 'In strategic thinking, dependence soon becomes a vulnerability and, by extension, a potential target'. *The Revolution in Strategic Affairs*, Adelphi Paper 318 (Oxford: Oxford University Press, 1998), p. 52.

4 Bitzinger and Gill (1996) outline four conventional scenarios in any conflict with Taiwan, from 'low-level intimidation' to invasion.

5 Examples of such Cold War propaganda can be found in Asian People's Anti-Communist League, *A Decade of Chinese Communist Tyranny*, Taipei: 1960, and in the annual *China Yearbooks*, later *Republic of China Yearbooks*, published by the Government Information Office in Taipei.

6 *Information Warfare and Military Revolution* [*Xinxi Zhanzheng yu Junshi Geming*] (Beijing: Military Sciences Publishing House, December 1995), p. 144.

> Major General Wang Pufeng is nominally the author of ... [what] appears to be the first full-length book on IW published in China.... Attaching his name to the book at least indicates that the subject is taken very seriously by the PLA High Command.
>
> (Jencks 1997: 161 n.12)

It is clear, however, that the coalition forces won victory over Iraq by using a carefully designed combination of information warfare and conventional methods of military attack (Waltz 1998: 7–8). For more on Chinese approaches to information warfare see Chen (1997) and You (1999).

7 There is evidence in the available Chinese literature that the authors have borrowed heavily from US discourse on Information Warfare. See James Mulvenon (1999: 178).

8 This strategy involved more active, but low-level intimidation of Taiwan (Gill 1997: 105–28).

9 Viruses can be considered 'Trojan horses', hidden within a host programme and triggered upon execution; worms 'obliterate or alter data as they bore through system memory'; and 'logic bombs' 'embed themselves in an executable file until activated by a specific event, such as a date' (Freedman 1998: 55).

10 Major-General Chen Wen-chien, deputy director of the Ministry of Defense's communication electronics and information bureau, quoted in AFP, 'Taiwan has 1,000 computer viruses to fight cyber war with China', 9 January 2000.

11

> The backbone of the PLA's missile forces opposite Taiwan are the Dongfeng-11 and Dongfeng-15 SRBMs. They are expected to be augmented in coming years with conventionally armed Dongfeng-21/25 medium-range ballistic missiles. China is also expected to develop cruise missiles for land attack to boost its ability to strike Taiwan.
>
> (Lague 2004: 26)

7 Information warfare operations within the concept of individual self-defence

Dimitrios Delibasis

> Cyber attacks defeat the basic national security paradigm that has existed in our country since the early nineteenth century.
>
> Colonel Chester H. Morgan (Morgan 2001: 5)

Introduction

Throughout the course of human history knowledge and information have always been considered to be tantamount to power (Kuehl 2004: 118). In contrast with the past, where the notion of power was thought to comprise solely military, economic and diplomatic factors, the current advent of the 'information revolution' has made it evident that another vital, and perhaps the most vital element of power is, and has always been, information. Information has always historically been a force multiplier. However modern rapid advances in computer technology and especially in networking have instigated a major as well as fundamental shift in national security affairs and have irreversibly ushered the world community into a new era in which information warfare is the most prominent of powers (Joint Command Control and Information Warfare School 2003: 118). As a direct consequence, the ability offered by modern technology to states to incorporate the full spectrum of information warfare tools and techniques in their respective arsenals, is currently affecting to an ever growing degree the means by which they would be going about their military as well as their civilian affairs in the new millennium (Joint Command Control and Information Warfare School 2003: 118).

Even more important is the fact that information warfare, along with global networking, has currently allowed any and all members of the international community to be in a position to benefit from the advantages of the information revolution by being able to utilize it in order to directly interact with one another irrespectively of their relative state of technological, economic or military development. As an immediate result, there is nowadays not a single world state that is not in a position from which it can have a significant effect to both the maintenance of international peace and security as well as the world's economic development (FM3–0, 1 January 2004). There currently are quite a few indications that potential state-sponsored as well as non-state-sponsored actors of aggression are showing a continuously and dangerously increasing appreciation for the employment of information warfare as the best means of achieving any specific gains they might have (Office of the Undersecretary of Defense for Acquisition, Technology and Logistics 2001: 1). Information warfare attacks perpetrated by trusted insiders, plain individual hackers, organized groups and finally and most importantly, various states have dramatically increased and they constantly explore new approaches that make them extremely hard to identify and be traced back to their source.

An ever-increasing number of members of the international community, has made explicitly clear that it will fully integrate information warfare as an asymmetric response in any future conflict it may be involved in. Various elements of information warfare, such as psychological operations, computer network attacks, as well as computer network defence, are steadily taking an ever more important place in the plans of modern actors of aggression.

It is currently extremely hard to make an accurate prediction as to how much of an actual threat information warfare will eventually pose to international peace and security and what exact response, especially in the regulatory field, the world will choose to give to it. Much will depend on the actual events that will eventually force the international community to turn its full attention to information warfare and whether it will eventually look at it as a potent threat or just as a peaceful and purely scientific achievement. However, there appears to be already enough room for concern. Advanced 'Commercial off the Shelf' technology has allowed high speed interconnected information networks with a continuously increasing real time ability to identify targets, create and transmit plans, disseminate and analyse data and finally make decisions and take the necessary actions in minutes, if not seconds, to become an integral part of the warfighting machine as well as of today's civilian national critical infrastructures of all modern states.

The local as well as global interconnectivity of modern high speed information systems is their greatest advantage and also their greatest potential vulnerability of such systems, as it provides the gate through which all unauthorized entries can, and usually do take place (Office of the Undersecretary of Defense for Acquisition, Technology and Logistics 2001: 1). Prudence requires that states consider all existing viruses and 'hacker attacks' as real information warfare operations and take the necessary steps to neutralize them as soon as such attacks are identified and traced. As a result, currently existing legal norms conceived with regard to the use of force in its traditional forms may not prove adequate in regulating such a unique and potentially extremely volatile for inter-state relations situation.

On the other hand, any new legal framework specifically conceived to regulate cyberspace warfare has to be based on a set of certain basic legal principles that will allow it not only to be effective but also, and perhaps primarily so, to shut the door to potential abuse on the part of states that find themselves at the unhappy receiving end of cyber-warfare attacks. The only set of international legal principles capable of serving such a twofold purpose and at the same time being accepted by the vast majority, if not by all members of the international community, can currently be found only within the legal norms comprising the concept of self-defence. Therefore, it stands to reason that any effort to develop a specialized legal framework specifically tailored to regulate potential forcible actions in cyberspace depends for its actual success on putting modern information warfare operations into perspective within the concept of individual self-defence.

The legal foundations

UN Charter Article 51 specifies that only an armed attack gives rise to the right of states to take recourse to forcible defensive action (The Charter of the UN 1945: Article 51). Therefore, and in examining information warfare within that context, the crucial issue requiring an answer would be whether a computer network attack could be classified as an armed attack and as such justify recourse to counter-force for self-defence purposes.

At first glance, by centring simply on the means being used in an information warfare attack, one might draw the conclusion that electronic signals do not closely resemble bombs, bullets, troops or other traditional types of weapons. On the other hand, the international community appears to have had no trouble over the years to consider the use of chemical or biological weapons as falling well within the definition of an armed attack, even though they also happen to be undetectable by unaided human senses. This is consistent with the view according to which the particular choice of weaponry relied upon by the perpetrator of an armed attack is immaterial, since Article 51 does not refer to any specific weapons and it applies to any armed attack irrespectively of the type of weaponry employed (Advisory Opinion on the Legality of the Threat or Use of Nuclear Weapons 1996: 226, 244).

This reflects events in the real world where a given armed attack may not, and usually it does not, comprise only traditional military weapons and tactics. In fact, it is only customary for potential actors of aggression in order not only to mount a successful offensive, but also to avoid being earmarked as perpetrators, thus escaping any possible repercussions of their action, to rely as heavily as possible on unorthodox or newly developed means and methods of attack falling outside the traditional realm of military weapons and tactics. Information warfare represents the almost ideal textbook example of such a form of armed attack comprising weapons and tactics, which are newly developed, unorthodox and, until their advent, virtually non-existent.

Eventually, and in accordance with the phrasing of Article 51, the international community is far more likely to deem a future successful information warfare attack as constituting an armed attack based on its potential consequences, rather than its specific mechanism. In such a case, it may not be too unrealistic to conclude that no member of the international community would challenge the victim state's logical deduction that it has been the target of an act amounting to an armed attack.

The primary feature of the UN Charter with regard to regulating the exact circumstances under which states are entitled, or not as the case may be, to resort to counter-force, is the specific language utilized by the drafters of those articles. The most important element of which, as well as the only condition for making such a resort lawful other than an authorization of the Security Council, is the term armed attack (The Charter of the UN 1945: Articles 39–42). At the same time, the use of the term 'armed attack' implies acceptance on part of the drafter of a fact which was correctly pointed out by the International Court of Justice in the Nicaragua case, namely, that no legal instrument is capable of fully and directly regulating all aspects of a given legal right or situation (Case Concerning the Military and Paramilitary Activities in and against Nicaragua 1986: 94).

Indeed, it is rather important to keep in mind that any potential forcible action taken by the world's states or armed attack launched against them comprises a legal as well as a technical element. The various means at the disposal of potential actors of aggression worldwide have a tendency of not remaining static and unchanged over the course of time. They do follow an evolutionary pattern, which is always strictly related to the specific technological advances that are constantly taking place on their surrounding environment.

As a result, the critical threshold, the violation of which constitutes an armed attack, is far more likely to be related to the consequences, rather than the means being used in any given act of aggression. This is what in the end makes the choice of weaponry by a potential illegally attacking state totally immaterial and unrelated to the attack and gives rise to the right of the victim state to act in self-defence, irrespectively of the exact nature and level of sophistication of the armaments employed by the aggressor (Advisory Opinion on the Legality of the Threat or Use of Nuclear Weapons 1996: 226, 244). In fact, as Professor Kelsen has put it, the conduct described in the relevant provision of Article 51 includes both the use of arms and a violation of international law, which involves an exercise of power in the territorial domain, but no use of arms in the traditional sense (Kelsen 1998: 57).

Information warfare represents perhaps the most classic paradigm of a totally new and until very recently completely unknown form of attack, which came into being simply as a result of a rapid technological advancement that took place mainly over the last fifteen years or so. The international community has faced similar situations in the past with the advent of technological innovations such as the airplane, the advent of biochemical weapons and finally nuclear fission. All these innovations had already managed to establish themselves as extremely potent instruments of peace or war, well before the UN Charter came into existence. Some, such as the airplane and chemical weapons were already the subject of international legal regulation with regard to their potential devastating effects, if employed as means of warfare (Roberts and Guelff 2000: 139 et seq.).

It is imperative to bear in mind that the international community has always been characterized by a slow, yet steady evolutionary process. As a result, new ways, situations and forms of conduct are constantly replacing older ones. It stands to reason that no legal framework can manage to successfully regulate all possible eventualities based solely on a specific, rigid and unchanged set of rules. All legal rules must be capable of adapting themselves continuously to new circumstances, in other words to be flexible enough to even cope with newly emerged situations for the exact regulations of which they may have not been initially intended. Whenever the world community faces the challenge of regulating a newly appeared contingency, it has no option, at least not until it sets forth a regulatory framework, specifically designed to deal with that previously nonexistent contingency, but to turn to the general principles of international law. Such general principles are usually being deduced by analogy from already existing rules, which are broad enough to cover more than one eventuality, if and when the relevant need arises.

As Professor D'Amato has pointed out, too rigid an interpretation of any given rule can often lead in a rupture in the system of international law. An absolutely rigid interpretation of any given rule will be no different than having a robot interpret a rule exactly by the letter, without taking into account any of its real life consequences (D'Amato 2000: 2).

The material disagreement existing in the academic community with regard to the potential interpretation of Article 51 and whether it has to be interpreted in a narrow or in a wide way is rather well known and the relevant analysis is well beyond the scope of this work. Nevertheless, it has to be stressed that the controversy over whether Article 51 allows for other patterns of self-defence of an anticipatory nature is totally irrelevant to information warfare. This is due to the specific nature of this form of warfare, calling for every single of the various elements comprising it to be dependent on cyberspace, thus forcing them to ensue in real time and virtually instantly. This makes it technically impossible, for even the best national means of verification employed by states, to spot even the slightest indication that a computer network attack is imminent, before the actual attack materializes, thus ruling out any option for recourse to anticipatory measures of self-defence.

It is also due to the same aforementioned real time, as well as instantaneous nature of information warfare, that the exact moment in time at which an armed attack, employing means and methods of information warfare, begins to take place can be pinpointed accurately, thus allowing for forcible counter-measures to become legitimate as self-defence.

This is established by application of the rule of 'the first shot' (Dinstein 2001: 170), namely becoming aware of which state, through its armed forces, was the first to commence firing. In contrast with armed attacks employing other means, and usually more conventional means, than information warfare, where the first use of force is often a prima facie evidence of aggression (General Assembly Resolution 3314 1974: 29(1) Resolutions adopted by The General Assembly 143), in armed attacks utilizing information warfare techniques and tools, their starting point cannot but coincide with the first use of force.

This special nature of information warfare which stems from its link to cyberspace is also responsible for ruling out the option of interceptive self-defence, with regard to information warfare operations constituting armed attacks, since the only technically possible way to realize that such attacks are under way is by watching them materialize, which happens only just as they strike their objectives.

Generally speaking an armed attack presupposes any or both of the following results: human casualties and serious destruction of property (Dinstein 2001: 174). Consequently, and in accordance with the relevant clarification introduced by the International Court of Justice (ICJ), the first set of features that distinguishes an information warfare attack, or any other attack as the case may be, constituting an armed attack is its 'scales and effects', a term which refers to the scale in place and time and also the scale of the impact of the attack (Case Concerning Military and Paramilitary Activities in and against Nicaragua 1986: 103). The second set of features, established by the ICJ that distinguishes an information warfare operation as an armed attack, is its 'circumstances and motivations' (Case Concerning Military and Paramilitary Activities in and against Nicaragua 1986: 103). This second set of features seems to imply that there can be no armed attack in circumstances where there has been no intent to carry out an armed attack.

The least vague, and as a result leading, criterion for classifying an information warfare attack as an armed attack is the 'scale and effects' concept. This criterion has been repeatedly affirmed by the ICJ, first, when it explicitly ruled that low intensity fighting, such as the sending of armed bands into the territory of another state, may count as an armed attack (Case Concerning Military and Paramilitary Activities in and against Nicaragua 1986: 103). Second, when with regard to the Iranian Oil Platforms Case, it held that a series of incidents allegedly amounting to armed attacks could not qualify as a 'most grave form' of the use of force, as per the relevant requirement established in the Nicaragua Case and therefore be deemed to constitute armed attacks (Iranian Oil Platforms Case 2003: 51, 64).

The process of distinguishing armed attacks from less serious incidents involving forcible action, which could not qualify as armed attacks, as affirmed by the ICJ, is of extreme importance if the concept of self-defence is not to be abused, especially with regard to information warfare operations, where alleged armed attacks, as a result of their comprising weaponry are made purely of electrons. Also utilizing the global interconnectivity offered by the World Wide Web, can assume a 'most grave form' of the use of force, just as easily as they can assume the form of a whole string of incidents involving recourse to force, having 'scale and effects' of a lesser and quite often variable magnitude.

The locale of any given illegal recourse to force, irrespectively of whether that illegal recourse to force is cross-border in nature or not, is not a requirement for its potential classification as an armed attack. Therefore it is also not a requirement for taking legitimate action in exercise of the right to self-defence (Case Concerning United States Diplomatic and Consular Staff in Tehran 1980: 29, 42, 43, also, Stein 1982: 499–500; Schachter 1985: 325, 328; Case Concerning Military and Paramilitary Activities in and against Nicaragua Dissenting opinion of Judge Schwebel 1986: 292). This is of particular relevance to information warfare attacks and their potential classification as armed attacks. Since all such attacks, due to their reliance on the World Wide Web in order to materialize, are capable of defying physical borders, literally at will (which is exactly what happens in most real-life situations). As a result, it is rather essential for the accurate potential classification of any such attack as an armed attack to leave no room for misinterpreting its locale as a prerequisite for a lawful resort to self-defence. Thus, not only will potential aggressor states be prevented from employing armed attacks comprising information warfare means with impunity, supposedly defending states will also be faced with a clear view of what constitutes an armed attack and what does not and therefore the relevant room for potential abuses of the concept of self-defence will be extremely limited.

The potential target of an armed attack, with regard to the state targeted by the attack, is usually either one of the following (Dinstein 2001: 179–80):

- any part of its territory, including persons or property within the area affected by the attack;
- any military unit of its armed forces which may be stationed, either within or outside its borders;
- any of its public installations, either military or civilian, which may be stationed outside its borders;
- any of its nationals, while in the territory of another state and not on any of its installations or vessels, as long as it satisfies the legal test put forth during the 1956 Suez military intervention (Marston 1988: 773, 795, 800).

In its ruling with regard to the Nicaragua Case, the International Court of Justice held that it may be considered to be agreed that 'an armed attack must be understood as including, not merely action by regular armed forces, but also the dispatch of armed bands or irregulars into the territory of another State' (Case Concerning Military and Paramilitary Activities in and against Nicaragua 1986: 103).

The issue of cross-border action by irregulars and whether such action can amount to an armed attack is extremely relevant to information warfare operations, due to the fact that computer network attacks can be launched by irregulars, armed bands, terrorists or any other private parties just as easily as they can be launched by a state's regular armed forces. This is going to be particularly the case in situations where information warfare attacks are being contemplated as the weapon of choice against far more powerful countries, against which the perpetrators of such attacks could never hope to level the playing field by reliance on any other more conventional means of warfare. By launching attacks through an irregular force, a terrorist group or any other private party, the state perpetrator of such attacks can have the advantage offered by plausible deniability.

Information warfare attacks mounted by irregular forces of any kind, which have either been sent by the state from the territory of which they operate or they are acting on its behalf cannot be deemed to constitute armed attacks, unless they are of sufficient gravity as to amount to an armed attack, if committed by regular troops (Case Concerning Military and Paramilitary Activities in and against Nicaragua 1986: 103). As specified by the court in the Nicaragua Case, the concept of armed attack does not include the supply of arms and any other logistical support to irregular forces, terrorist groups or any other private parties (Case Concerning Military and Paramilitary Activities in and against Nicaragua 1986: 103).

In information warfare attacks, the provision on the part of a state of logistical support to a private group being utilized by that same state to launch such attacks against the territory of another is inconsequential and, therefore, of no importance with regard to the potential classification of such attacks as armed attacks. This is due to two factors. First, the vast majority of the technological means needed to mount an effective computer network attack can easily be obtained in the open market. Second, the military of the various states having an active interest in this form of information warfare have a very strong interest in the non-proliferation of the information warfare weapons they develop. Such weapons are always classified, because, as soon as their exact nature is revealed, they immediately lose their value, as potential adversaries can develop the means to neutralize them, and they are also potentially too destructive, especially if they were to be allowed to spread indiscriminately in the World Wide Web to be supplied to irregulars.

On the other hand, there may be instances where groups of irregulars or terrorists engaged in information warfare attacks, which are of sufficient gravity to amount to armed attacks, are deemed to be de facto organs of the state sponsoring them, regardless of any specific instruction by the controlling state concerning the commissioning of the individual acts comprising these attacks (Judgment I.C.T.Y. Case No. IT-94–1-A Appeals Chamber 1999: 38 ILM 1518, 1545). The critical factor here, as first established in the Tadic Case, is the subordination of a given irregular group to the overall control of the state sponsoring it, without requiring the sponsoring state to single-handedly direct every action of such a group.

Such subordination, exactly as was envisioned by the Court in the Tadic Case, is always bound to be an inherent element of any information warfare attack executed by irregulars sponsored by a specific state, because it is directly related to how close the attack is eventually going to get to having maximum possible effect. At this point, it has to be noted, that the reason for this is that information warfare attacks depend, in order to have the maximum possible effect in relation with their objective, on accurate charts of the World Wide Web and of the particular systems which form their objective.

Last but certainly not least, there is the issue of whether a lesser degree of state involvement in information warfare operations undertaken by irregular groups, such as acquiescence or even inability to control such groups operating from a state's territory could ever constitute an armed attack.

The important legal norm to remember with regard to this issue is that currently the concept of armed attack does not include state involvement lesser than the sending, by or on behalf of a state into the territory of another, of irregular forces (Case Concerning Military and Paramilitary Activities in and against Nicaragua 1986: 103). This legal norm has recently been re-affirmed by the ICJ in the Palestinian Wall Case (Advisory Opinion on the Legal Consequences of the Construction of a Wall in the Occupied Palestinian Territories 2004: 139) and is also shared by states which have fallen victims to incursions by irregular groups. Such states also appear to be of the view that, only when the state hosting irregular groups mounting attacks in the territory of another state is actively involved in their actions, is recourse to self-defence justifiable (Gray 2004: 111).

It is obvious from the reasoning of the court both in the Nicaragua Case and in the Palestinian Wall Case (Case Concerning Military and Paramilitary Activities in and against Nicaragua 1986: 103; Advisory Opinion on the Legal Consequences of the Construction of a Wall in the Occupied Palestinian Territories 2004: 139), that the main concern behind the court's reasoning was to leave no room for potential abuses of the right to self-defence by states which would use the action of irregulars as a pretext. And at the same time, it had to balance the need to safeguard against such abuses with the necessity to avoid extenuating a real armed attack by the subterfuge of indirect aggression or by reliance on a surrogate (Harry 1986: 1289, 1299).

Nowhere is this need for balance more apparent than in the field of information warfare operations, as a result of the fact that information warfare attacks occur in real time and allow for no deliberation at all on part of the defender. Hence, it is extremely likely that states which find themselves facing a serious information warfare attack, even if the attack at hand looks like the work of just an irregular group, will seek recourse to counter-force immediately, without taking the necessary time to establish whether the attack at hand constitutes an armed attack. Such an occurrence could be a potentially major destabilizing factor for international peace and security, as it will practically leave the door open to abuse. At the same time, it is imperative that potential aggressors are prevented from utilizing the tools and methods of information warfare to mount armed attacks with impunity since such an occurrence will also be destabilizing for the international legal order in the long term.

The legal test established by the ICJ in order to determine the exact boundaries of the concept of armed attack with regard to armed bands and irregulars has been repeatedly affirmed by the court as being applicable to the forcible action undertaken by such groups irrespective of the type and nature of weaponry it may comprise. It therefore represents the best means of achieving the perfect balance between curtailing aggression and safeguarding international legal order from abuse, even with regard to uses of force consisting of a new and previously unheard of nature, such as information warfare.

Information warfare operations within the optional modes of individual self-defence

The unique nature of information warfare operations within the modality of individual self-defence

Information warfare operations take advantage of the 'network-centric' architecture integrated in all modern information resources, military and civilian alike, in order to gain access to them and to ultimately deny them to their user (Dunnigan 2002: 208). However, it is essential not to lose sight of the fact that gaining access in such a way to any state's information cycle is in essence tantamount to nothing less than the potential acquisition of a completely new means of applying armed force, which can be employed at will against that state's national critical infrastructure, military as well as civilian. This is due to the fact, that as soon as access in any state's information cycle is secured, the current level of computer technology allows the deployment of information warfare weapons. Such weapons comprise specially developed software, and once deployed are fully capable not only of disrupting, but also of destroying all assets which happen to be dependent on the information cycle which has been breached (Denning 2002: 28–30; also, Dunnigan 2002: 9; Joint Command Control and Information Warfare School 2003: 62 et seq.).

All in all, and as a result of their aforementioned unique nature, information warfare operations offer unparalleled flexibility when relied upon as means of applying counter-force during the course of exercising self-defence. First, they allow the application of counter-force literally at a moment's notice and at virtually any time and place. Thus, the defending state can do its best to exhaust all other avenues of defusing a given crisis instigated by an armed attack, before it resorts to self-defence and still be capable of employing counter-force in a most effective manner, if every other option fails without having to risk running afoul of the requirements of necessity and of immediacy. Second, they offer the defending state the ability to vary the level of counter-force it chooses to apply practically at will. Hence, they make it rather effortless for the defending state choosing to rely on them to match the scale and effects of the counter-force it will eventually employ with the scale and effects of the armed attack, which instigated any such recourse to counter-force in the first place and therefore satisfy with relative ease the requirement of proportionality.

Information warfare operations in response to an armed attack by a state

Measures short of war

The first category of self-defence falling under the classification of measures short of war is the 'on the spot reaction', which is defined as a spontaneous and 'in situ' recourse to counter-force, instigated by an armed attack of usually small scale and undertaken either by the victim state's military assets under attack, or by any other military assets of the victim state that happen to be in the vicinity of the armed attack (Dinstein 2001: 192). The validity of the 'on-the-spot reaction' has been acknowledged by the International Court of Justice in the Corfu Channel Case where the court appeared to have taken for granted that warships passing through international waterways are entitled to retaliate quickly, if fired upon by coastal batteries (Corfu Channel Case 1949: 31).

Information warfare operations are ideally suited to be relied upon as the means of mounting an on-the-spot reaction. First of all, they offer an immediate response capability not only on a strategic, but also on a tactical level, hence providing counter-force whose employment is literally consecutively linked to the armed attack triggering it, and as such easier to satisfy the requirement of immediacy. At the same time, it is this unique immediate response capability inherent in them which allows the local commander, in the vicinity of a small-scale armed attack, to explore alternative courses of action and still have the time to mount an effective on-the-spot reaction, if there are no alternative ways to defuse the situation at hand. Last, but certainly not least, and as a result of the unparalleled flexibility in the amount of force that can be applied through them, information warfare operations are the best means for applying counter-force with 'scale and effects' (Case on Military and Paramilitary Activities in and against Nicaragua 1986: 103) similar to those of the armed attack at hand.

The second category of self-defence falling under the classification of measures short of war is the 'defensive armed reprisals'. The term, as used here, refers to measures of counter-force, short of war, taken by one state against another, in response to a prior act which constituted a violation of international law (Dinstein 2001: 194–5; Schachter 1982: 168).

The distinctive character of information warfare operations, allows them to be employed as defensive armed reprisals. First, the actual choice of the time and place for their employment, as well as the objective they will be eventually employed against rests entirely with the defending state, just as it is required from any lawful recourse to defensive armed reprisals (Dinstein 2001: 194–5; also, Schachter 1985: 168). Second, information warfare operations can be relied upon during the course of resorting to defensive armed reprisals even if they do not necessarily mirror the offensive measures employed by the aggressor (Case on Military and Paramilitary Activities in and against Nicaragua Dissenting Opinion of Judge Schwebel 1986: 379). Hence, the defending state is allowed some extra room to manoeuvre with regard to its final choice of the type of counter-measures and less likely to resort to defensive armed reprisals that may very well end up being disproportionate. Finally, utilization of information warfare operations as defensive armed reprisals allows the defending state, more than any other type of counter-force (Denning 2002: 28–30; also, Dunnigan 2002: 9 et seq.; Joint Command Control and Information Warfare School 2003: 62 et seq.), to ensure that no rights of third states are put at risk (Naulilaa Case 1928: 1011, 1026).

Furthermore, potential reliance on information warfare operations during the

course of seeking recourse to defensive armed reprisals is the best way of applying just the amount of counter-force required under the circumstances at hand,
thus ensuring that it will not be excessively disproportionate and therefore be
deemed as unlawful (Naulilaa Case 1928: 1011, 1026). Even more important,
the employment of information warfare operations as defensive armed reprisals
allows the defending state to make a potential calculation of the casualties, as
well as of the damage that may be caused by the specific counter-measures it
contemplates with unmatched accuracy. This is due to the fact that the precision
inherent in information warfare operations practically nullifies the element of
chance embodied in all military entanglements (Denning 2002: 28–30; also,
Dunnigan 2002: 9 et seq.; Joint Command, Control and Information Warfare
School 2003: 62 et seq.).

It has been long established with regard to defensive armed reprisals, which
are always supposed to ensue after a certain amount of time has passed from the
armed attack that triggered them, that for the defending state to satisfy the
requirement of necessity it has to exhaust all possible avenues of seeking a
peaceful solution to the situation at hand before it seeks recourse to counter-
force (Naulilaa Case 1928: 1011, 1026; also, Case Concerning Military and
Paramilitary in and against Nicaragua 1986: 1026–7). Information warfare
operations, through their utilization of cyberspace, allow for the immediate
application of precisely the amount of counter-force opted for on part of states
contemplating them as defensive armed reprisals, instantaneously, as soon as
such states decide to employ them (Denning 2002: 28–30; also, Dunnigan 2002:
9 et seq.). As a consequence, the requirement of necessity is far more likely to
be satisfied and abuses will be less possible.

The right of a state, facing an armed attack, to avoid being embroiled in
endless negotiations, which can very well constitute nothing more than an
attempt on part of the attacking state to stall for time, is interwoven with the
requirement of immediacy, which all defensive armed reprisals have to meet
(Dinstein 2001: 198). Once again, the immediate response capability provided
by information warfare operations is essential for allowing states to satisfy this
requirement (Dinstein 2001: 198), which is the matrix of the legitimacy of any
such reprisals (Dinstein 2001: 198). The third category of self-defence falling
under the classification of measures short of war is the protection of nationals
abroad. During the course of the last fifty years, international state practice
shows quite a few cases involving recourse to forcible action for the alleged protection of nationals abroad (Arend and Beck 1993: 93 et seq.). According to the
relevant legal test (Marston 1988: 773, 795, 800), which has to be strictly
adhered to, there must be an imminent threat of injury to nationals. There must
also be an inability, failure or unwillingness on part of the territorial sovereign to
protect the foreign nationals under threat. Finally, the forcible counter-measures
employed must be strictly limited to the purpose of protecting the nationals
under threat and they must be terminated, as soon as possible, with the smallest
possible infringement of foreign territory.

It is this necessity of satisfying the aforementioned legal test, which makes information warfare operations practically indispensable during the course of any recourse to forcible counter-measures for the protection of nationals. Information warfare allows states to fully exploit all their assets during any such recourse. Assets become virtually amalgamated into one fully automatic, as well as, interactive information network based on the basic principles of the World Wide Web (Joint Chiefs of Staff 2003: 3 et seq. also, Joint Command Control and Information Warfare School 2003: 11–12). As a direct consequence, all crucial pieces of information, including voice communication, photo and video imaging, can be exchanged in real time, thus providing all elements of the 'National Command Authority' of the state engaged in employing forcible counter-measures to protect nationals abroad with complete situational awareness (Joint Chiefs of Staff 2003: 3 et seq.; also, Joint Command Control and Information Warfare School 2003: 11–12).

Complete situational awareness under such circumstances is essential for an accurate factual review, which will eventually permit:

1 to assess the true magnitude of the threat at hand, as well as its imminence;
2 to assess and in the end confirm any potential failure, inability, or even unwillingness on part of the territorial sovereign to protect the nationals under threat;
3 to employ the most appropriate forcible counter-measures for protecting the nationals under threat and at the same time ensure the minimum possible infringement of foreign sovereignty, hence making the potential for abuse less likely (Joint Chiefs of Staff 2003: 3 et seq. also Joint Command Control and Information Warfare School 2003: 11–12).

War

War as an act of self-defence denotes comprehensive use of counter-force in response to an armed attack (Dinstein 2001: 207). Information warfare operations, as a result of their specific features, can play a major role within the context of such a war, even up to the point of almost literally single-handedly shaping its final outcome (Joint Chiefs of Staff 2003: 16 et seq.). The potential legitimacy of any information warfare operations resorted to within the context of a war of self-defence relates to the satisfaction of two criteria: the first one (which will be the main focus of discussion in the section at hand), is the three conditions of necessity, proportionality and immediacy; the second one (which is beyond the scope of the work at hand), comprises the legal requirements of the 'jus in bello'.

Recourse on the part of a state to a war of self-defence comprising mainly, or even strictly information warfare operations, following a full-scale military strike or invasion would satisfy the condition of necessity beyond any doubt. After all, no state can be expected to allow an invasion to proceed without resistance on the pretext that it should first exhaust all available means of seeking a peaceful settlement (Schachter 1984: 1620, 1635). On the other hand, when a war comprising information warfare operations begins following an isolated armed attack, the condition of necessity becomes much harder to satisfy. No such recourse is allowed unless the state contemplating it establishes that no other settlement of the crisis at hand can be attained in any other amicable way.

A war of self-defence, particularly one relying on successfully waged information warfare operations, has the actual potential of being the more extreme, as well as, destructive form of self-defence open to states. This is due to the fact that it is shaped around the unique, and potentially lethal, advantage of offering full access to the attacking state's information as well as to its decision cycle, which can thus be controlled and ultimately manipulated at will, along with all the military assets interconnected to it, without that state realizing it until it is too late. It therefore stands to reason that satisfying the condition of proportionality becomes especially important within this context.

Consequently, the following specific criteria must be met (Schachter 1984: 1637; also, Ago 1980: 13, 69). One, the comparative evaluation of force and counter-force must take place at the inception of the exercise of self-defence and not at its termination. Two, recourse to a war comprising information warfare operations as a measure of self-defence can only be justified and therefore be judged as being legitimate, only when it is predicated on the gravity, as well as the critical character, of the armed attack at hand. Finally, once such a war has commenced lawfully, it can be fought to the end, since the action needed to halt and repulse the attack, may well have to assume dimensions disproportionate to those of the attack suffered.

The applicability of the principle of proportionality to a war of self-defence comprising Information operations does not appear to be affected by the special nature and characteristics inherent in information warfare operations. By analogy to the 1996 Advisory Opinion issued by the ICJ with regard to the Legality of the Threat or Use of Nuclear Weapons (Advisory Opinion on the Threat or Use of Nuclear Weapons 1996: 256–7), the following analysis is deduced.

At present there is no customary or conventional international law prohibiting recourse to information warfare operations in the course of a war of self-defence. As a result, it could only be considered as illegal in light of a possible violation of general humanitarian law; especially with regard to the distinction between combatants and non-combatants and the prohibition to cause unnecessary suffering. In the end, and that has been made clear by the Court (Advisory Opinion on the Threat or Use of Nuclear Weapons 1996: 266), the eventual legality of any potential recourse to information warfare operations during the course of a war of self-defence will be dependent on whether the specific circumstances of self-defence which triggered it are such that they jeopardize the very survival of the state seeking such recourse.

As far as the principle of proportionality is concerned, it is subject neither to any geographical limitations nor to any misconceptions that would call for a war of self-defence to end immediately upon the aggressor state losing its willingness to continue the hostilities it initiated. As a result, information warfare operations can legitimately take place anywhere within the region of war, always in self-defence, and they may carry the combat to the source of the aggression (Case on Military and Paramilitary Activities in and against Nicaragua Dissenting Opinion of Judge Schwebel 1986: 371). Moreover, they may very well not be concluded as soon as the aggressor is repulsed and they may be continued on part of the defending state, until final victory is achieved (Kunz 1947: 872, 876; also, Zourek 1974: 49–50).

The final condition any information warfare operations, undertaken within the context of a lawful war of self-defence, must satisfy is the requirement of immediacy. Information warfare operations, with their inherent capability of providing an immediate forcible response practically as soon as the decision to seek recourse to them is taken, allow for an easy fulfilment of the condition of immediacy (Joint Chiefs of Staff 2003: 16 et seq.).

Information warfare operations in response to an armed attack from a state

An armed attack from, and not by, a state refers to the possibility of armed bands, irregulars or terrorist groups launching attacks against a state, from a base of operations situated within the territory of another state, without being sponsored or encouraged in any way by that state's government.

Only if a host country allows the use of its territory as a safe haven or staging area for armed attacks by private groups, when it could shut those operations down and does not exercise due diligence by taking all reasonable measures to take care of the situation at hand, while at the same time refuses requests to take action, the state targeted by those armed attacks can seek recourse to counter-force in self-defence (Wedgwood 1999: 559, 565; also, Fawcett 1961: 343, 363; Lillich 1976: 268–9). Any recourse to counter-force sought under the aforementioned condition, which can otherwise be referred to as 'extra-territorial law enforcement', can comprise any means of applying counter-force, as long as such means are not prohibited by international humanitarian law, including information warfare operations.

Recourse to information warfare operations, immediately after an armed attack mounted from a private group operating from the territory of a third state, can provide access to whatever information recourses that group is bound to be dependent upon, thus helping to assess the exact circumstances at hand and verify the potential existence of any subsequent necessity to infringe upon the sovereignty of that third state. This will also ensure that any forcible measures of counter-force eventually employed are not of an anticipatory measure, and that they are taken only in response to a real armed attack, a repetition of which can be expected. Access to the 'information cycle' of the private group responsible for the armed attacks will also play a crucial role in finally determining whether there are no alternative means for ending the group's activities.

Reliance on information warfare operations during the course of 'extra-territorial law enforcement' provides the defending state with a practically immediate response capability as soon as the armed attack suffered is completed. Hence, the cause (armed attack) and effect (self-defence) will be obvious beyond any doubt and the condition of immediacy, which requires a certain degree of urgency for any recourse to self-defence to be lawful, will be satisfied.

Last but not least, only information warfare operations can provide the precision required in order to ensure that any operation undertaken during recourse to 'extra-territorial law enforcement' will be directed exclusively against the armed bands, irregulars or terrorists using the territory of a third state as safe haven to launch armed attacks against the defending state and not against that state's military or against its civilian population.

Conclusion

Legislators in general, and international legislators in particular, in their constant quest for developing legal rules, in order to regulate all major aspects of the behaviour of individuals, as well as of states, very seldom tend to identify potential problems before they arise and put into place the relevant legislative solutions to those problems, before such solutions are needed. As a result, the actual eventual shape a given legislative answer developed in part of the international community in order to regulate a specific and previously unheard of issue may take often depends up, to a great extent, to the exact circumstances under which the issue to be regulated will manifest itself (Johnson 1999: 1–2).

The issue of information warfare operations in all their respective forms and with all their possible implications for the members of the international community, as well as for international peace and security, has practically barely began making its entry to the world stage as well as catching the eye of the protagonists of this stage and its full technical, military and legal aspects are far from being fully explored and appreciated.

In the coming decades, and in a highly unstable world environment, international peace and security may come face-to-face with a multitude of threats as well as challenges. However, none will be so likely to pose such a dramatic challenge, for both the best and the worst, as the one posed by the advent of the information revolution and especially by information warfare. The only way for the members of the international community to stand up successfully to this enormous challenge is by the adoption of an international legal network specifically designed to regulate all its potential aspects and therefore minimize the risks accompanying it.

This work was conceived and eventually put together with a very specific purpose in mind. To outline some of the challenges set by the advent of information warfare which is a completely new and mostly untried concept and as such is inevitably going to reach a point where it will require a regulatory framework. Nevertheless, a necessary prerequisite for the successful undertaking of such a feat is to begin by attempting to place modern information operations within the context of current legal norms relating to the use of force. Currently, existing legal norms on the use of force appear to be marginally capable of being that regulatory framework, and only because of the absence of a legal regime specifically tailored to deal with the issue at hand. On the other hand, they do offer a single yet significant advantage: they comprise the only set of basic, and at the same time commonly accepted, principles relating to the potential regulation of state forcible actions, which can easily serve as the basis for the actual development of the aforementioned specialized international legal regime.

Time can only tell how much of a threat information warfare will eventually prove to be in the years to come. However, it has undoubtedly given a completely new meaning to the term warfare and nullified traditional borders between states. These are only two of several new regulatory challenges, the successful answering of which will undoubtedly eventually call for the creation of a new paradigm with regard to the legal norms relating to forcible action. And the actual success of failure of any such new paradigm will depend on two factors, which they alone will decide whether it will be easily and unanimously accepted by all members of the international community:

1 its ability to guarantee the effective countering of a new and totally asymmetrical threat;
2 to prevent any potential abuses, by not allowing the states that may find themselves faced with that particular threat from reaching the conclusion that there is no alternative at their disposal, other than putting themselves above the rule of international law.

This is an issue, which sooner or later the international legal community will have no choice but to face. And before it finally does so, perhaps it should remember the words of James Thurbur (US Department of Defense 2001: 85): 'In times of change, learners shall inherit the earth, while the learned are beautifully equipped for a world that no longer exists.'

Part III
Ethno/religio/cultural cyberconflicts

8   The Internet and militant jihadism

Global to local re-imaginings

Frazer Egerton

Introduction

Although much has been written on the Internet's interaction with, and impact on, militant jihadism (Hoffman 2006b; Weimann 2006), one aspect of that relationship that has been under-explored is the way in which the Internet contributes to a greater array of possibilities in which individuals might imagine themselves. Such a (re)imagination is central to the story of militant jihadism in the West, a phenomenon that depends upon a reconfiguration in the way in which individuals self-identify and subsequently resituate themselves. This chapter seeks some measure of redress. It looks, using the Netherlands as a case study, at the effect of the Internet, and the images therein, in the creation of a particular self-conception that is at the centre of militant jihadism in the West. 'The revolution in communication technology in the 1990s ... coincided with the rise of the global Salafi jihad' (Sageman 2004: 158).

The assertion of the particular importance of the Internet in the study of militant jihadism rests on two arguments. First, the political imaginary has assumed a new significance in global politics today. This represents

> something new in global cultural processes: *the imagination as a social practice.* No longer mere fantasy (opium for the masses), no longer simple escape (from a world defined principally by more concrete purposes and structures), no longer elite pastime (thus not relevant to the lives of ordinary people), and no longer mere contemplation (irrelevant for new forms of desire and subjectivity), the imagination has become an organised field of social practices, a form of work (in the sense of both labour and culturally organized practice), and a form of negotiation between sites of agency (individuals) and globally defined fields of possibility.... *The imagination is now central to all forms of agency, is itself a social fact, and is the key component of the new global order.*
>
> (Appadurai 1996: 31, italics added)

There are few cases where this is more apparent than in the case of militant jihadism in the West, where the articulation of a new identification and the subsequent assertion that such an identity is under real threat, a process that may take place over a very short period of time, represents a particularly profound leap.

Second, there are many significant forces that facilitate an array of political imaginaries (Appadurai 1996; Rosenau 1990). There is no one dynamic that, taken in isolation, gives rise to a self-conception of individuals as representatives of a global ummah under threat from the West, and in whose defence they are obliged to wage jihad. However, an acknowledgement that there are several such forces at play should not detract from the fact that the Internet, and the images it transmits, is a significant one of them.

This chapter is divided into two sections. The first details the importance of the Internet for one particular group of militant jihadists in the Netherlands, in particular in the profusion of (a particular type of) images it offers. The second offers an analysis as to why the Internet and the images therein are so indispensable to the movement as it appears in the West.

The Hofstad group

The Hofstad group was named by the AIVD, the Dutch secret service. Hofstad translates as 'Court City', a reference to The Hague, the city in which they originally began to meet. It was a loose group, haphazardly and contingently constituted (Peters 2007).

Largely made up of second generation Dutch of Moroccan background, the group was watched by the AIVD since at least 2002. They rose to particular prominence when one of their numbers, Mohammed Bouyeri, killed Theo Van Gogh, on his way to work in Amsterdam in a ritualistic manner.[1] In accordance with his self-ascribed role as a provocateur, Van Gogh had issued various insulting diatribes aimed at almost every conceivable collective, including Islam. Since the prosecution of Bouyeri, who had hoped Dutch police would grant him his wish for martyrdom, many of the activities and plans of the group, and the individuals within it, have come to light. These include plots for further attacks, links with militants in other countries, and further efforts to kill and be killed (Nesser 2004: 12–14).

The Internet played a central role in the militancy of the members of the Hofstad group and it did so in a number of different forums in which the members participated and communities of which they were a part. The following account reflects that, examining its use in three areas:

1 group meetings;
2 the Hofstad group Internet community;
3 Internet communities between members and other militants.

Meetings

Members of the Hofstad group would meet twice weekly, in a phone centre in Schiedam and then in Bouyeri's house, where the living room served as a classroom and pulpit. In these meetings sermons were delivered by the Syrian Redouan al-Issa, who played a key role in the early days of the group. When he was absent, Mohammed Bouyeri assumed responsibility (Peters 2007).

In addition to embracing the wisdom of al-Issa and Bouyeri and discussing issues amongst themselves, the Hofstad group also used to watch film footage purportedly demonstrating the persecution of Muslims throughout the world, and the subsequent resistance offered by some. Recordings from Chechnya and Iraq appear to have been particularly prevalent. There was also a preoccupation, almost a fixation for some, with beheadings (Vermaat 2005). So central to the meetings were such films and clippings that many members would bring laptops to the meetings which they would use to watch material downloaded from Islamist websites. These sites

> showed executions in the Middle East, foreign infidels having their throats cut by holy warriors wrapped in scarves and balaclavas. Mohammed, according to a man who attended these sessions, got visibly excited by these grisly spectacles. Nouredine[2] spent his wedding night on a mattress in Mohammed's apartment, together with his bride, watching infidels being slaughtered.
>
> (Buruma 2006: 212)

After the murder of Van Gogh, police raided Bouyeri's apartment. There they found

> [a] CD-ROM disc ... with video film of more than twenty-three killings of 'the enemies of Allah,' including the American reporter Daniel Pearl. These were taken from a Saudi website edited in London. Apart from detailed images of men of various nationalities being beheaded, the CD contained pictures of a struggling man slowly having his head sawed off, taken from a Dutch porn site.
>
> (Buruma 2006: 4)

Hofstad Internet community

The Hofstad group ran an Internet community within which films, translations and information – 'snatches of revolutionary texts, calls for jihad, glorifications of martyrdom' (Buruma 2006: 194) – could be shared. This was done through an MSN group that was set up and controlled by one if its members Ahmed Hamdi. It was Hamdi who dictated who was allowed to join, and having done so engage in the exchanges that took place therein (Vermaat 2006). He was also the IT expert to whom other group members would turn to maximise their efforts and to offer a degree of security from the authorities (Benschop 2004).

Because of their acquaintance, even intimacy, with one another, and because of the presence of a gatekeeper in Hamdi who studiously vetted membership, this community was the electronic mirror of the living-room meetings. The same activities were undertaken by the same known individuals – texts were translated and distributed, conflict footage (including the beheadings) exchanged, usually from English language websites and threatening letters to key Dutch political figures drafted (Buruma 2006: 194).

Other Internet communities

> The members of this network used (the) Internet to express their process of radicalisation, to convince others ... of the blessings of the holy jihad, in order to cultivate the group feeling of the chosen ones, and to give themselves a political identity.
>
> (Benschop 2004)

The Hofstad group neither demanded nor received exclusive loyalty from its members. Many, if not all, were involved with other groups of militants, often loose coalitions who came together in Internet chatrooms. Perhaps the best way to conceive of the militant milieu in the Netherlands in the early twenty-first century is of several fluid and overlapping groups, all of whom shared some information and memberships.

> A few members of the Hofstad group set up and maintained a number of MSN groups. In this way they made their own web pages with MSN groups, for example under the name 5343, the tawheedwaljihad and the MSN group Muwahidin/dewareMoslims. Based on Peters'[3] analysis of the literature from members of the Hofstad group ... and the analysis of the dissemination pattern of a number of documents from this literature, we can say that many of the MSN groups were clearly influenced directly or indirectly by the Hofstad group.
>
> (Joustra 2007: 64)

Bouyeri, for example, hosted the afore-mentioned MSN group Muwahidin. Hamdi's expertise was again utilised and he served as the assistant webmaster of the group (Benschop 2004). Using his alias, Abu Zubair, Bouyeri wrote articles about (militant) Islam and translated texts of influential radical Islamist thinkers, including Abul Ala Mawdudi[4] and Sayyid Qutb.[5] His writings also referenced contemporary figures, including Omar Addur-Rahman[6] and Abu Hamza al-Masri.[7] He also offered familiar militant diatribes against the West, called for jihad to be waged in Iraq, for prominent Dutch figures to be killed, and for a re-establishment of the caliphate as a guarantor of Muslim rights in the face of Western hostility.

Another member of the Hofstad group was Rashid Bousana. He is described as spending much of his day in front of a computer visiting militant jihadist sites. Through (and because of) these, he sought to recruit others to the case of militant jihadism, as well as to collect funds for the Al-Aqsa Foundation in Rotterdam[8] (Benschop 2004).

Bilal Lamrani was an additional member of the group and someone who actively recruited, both for the Hofstad group and for the wider violent jihadi cause. He also made much use of the Internet in his efforts to convince others of the obligation to, and desirability of, waging jihad.[9] In one MSN group he responded to the question as to whether one who abuses the prophet Mohammed should be punished by death. His answer is unambiguous:

> It is an obligation to kill he who abuses the Prophet whether he is Muslim or Kaafir. And Hirsi Ali and Theo van Gogh, these pigs who have abused the prophet their punishment is death and their day will come with Allah's will![10]
>
> (cited in Benschop 2004).

Similarly, in the site 'Jama'at Al-Tawheed Wal Jihaad', he wrote that

> those who combat Muslims or support the combat of Muslims in any way are regarded as one joint enemy. And unfortunately the Netherlands hasn't learnt anything from the blessed attacks in Madrid.... We Muslims accept no humiliation!!... And Geert Wilders and Hirsi Ali[11] and the Dutch government, the Mujahidin are on their way. Oh, Allah, let our death resurrect the Ummah again ... Amen.
>
> (Benschop 2004)

Lamrani maintained two MSN groups himself. Particularly prevalent in these were death threats against Mr Wilders (Joustra 2007: 64). Indeed, this seems to have been something of a preoccupation for Lamrani. A professionally edited video of his from January 2005 began with a pledge of support for Bouyeri and ended with the message 'A small present for Geert Wilders. We have already sharpened our swords, dog'. In the background there was the sound of knives being sharpened (Joustra 2007: 73). When he was arrested for the first time police found 140 pictures of Bin Laden on his computer (Benschop 2004).

Two other members of the Hofstad group were brothers Jason and Jermaine Walters, the sons of an American father and Dutch mother. At the age of sixteen Jason converted to Islam with real enthusiasm, and pursued a radical interpretation shortly afterwards. Jermaine followed a similar trajectory. According to a familiar pattern, Jason made extensive use of the Internet. The content of that which he engaged with is not dramatically different from those the others did – radical texts and war footage. However, there are also records of interesting discussions he has with other individuals, in which the righteousness of theft and murder are discussed.[12]

Thus far the story has been about those who already accept militancy. However, it is not only committed followers that utilise the Internet, but also those who later turn to militancy. Media matters in the formative stages of militancy. For example, upon release from a spell in prison, Mohammed Bouyeri immediately began using the Internet in his search for 'the truth' (Benschop 2004). That was his first port of call. Indeed for Bouyeri, who was largely self-taught in Islam and the radical version he embraced, the majority of his know-ledge, much of which he in turn sought to impart via the Internet and the living-room sermons, 'came from English translations of Arabic texts down-loaded from the Internet' (Buruma 2006: 3–4).

The Internet as a tool in the exploration of a religion, and the reformulation of identity, was common to many others. During the hearing of Soumaya Sahla[13] who was detained in Amsterdam at the same time as Nouredine el Fatmi and Martine van der Oeven,[14] she detailed how she regularly visited Internet cafes in Amsterdam and The Hague, in an effort to acquire information concerning her faith. In one incident, when she began wearing a burqa her father tore it up. Sympathisers who heard of her plight ordered replacements and had them mailed to her home (Button 2005). Via the Internet she searched radical sights including al-islaam, al-yaqeen and islamway.com (Benschop 2004). She also regularly chatted with Nouredine via MSN, after he got in touch with her after her various Internet postings (Benschop 2004; Joustra 2007: 65). It was to the Internet that Sahla turned in her pursuit of a radical interpretation of Islam. As far as is known she did not turn to a local figure or institution but to the elec-tronic media and all that it offers.

Similarly, Joustra reports that

> the autobiographical sketches of Samir A(zzouz),[15] that the Dutch National Criminal Investigation Team discovered on his computer under the title 'Deurwaarders' (Bailiffs), contain an extreme description of his searching procedures on the Internet and the part played by the Internet in his radicali-sation process.
>
> (Joustra 2007: 74)

Another example of this process is Bilal Lamrani. He described his burgeoning interest in Islam in the following way:

> I will not deny it. I am interested in the jihad. But eight months ago I wasn't religious at all. I know very little about islam. Someone mailed me: 'If you consider yourself a muslim, read this, and read that'. And he sent me videos of the events in the Middle East and some books. I don't know who that person is. I get this sort of thing a lot on the internet.
>
> (Bilial Lamrani, cited in Benschop 2004)

Then there is the story of Yaya K,[16] an eighteen-year-old student from Sas von Gent who was detained after making threats against Hirshi Ali and the AIVD. Joustra reports that

> [d]uring his arrest he was found in possession of home-made explosives that he had assembled using knowledge derived from the internet. He had under-

gone the entire radicalisation process from in front of this computer screen in the virtual world as well.

(Joustra 2007: 82).

Yaya was not a member of the Hofstad group, but his story of radicalisation and the role of the Internet on it is a superb example of that which impacted many of those who were connected to the Hofstad group. It is also very similar to that of Michael R, a seventeen-year-old descendent of British and Dutch parents who converted to Islam at the age of fourteen. He had been the administrator of various MSN groups in which he disseminated 'fundamentalist texts and threatening appeals, films and images.... (He) published hundreds of texts on his websites, with speeches of Osama bin Laden and members of the Hofstadgroup.... He made links to jihadist photos and videos' (Benschop 2004).

The examples above illustrate the importance of the Internet to militant jihadists in the Netherlands. It seems highly likely that such 'imagery shooting around the world' (Buruma 2006: 4), accessed and shared by the Hofstad group, contributed to a process whereby men and women felt themselves to occupy a certain role, one that called upon them to avenge those who had transgressed, as Van Gogh had done. In the remainder of this chapter one particular reason why this might be so is explored – the transformative effect it may exert on individuals because of the particular images circulating through cyberspace.

Opening up the conditions of possibility – the role of images

'In both sites however, the bulk of the threads are pictures of Jihad. Actual discussion among members is not very deep; the pictures and news are looked at and praised more than they are actually debated on' (Taboul 2005). Almost an aside, this represents a crucial element of the effect of the Internet on militant jihadism. In her study of radical Francophone Islamist websites, Taboul examines two particular sites. Despite considerable differences in their emphases,[17] both are nonetheless dominated by images of violent jihad. There are many other things that might have received greater attention. Discussions on what it is prescribed for Muslims to do in a variety of different circumstances, appeals for the satisfaction of the social needs of other Muslims and accounts of the history of Islam all figure in the two sites, along with numerous other topics and debates. However, these are all overshadowed by images of Muslims being killed and mistreated around the world and the efforts of some mujahideen to respond in kind, albeit one prescribed by God. In addition to the dominance of such images, another marked feature is that they also provoke limited discussion. There is very little, if any, debate as to what they represent, who the apparent victims are/were and what reasons led to this state of affairs. This is assumed superfluous – the answers are taken as clear. The abundance of images meets with both approval and a particular understanding.

Such an acceptance of the meaning of pictures and videos is not peculiar to the story of militant jihadism, or even Islamism. The main portal for those members of the Sikh diaspora who support the creation of a homeland, Khalistan, in what is today India, is www.khalistan.net. There one can find numerous images of the victim, again, with little explanation deemed necessary:

> The production of the image of the tortured body constitutes the Sikh subject through gruesome spectacle, one whose contours are quite familiar to those involved in, for example, Palestinian or Kashmiri struggles. The authority of the spectacle, moreover, is elaborated through reference to a monstrous inhuman Other, the Indian nation-state.
>
> (Axel 2002: 415)

In the Sikh example, the dead bodies represent the suffering of the Sikh people at the hands of an Indian state that is unwavering in its opposition, something that, in the name of the preservation and protection of Sikhs, necessitates the establishment of a homeland. In the Islamist example, footage of conflict is taken to demonstrate the existence of a battle, waged by the West against Muslims, and the response in the face of an asymmetric power difference of some righteous believers, again with a focus on dead bodies. Thus, for VCD's released by Muslim partisans to the conflicts in Ambon, Indonesia, their

> appeal depends upon their sympathetic, almost tactile engagement with victims and their bodies, on close-ups of oozing wounds, bullets protruding from body parts, maimed and charred corpses, and the bodily contortions, moans and screams of people's suffering too painful to watch.
>
> (Spyer 2002: 12)

Images play a role here that encompasses, but moves beyond, propaganda. They offer something that is materially different to that which may be produced by other forms of communication, for, as Marshall McLuhan (2001) persuasively argues, the medium affects the message. Medium theory, championed by McLuhan and his intellectual predecessor Harold Innis (1999), 'holds that communication is a sphere where the technology involved may have an immense significance for the society in which it occurs, and perhaps radically affect the concurrent forms of social and economic organisation' (Deibert 1997: 21).[18]

The expression of the belief in a global conflict between Islam and the West and stories of horrors perpetuated against Muslims from around the world may have an effect on audiences, but it is quite different from that which can result from witnessing and absorbing images which purportedly carry the same claims. The images and videos that proliferate on militant jihadists sites are dominated by one idea – jihad in the face of Western aggression.[19]

Such footage is highly emotive, but its significance goes beyond that. Much of the power of these images lies in their transformative effect. They present both the familiar militant worldview of Western aggression and a justified Islamic response, but importantly also allow for a ready accommodation of the individual within that global understanding. In the earlier Sikh example, the images presented the idea of Indian hostility and, crucially, allowed diasporic Sikhs to vicariously experience what they never had directly, and to reimagine themselves as an integral part of that supposed battle. The same story can be told for numerous movements. The anti-globalisation movement to which the militant jihadist one has more than a passing resemblance (as noted in Burke 2003) has enabled individuals from a wealth of backgrounds not only to protest the inequities and unfairness to which globalisation is alleged to give rise, but also to conceive of themselves as necessarily involved in reversing that trend not as external actors motivated by morality but as integral actors motivated also by identity.[20] Images of battles involving Muslims can have the similar effect, convincing some in Paris and Berlin that the conflicts in Palestine and Baghdad are not distant conflicts involving actors for whom they may have a great deal of sympathy, but little in common, that in fact they share the same plight.

This is possible in large part because of the nature of images, which, by their nature present an unanalysed, decontextualised snapshot. The recipient does not interact with them in the way they do a sustained written argument. They are more free-floating, to be taken, understood and used not according to the facts of the argument but rather the preferences of the consumer. It includes no historical perspective. In the absence of continuity and context, as Postman cites Terence Moran, 'bits of information cannot be integrated into an intelligent and consistent whole' (Postman 1984: 137). As Postman himself comments

> [m]eaning is distorted when a word or sentence is, as we say, taken out of context; when a reader or listener is deprived of what was said before, and after. But there is no such thing as a photograph taken out of context, for a photograph does not require one. In fact, the point of photography is to isolate images from context, so as to make them visible in a different way.... Like telegraphy, photography recreates the world as a series of idiosyncratic events. There is no beginning, middle, or end in a world of photographs, as there is none implied by telegraphy. The world is atomised. There is only a present and it need not be part of any story that can be told.
>
> (Postman 1984: 74)

Appadurai similarly writes that what images have to offer

> to those who experience and transform them is a series of elements (such as characters, plots and textual forms) out of which scripts can be formed of imagined lives, their own as well as those of others living in other places.
>
> (1996: 35)

In a world where photographic images dominate, anything can be made separate from, or connected to, anything else. They are able to 'perform a peculiar kind of dismembering of reality, a wrenching of moments out of their contexts, and a juxtaposing of events and things that have no logical or historical connection with each other' (Postman 1984: 74). Thus the fragments of the lives of others offered by the images circulating on the Internet and accessed around the world has meaning ascribed largely according to the desires of the film editor, the consumer, the future militant jihadist.

The failure to engage with the footage is not simply intellectual apathy. It is the direct result of the ahistoricism and decontextualisation of images (see also Naficy 1991). They are taken by the consumer and meaning conferred upon them as the individual constructs a story within which they might be placed, one which imagines their own lives as well as others, often in disparate locations and diverse situations. The 'images and messages have a binding effect on prepared participants, as these select and interpret the content within the framework of already existing commitments to a transcendent project' (Cetina 2005: 222). These images are sewn together by the recipients in accordance with, and production of, a particular narrative of right and wrong, suffering and resistance, allowing for the construction of a story within which they might be placed, one which imagines their own lives as well as those of others, often in disparate locations and diverse situations. That they are able to do so, is because the images themselves 'provide little perspective on events and often make no pretension to having a narrative, besides, that is, the insistent, repetitive narrative of victimisation resurrected on and out of body parts' (Spyer 2002: 12). The picture of a dead woman in Srebenicia can thus become part of the same story as the picture of a dead child in Fallujah. Marked differences between the Muslims in Bosnia and those in Iraq, as well as within the two countries need not enter the equation. The same applies for the supposed aggressors.[21] The conflicts do not need to be placed in a broader historical context – there is no need for reference to and exploration of the effects of the rise of the neo-conservatives in the United States, the demise of Yugoslavia, the belligerence of Saddam Hussein etc. There are limits of course – the image of a dead body is the image of a dead body, and a narrative that seeks to explain how that came about cannot explain it as being something wholly different. Intellectually, however, the explanation for that dead body may include the clash of (religious) civilisations, the inherent violent misogyny of men, the imperatives of a state system in a condition of anarchy or the unfortunate side effects of a humanitarian-inspired enterprise to rid a nation of a dictator. However, for those accessing these sites there is minimal, if any, consideration of such differing explanations. No such views are animating discussion amongst those accessing jihadist footage. Rather, there is a clear consensus as to what is being witnessed, and so 'Ambon's VCDs look much like Kashmir's, Bosnia's, and those of Palestine shown in Malaysia and elsewhere' (Spyer 2002: 12). Moreover, because of the role of the electronic media, the people in the images are 'experienced as intimates' (Meyrowitz 1986: 137), that is, a close connection is drawn between the viewer and the viewed. A link is drawn between the two with an understanding that they are both warriors in the same war.

Images of jihad are accommodated into a narrative constructed by individuals in a way that allows them to be part of it, something that would be difficult, if not inconceivable, without them. The images allow for self-conceptions of groups in the Netherlands, Italy and Sweden as being the same as that they have conferred on others in Afghanistan, Bosnia and Iraq. Pictures of blood-stained niqab-wearing bodies affirm the existence of a conspiracy against Muslims. Images of a man in orange being beheaded to the background of Koranic scriptures and the soundtrack of Arabic music acts as confirmation of the ummah and its willingness to fight back. In such a dichotomous world it is a much easier task to accommodate oneself, even if your experience of Islam consists of little more than occasional visits with your uncle to a mosque when you were young, meetings with other militants and hours spent reading radical texts (about jihad) and watching videos in which it is apparently being waged by your co-religionists.

The near synonymous growth of the Internet and the phenomenon of militant jihadism in the West is not a coincidence. The latter requires a leap of the political imaginary that is facilitated in part by the former. The Internet, with images as a prime currency, help to make possible identification as part of a global Islamic community under sustained attack by a non-believing opponent. Without the instantaneous, interactive forum of the Internet and the access to images it provides, the reimagination on Western individuals as mujahideen would be an infinitely more difficult affair.

Notes

1 Van Gogh was a descendent of the artist Vincent, as well as a prominent Amsterdam writer and filmmaker in his own right. Bouyeri first shot Van Gogh, and then tried to behead him with a knife. He planted a note on his body with another knife.
2 Nouredine el Fatmi was an illegal immigrant in the Netherlands who shared a house and membership of the Hofstad group with Bouyeri. After Van Gogh's capture Nouredine and Samir Azzouz both tried to begin other similar cells. His Koranic knowledge was negligible and so he relied upon the Internet to read aloud 'Qur'anic verses and other details about what he called "pure Islam". The girls to whom he was preaching were also "shown videos of decapitations"' (Neurink 2005) '"Mujahideen of the lowlands" on trial in the Netherlands' (*Terrorism Monitor*, 3, pp. 6–8, p. 7).
3 Professor Ruud Peters analysed Mohammed Bouyeri's thoughts for the court that tried him.
4 Founder of the Jamaat-e-Islami Pakistani political party.
5 An Egyptian, ultimately tortured and hanged by Nasser's regime, Qutb radicalised after a two and a half year spell in the US. Upon his return he joined the Muslim Brotherhood. His works include *In the Shade of the Qu'aran* and *Milestones*.
6 The 'blind Sheikh', imprisoned for his role in the WTC bombings of 1993.
7 Egyptian-born preacher currently serving a seven-year sentence for crimes that include inciting terror. Hamza was the imam at the notorious Finsbury Park mosque in North London. O'Neill and McGrory (2006) *The Suicide Factory: Abu Hamza and the Finsbury Park Mosque*.
8 The foundation was outlawed in 2003 after the AIVD published its 2002 annual report. The report says that foundation money was transferred to Hamas to buy weapons and train suicide bombers.
9 For example, in April 2004 he advised people to take shooting lessons as good preparation for conflict and counselled them as to how they may best avoid detection. He provided the details of a number of possible venues and offered the following advice as to how to appear as inconspicuous as possible.

> Try to keep this kind of activities a secret, so that you may depart from a pure niyya (intention). At the shooting range, keep your opinions and convictions to yourself, and don't go in conclave with the others that are present. Don't talk about Islam and perform your salaat in secret. You are going to the shooting range as a preparation for the Jihad and not to invite people to Islam.

> (Benschop 2004)

10 The text he quotes, 'Verplichting van het doden van degene die de profeet uitscheld' [Obligation to kill those who revile the prophet], was from a collection of texts from a fourteenth-century document which had been translated by Mohammed Bouyeri in July 2004.

11 Both are politicians and both have excited much hostility amongst Dutch Muslims.

12 In one example a conversation takes place between Jason and another unidentified discussant. In it the two discuss what is permitted and esteemed by Islam, including theft and murder. The interpretation of these moral questions is that of Abdul-Jabbar van de Ven, a convert and preacher at a mosque in Eindhoven. In one forum, with Walters writing under a pseudonym, he requested that the other person ask van de Ven whether he was justified in killing and stealing from non-Muslims, in his words, whether (Van de Ven's interpretation of) Islam would 'permit slaughtering the "kufaar" (the disbelievers) and/or stealing their riches'. Later Walters, who between the two correspondences has met with van de Ven, excitedly tells another anonymous chatroom participant that the Imam authorises violence against the Dutch Benschop. Van de Ven attracted considerable attention in the Netherlands for an interview in which he expressed the desire that the MP Geert Wilders die within two years, that Osama Bin Laden was a 'brother' and that 'the Netherlands is a cancer'. His later protestations that he was not authorised to issue fatwas and that his relationship with Jason was slight was generally dismissed, but one who knows him, and Walters, better than most described him as the most apolitical salafist he had ever met (Peters 2007; Interview with author).

13 Sahla came from a traditional Moroccan family in The Hague but rejected their traditionalism for the very modern militant jihadism she pursued.

14 A Dutch convert.

15 Azzouz, a Dutchman born of Moroccan parents, became a militant very early in his life. He is currently in prison after a third prosecution proved successful.

16 Dutch law prohibits the publishing of a defendant's full name (Mohammed Bouyeri, for example was referred to for a long time as Mohammed B). Successful prosecution removes that injunction, and the difficulty in policing the Internet often circumvents the rule. Yaya K's full name remains out of the public arena however.

17 'Voice of the Oppressed ... is aggressive, political and uses heavy propaganda. The other, Al Mourabitoune, uses a more subtle and societal approach and relies heavily on religious teachings' (Taboul 2005).

18 Innis argued that different media have different potential power for control. Thus a medium that is either in short supply, or complicated to operate, is more likely to be used by those within society who have the resources of time, finances and education to do so. A more democratising process may be anticipated by a more widely available form of media. Further, Innis argued that each manner of communication has a bias either towards durability or distance. The former, such as stone hieroglyphics, last a long time and tend to lead towards small and stable societies. The latter, for example papyrus, facilitates larger and less stable societies. To Innis's work, McLuhan added the notion of media as extensions of human processes and senses. Different periods of history – there are three for McLuhan, namely oral, writing/printing and electronic – are characterised by a different interplay between those forms of media and the senses and therefore by alternative forms of thought and communication (Meyrowitz 1986).

19 This is not limited to direct military actions. The roots of Muslim suffering in Saudi Arabia, Algeria and Palestine are thus the responsibility of Western countries who support the occupiers and governments that allow this oppression to happen.
20 See also Scholte (1996) and Tololyan (2001).
21 As witnessed by the transformation of the United States, Britain and others from rescuer, perhaps belatedly, in Bosnia, to the aggressors in Iraq.

9 How small are small numbers in cyberspace?

Small, virtual, wannabe 'states', minorities and their cyberconflicts

Athina Karatzogianni

Introduction

This chapters argues, first, that established mainstream media and their online equivalents usually support what different theorists call state-like, hierarchical, or vertebrate political forms of organization crucial to state/status quo survival. Second, that independent, alternative or peer-to-peer, networked media, usually support transnational, rhizomatic, cellular networks, such as ethnoreligious and sociopolitical movements or diasporic minorities and dissident networks within. Third, that small states and minorities are especially vulnerable to both these modalities, as they are frequently too small, too new or too insignificant to have been adequately mass-mediated in the past, so any representations by the mass media are registered automatically as negotiated in the global public sphere.

Further, by examining small states' and minorities' online representations, this chapter seeks to contribute empirically to Appadurai's notion that a geography of anger is fuelled by the media, but its sparks are the uncertainty about the enemy within and the anxiety about the always incomplete project of national purity so that 'these geographies are the spatial outcome of complex interactions between faraway events and proximate fears, between old histories and new provocations, between rewritten borders and unwritten orders' (Appadurai 2006: 100).

Small states

As Jeanne Hey argues, despite decades of study, no satisfactory definition has been found, rendering smallness useless as an analytical tool, as some scholars can have in mind microstates with a population of less than one million, small states in the developed world, and small states in the third world or former colonies (Hey 2003). Stereotyping small states means conceptualizing them as insular, insecure, underdeveloped, unstable, vulnerable, limited in foreign policy, passive and reactive states, incapable of instigating change in the world system. Exceptions to these descriptions refer to the flexible, creative, networking/alliance-building capacity and risky behaviour, under specific local and systemic opportunities some of these states display, such as Luxemburg.

If we were to accept Hey's solution to this definitional problem and its repercussions, that 'if a state is perceived as small either by its own people or by others, it should be considered a small state', then we would have to rigorously engage with issues very much related to how some of these states are represented, perceived and mediated in the global public sphere; what that means for their capacity-building capabilities; how their image is mediated by the global media and communications; what are the circumstances behind these representations on the systemic, global politico-economic climate of both international, transnational, regional and local levels of societies, corporations, cultures and individuals; and even more significantly for this particular discussion what are the structurational dynamics in relation to media networks and their current transformations due to competitions created through the new information communications technologies, for instance alternative or grassroots media, independent direct publishing, digitization, and copyright and financial challenges to name a few.

Currently, states are asked to operate in an environment of importation logic, aggravated by the consequences of internal and external protest in the global scene as 'the protesting actor irrupts onto a scene that is already affected by a loss of meaning, that is destabilized and challenged by the crisis affecting the universality of political models' (Badie 2000: 201) namely then from multi-variant tensions deriving from dependence and diffusion of the Western model of government. Following Badie's argument, individuals uncertain of the failure of states and their diplomatic and military monopoly, which already feels foreign, choose to ally themselves to networks of global solidarity, where citizenships, nationalities and identities converge, compete or collide. The weakening of the periphery through Westernization/importation 'accelerates the relativization of citizenship allegiances … [has] the unusual effect of reactivating transnational cultural actors' and this reactivation has much to do with 'the call of empty social spaces linked to the bankruptcy of imported states' (ibid.: 203).

If 'traditional culture is associated with the media and encouraged politically to inflame the allegiance of the receiving public and to prevent the traditional culture from serving the ends of protest activity' (ibid.: 207), then to what extent is this successful in relation to smaller states, their representations and their cultures, especially under the current transformation of the global media due to the challenges of fast virtual communications and enhanced capabilities these afford the receiving public?

This chapter engages with these questions by looking at online discourses and images produced by the global media, mainstream and independent/grassroots media, official/unofficial websites of small states, wannabe small states, minorities seeking independence and statehood, secessionist movements, individuals and collectivities from these communities. The regions used here as empirical examples are Transistria/Pridnestrovie, Vanuatu, Papua, Lebanon and Estonia and the main media examined for all cases are BBConline, CNNonline, English.aljazeera.net, the *Guardian* online and for each case individually relevant local and regional online publications, by the groups and individuals described above. Methodologically and theoretically, this work expands research on ethnoreligious and sociopolitical cyberconflicts and the cyberconflict model to include cultural cyberconflict (Karatzogianni 2006) through engaging the work of Arjun Appadurai (2006).

The 'virtual state' in wannabe states: the case of Pridnestrovie

> People simply presume that the terminal entity for loyalties, policy decisions, and moral authority is, for better and worse, the state. This presumption is so deeply ingrained in the culture of modernity that is not treated as problematic. ... Thus with the state deeply ensconced as a cast of mind, as an organizing premise, the initial – indeed the only – response to the collapse of states due to war, internal strife, or other calamities is to rebuild them.... The state-preserving habit opposes partition and favors forcing antagonistic groups to remain together on the grounds that a rebuild society and state will lead to degrees of stability and progress such that the antagonisms and hatreds will give way as conditions improve, as if hatred derives from rational calculation as to what is in the best interest of those who hate.
>
> (Rosenau 2003: 342)

The *Guardian*, in 'Welcome to Nowhere' informs us that we will struggle to find Transistria or Somaliland in an atlas, because they do not officially exist. Gwyn Topham, the author, asks 'But can you holiday there?' His reference is a series of the BBC, *Holidays in the Danger Zone*:

> another level of non-existence: a whole swath of regions, conflict areas and breakaway states, off the political map, unrecognised by the international community, where people stubbornly continue to live. These are the sort of places Simon Reeve has chosen to visit.

According to Reeve, if you are an eighteen-year-old, you go to Peru and Thailand because it is exotic, so if you want to push the boundaries, this is your next destination: the unrecognized regions 'where gunmen and poverty are recurring themes' and 'the scenery is pretty special. Azerbaijan, Armenia, Georgia, the central highlands of Taiwan – they're stunning, the sort of stuff that makes you go – [mimes jaw dropping]'. We encouraged to visit these places as tourist destinations, since the trips to Peru and Thailand, which of course everyone can afford, are not 'special' anymore.

For example, this is Transistria, Trasnister or Pridnestrovie – depending on your political mood – described by Reeve:

> You could probably get here for a long weekend. From Chisinau, the Moldovan capital, you can just get a bus or a taxi to Transnistria for the

price of a bag of chips. If you're on the bus, just sit at the back and keep quiet. But even being stopped by the Transnistria immigration officials is going to be a fun experience; if you're the sort of person who's prepared to go there then you want that sort of thing.

(*Guardian*, 28 April 2005)

His tips are

in these countries $5 goes a long way; if you want to see something, you might find there are 'special entrance fees' that will get you in; you probably need a visa – but the rules are fairly flexible, you aren't going to Sweden.

Also: 'here have been some fabulous traveller's tales and encounters en route – from buying fake passports and drinking snake's blood to finding a field full of abandoned missiles' (ibid.). Again in the *Guardian*, another wonderful article on the region:

for the surreal breakaway para-state of Transnistria on the east bank of the river Dniestr looks at first glance like a miniature version of the old Soviet Union. In the heart of the capital, Tiraspol, a giant redstone Lenin stands proudly before the Supreme Soviet. It makes me feel almost nostalgic....
  What does Transnistria matter to anyone who is not, as I am, a lover of the Tintinesque and a connoisseur of obscure east European conflicts?'

(Ash, 19 May 2005)

Similarly, photographs of the region in cyberspace are often followed with 'Forget Cuba, there is only one place you can experience Soviet-style communism as it really was' (Kirk, undated). Remarkably, a tourist unable to visit inside military facilities comments on globalvoices.org: 'The old Bendery fortress located inside a military base. We were not allowed to visit it [...]. Too bad. I think that because of paranoically keeping itself closed, [Transnistria] loses lots of tourists – and not just the political ones' (Khokhlova, 22 September 2006).
  A rather different approach on the issue is taken by Global Security, an online thinktank which advertises 'reliable security information' on its site, that Moldova has sought peaceful solutions to its ethnic and security problems including offering the largely Russian population of the separatist Transdniester region broad autonomy. Alas, 'bolstered by the presence of Russian troops, Transdniester continues to hold out for independence, thus denying Moldova control over significant industrial assets and its border with Ukraine'. These 'separatists' are involved in 'money-laundering and the manufacturing and smuggling of weapons, as well as trafficking in human beings and drugs' (globalsecurity.org). Along the same lines, Tom Casey, Washington spokesman, commenting on a referendum held in the region favouring independence (97 per cent voted for independence), states that the

US does not recognize the independence referendum held yesterday in the Transnistrian region of Moldova. … As the international community has made clear, Transnistria is a part of Moldova, and yesterday's efforts by the Transnistrian regime should not be recognized as anything other than an attempt to destabilize Moldova.

(Casey, 18 September 2006)

Although the 'Moldovan Dniester Republic' (MDR) is not recognized by the international community, the BBC reports that Russia has called this referendum free and fair, a number of deputies in the Russian parliament, the State Duma, have called for recognition and that 'critics argue that polls were not free and fair on the grounds that, by international standards, Trans-Dniester does not have a free press or a multi-party democracy' (Petru, 11 December 2006). To enlighten us, Al-Jazeera English constructs the conflict this way:

Trans-Dniestr declared independence in 1990 in Soviet times in response to fears that Moldova's Romanian-speaking majority would join up again with their Romanian neighbours to the south. A brief war erupted between the two sides in 1992, halted by Russian troops who remain despite promises to leave, guarding de facto crossing points and 20,000 tonnes of Soviet-era munitions.

(Al-Jazeera English, 20 September 2006)

Or according to the *Washington Times*, it is 'a black hole – a part of Moldova over which Moldovan authorities exercise no control' that 'diminishes the prospect of integration with European and transatlantic institutions, and it also serves as an all-purpose excuse for the failure to produce results' (Lindberg, 1 June 2004). And not surprisingly, NGOs are there yet again to offer and publicize online their invaluable services to the region 'controlled by the clan of its president':

In 2006, People in Need introduced a project to support Transnistrian non-governmental organizations. In close cooperation with its Ukrainian and Moldavian partners, PIN will identify potential participants of the project who will subsequently be provided with management training specifically focused on non-governmental organizations and effective support for their activities.

(People in Need)

This so far portrayed as special, fun, unimportant, criminal, undemocratic, destabilizing, steeped-in-cultural-conflict region is a product of a process that many nation-states had to face in the 1980s and 1990s:

the pressure to open up their markets to foreign investment, commodities, and images and the pressure to manage the capacity of their own cultural minorities to use the globalized language of human rights to argue for their own claims for cultural dignity and recognition.

(Appaduarai 2006: 65)

In the Caucasus it happened to Moldova with Transdniester, to Georgia with South Ossetia and Abkhazia, to Russia with Chechnya, the latter readily supporting the wannabe independent states, but shy of discussing the 'enemies' within. The obvious alliance between the three de facto independent states is presented by the *Tiraspol Times* (Tiraspol is the country's capital) as follows:

> According to the memorandum filed by the three non-UN members, Georgia and Moldova are presenting a threat to the world's security since they are carrying out military and political provocations against the already de facto independent republics and imposing economic blockades on them.
>
> (*Tiraspol Times*, 30 November 2006)

As Appadurai argues such state insecurity is especially marked

> where the states have lost clear links to mass politics, where ambiguous or selectively favourable economic policies are imposed on behalf of wider global interests or forces, and where states have begun to substitute fundamentally culturalist policies for developmentalist ones.
>
> (Appadurai 2006: 104)

This cultural struggle, which integrates war and politics at the borders with vigilance and purification at the centres, is exacerbated by the media in general and by new communication technologies in particular. The fight to win the global war of messages, propaganda and ideas has often produced unpredictable results, especially in cyberspace.

For instance, the answer to the aforementioned discourses on the Pridnestrovie is the official site of the Moldovan Dniester Republic set up specifically to counter most of what they see as Moldova's disinformation campaign (http://www.pridne strovie.net). It is a site that deliberately attempts to contradict these descriptions, which utilizes the latest web technologies and explains the MDR position professionally one by one, using the language of political marketing and national rhetoric:

> 10 Things you didn't know about Europe's newest country: Double of Iceland's population, Multi-party democracy, Signed UN human rights charters, Market based economy, A total of 35 nationalities live here, OSCE-ruled elections, 'Clean' report from EU border monitors, Historically never part of Moldova, Industrial powerhouse, Government success.

Each one of these links leads to much longer versions, directly addressing thematically the negative reports of the region and the administration's performance in the global media. We are informed that on the smuggling front:

A border monitoring mission from the European Union has been checking the transit of goods on Pridnestrovie's borders since 2005, filing monthly reports on its finding. The result? A 'clean' bill of health for Pridnestrovie, confirming similar reports by officials from the European Union and the Organization for Security and Cooperation in Europe (OSCE) saying that there is no evidence that Pridnestrovie has ever trafficked arms or nuclear material.

(http://www.pridnestrovie.net)

The case of Pridnestrovie is a contemporary example of the geography of anger Appadurai identifies as produced in the volatile relationship, between the maps of national and global politics (largely produced by official institutions and procedures) and the maps of sacred national space (produced by political and religious movements). In this particular case, Pridnestrovie is seen as a destabilizing region for Moldova and the neighbouring countries, the EU enlargement project and the US hegemonic order, especially in relation to Russia's hegemonic aspirations, energy disputes and legacy in the region. As such, it is represented by mainstream media as forgotten, a Soviet-era tourist destination, stubbornly seeking independence and protecting its Soviet population from Moldova and its neighbours. The speed and insecurity of virtual communications has put the unrecognized state on the defensive on the one hand, but on the other has allowed for online representations that attempt to counter-balance the online discourses and 'misinformation' as they see it from the established media, online equivalents and several other organizations framing the issue, such as Global Security. As today's ethnic groups number in the hundreds and thousands, their mixtures, cultural style and media representations 'create profound doubts about who exactly are among the "we" and who are among the "they" in the context of rapid migration or refugee movements, how many of "them are now among us"' (Appadurai 2006: 5). Pidnestrovie reflects this problem, in the effort by the inhabitants of the region to defend their culture and their majority against Latin, Romanian and Moldovian state culture of what they see as 'historically never part' of Moldova, feeling they entered 'a forced marriage' (www.pridnestrovie.net) when they were assigned to Moldova under global institutions and agreements. In essence, they are then defending the purity of their national space, and they do so by skilfully using online media technologies. To put it simply, following Appadurai, globalization and its technologies can expose pathologies in the sacred ideologies of nationhood.

Rapid urbanization on the 'happiest place on earth': the case of Vanuatu

How can friend kill friend, neighbor kill neighbor, even kinsman kill kinsman? These new forms of intimate violence seem especially puzzling in an era of fast technologies, abstract financial instruments, remote forms of power, and large scale flows of techniques and ideologies.... Such violence, in this perspective, is not about old hatreds and primordial fears. It is an effort to exorcise the new, the emergent, and the uncertain, one name for which is globalization.

(Appadurai 2006: 47)

In the pacific island of Tanna in the state of Vanuatu every fifteenth of February for more than fifty years now young men play the 'Star Spangled Banner' on bamboo flutes and dress up as American soldiers. Villagers at Sulphur Bay worship a mystic figure John Frum, who is often explained as the wartime GIs who introduced themselves as 'John from America'. The BBC reports that

> devotees say that the ghost of a mystical white man first appeared before tribal elders in the 1930s. It urged them to rebel against the aggressive teachings of Christian missionaries and the influence of Vanuatu's British and French colonial masters. The apparition told villagers to do all they could to retain their own traditions.
>
> (Mercer, 17 February 2007)

Through this homage to the US, disciples hope their ethereal saviour can be encouraged to return. 'It's a little bit weird but it makes me feel really patriotic' is one of the comments by an American visitor who travelled to Tanna to see the festivities. In the same BBC article we are informed that about 20 per cent of Tanna's population of 30,000 follow the teachings of one of the world's last remaining cargo cults and that other islanders can barely disguise their contempt for it:

> A Christian youth worker told me how he thought the cult was childish. 'It's like a baby playing games,' he insisted. 'Those people are holding on to a dream that will never come true,' he said. I put this view to Rutha, who's married to Chief Isaac's son. She was unfazed. 'I don't care what they think,' she says gently without a hint of displeasure. 'John is our Jesus and he will come back.' The John Frum Movement is still trying to entice another delivery of cargo from its supernatural American god.
>
> (ibid.)

In another BBC article, Vanuatu is featured as a story, due to its ranking as first among the 'happiest places' on earth (the others were Colombia, Costa Rica, Dominica and Panama) (Winterman, 13 July 2006). This time we get a different story on the cargo cult, it is not the Americans they are worshipping, it is the English:

> Up until now Vanuatu's biggest claim to fame was the island of Tanna, where locals worship the Duke of Edinburgh as their divine leader. Why? Because local legend tells how their spiritual ancestor ended up in England and eventually married a queen.
>
> (ibid.)

It is very useful also to be informed, predictably, as in most representations of these islands: 'But it is far from paradise lost, with limited employment opportunities and poverty' (ibid.). To the credit of the reporter, we get to read interviews from environmental volunteers, the British Friends of Vanuatu and others. Another interesting aspect were responses to the online article with many readers leaving messages of how puzzled they were about Colombia: 'drug cartels, left wing guerrillas and right wing death squads do not sound like my idea of happiness'. This links to the constructions of images of places in the global public sphere and the stereotypifications constantly produced and reproduced by the global media, especially since the retooling of American hegemony in the media sphere.

The impression we receive from these two articles is that there is a cargo cult, different details of what it is about, but the first article quotes an anthropologist explaining it as cultural preservation against the missionaries and what they saw as oppression. However, the reasons they are praying for more cargos full of American commodities to arrive are not discussed. During this research on the 'happiest place with the third world economy and an interesting cult', Al-Jazeera English featured a story about Vanuatu being in a state of emergency in March 2007. The lead of the article starts with 'Ethnic violence has been stoked after the recent death of a woman was blamed on witchcraft' (Al-Jazeera, 5 March 2007). A state of emergency was declared after 'clashes between islanders' killed two and injured ten people, while 140 were arrested by police. Policemen are interviewed for the piece, and the council's representative who is worried about tourism. The only other worthy information is that 'Vanuatu, with a population of about 200,000 people, comprises more than 80 islands and lies about three-quarters of the way from Hawaii to Australia' (ibid.)

Further, the representations of these articles refrain to discuss further the realities and causalities behind the cult, the history of colonization and post-colonization (Vanuatu served as a base for the Allies during the Second World War, images of the island during the time can be found online, and was decolonized in 1980), while the current clashes between islanders are 'ethnic' explained in relation to 'witchcraft', instead of being unsettled by rapid urbanization and mixing of their populations. Ethnic identity as explained by Appadurai is:

> a special flash point for the uncertainty brought by wider processes of demographic change, economic fear, and population shifts, exacerbated by the excesses of mass mediation and state or quasi-state propaganda machines ... the mix of social certainty and uncertainty becomes volatile and metastatic violence can develop.
>
> (Appadurai 2006: 104)

To the outside world reading about Vanuatu, these issues are still dealt with explanations that are inadequate and dangerous. Small numbers and their idiosyncrasies are themselves produced by socioeconomic and cultural processes in which the media, and the 'great powers' before them and with them are complicit. Sadly, Vanuatu, the periphery of the periphery, is also a case very much 'unreported' and untouched by the anti-globalization movement and the independent media traditionally siding with the oppressed.

Capturing the liberal imagination: the case of Papua

> Small numbers are also a worry because they raise the spectre of conspiracy, of the cell, of the cell, the spy, the traitor, the dissident, or the revolutionary. Small numbers introduce the intrusion of the private into the public sphere, and with it the associated dangers of nepotism, collusion, subversion, and deception. They harbor the potential for secrecy and privacy, both anathema to the ideas of publicity and transparency that are vital to liberal ideas of rational communication and open deliberation.
>
> Minorities are the only powerful instance of small numbers which excite sympathy rather than distrust in the liberal imagination, and that is because they incarnate that numerical smallness of which the prime case is the number one, the individual.
>
> (Appadurai 2006: 62)

Referring to the Free Papua Movement (Organisasi Papua Merdeka OPM) and the 'opposition to Indonesian control', the Global Security website puts it down to cultural differences between Indonesians and the indigenous population:

> complaints about the Javanization of Irian Jaya exacerbated tensions. The cultural conflict was aggravated by indigenous people's perceptions that they were being left behind economically by a flood of Indonesian immigrants coming in via the central government sponsored transmigration program.
>
> (http://www.globalsecurity.org/military/world/para/papua.htm)

Notice the use of the words 'complaints' and the indigenous people's 'perceptions' that they were being left behind. Of course, yet again, as in the case of Pridnestrovie, we are not left wondering what the American position is on the issue: 'The US Government asserts that the Free Papua Movement has committed human rights abuses including hostage-taking and summary executions, and it may be targeting US citizens or US companies in Irian Jaya Province for hostage taking or for sabotage' (ibid.) To appear balanced, we are also informed that the independence movement is accusing the Indonesian government of the same and US mining conglomerate Freeport McMoRan for environmental abuses in West Papua. Interestingly, a small touch is added in the end of how 'some critics, however, say there are other motives. What there is now is outrage of an unprecedented level with Jakarta for this effort to divide the province with an almost explicitly stated motivation of weakening the political independence movement' (ibid.).

In an article commenting on the Papua 'unrest' against the US-based Freeport McMoRan, the BBC reports from Jakarta that 'the roots of Papuan discontent are deeper and more intractable' (Johnston, 23 March 2003). Even if we are not told what these roots are (we are given a bit of a clue after a three-line historical background mentioning Dutch colonization and Indonesian annexation not honouring Papua self-rule granted by the Dutch), the International Crisis Group is quoted explaining that the Freeport protests reflected broader frustration and anger over the role of the military in Papua, lack of justice for past abuses and the failure of special autonomy to improve the welfare of the people. The report also refers to the issue of asylum seekers from Papua to Australia and

> a prominent Papuan nationalist, Edison Waromi, says that the recent arrival of 43 Papuan asylum seekers in Australia was designed to bring attention to the problems in the province. The boat they arrived on carried a banner saying in English: 'Save West Papua people souls from genocide, intimidation and terrorist from military government of Indonesia'.
>
> (ibid.)

This report gets even better when it mentions that Condoleezza Rice and Tony Blair visiting Jakarta are required to make a statement that they are committed to 'the unitary state of Indonesia', indicating they do not support independence for Papua or any other part of the country. This is an example of good reporting using sources that are discussing the issue domestically on the different parties, regionally, and in geopolitical terms.

Here is another BBC reporter, based in Sydney this time, on the Australian camps set up as disincentives for the Papuan refugees: 'The Prime Minister, John Howard, has insisted this is not the end of the road for the detention centre on Nauru.' Then he explains that Australia 'was worried about the number of people heading for its shores from Indonesia' and that

> the thinking was that the prospect of being shipped off to an isolated corner of the South Pacific would be a powerful deterrent to asylum seekers. The Australian government has said the policy has been an outstanding success and that the flow of people has been reduced to barely a trickle.
>
> (Mercer, 14 October 2005)

Lastly, we are told that the UN 'complained' about the conditions of detainees and welcomes the decision to remove detainees from Nauru. Nowhere in this piece any other side of the story except that of the Australian government is aired or discussed. Of course Australia has to deal with its own history with the indigenous populations. 'Minorities, refugees and oppressed peoples are marks of failure and coercion: They are embarrassments to any sponsored image of national purity and state fairness' (Appadurai 2006: 42).

Interestingly, Al-Jazeera reports on Australia's decision to revise its refugee evaluation after outraging Jakarta by granting asylum to forty-two people from Papua. Again, Howard is featured as saying that Jakarta's record is improving and that Australia should not encourage the region's independence However, in an article on the protest against the mine mentioned earlier, Al-Jazeera chooses to quote the Human Rights Watch urging Indonesia's government 'to allow an independent investigation into the violence in the region and to ease restrictions on foreign journalists and aid agencies entering the province' (Al-Jazeera English, 9 April 2006). On the asylum seekers issue, CNN quotes a refugee advocate, and does not fail to mention that Howard's tough stand against illegal immigration has been at the centre of his four consecutive election victories and that he is facing one in 2007 (CNN, 23 February 2007).

The pro-independence sites, such as www.freewestpapua.org; www.west papuaaction.buz.org; www.greenleft.org.au/2007/700/36334; www.fas.org/irp/ world/para/papua.htm; and www.eco-action.org/opm/wpau/00/wpau00.html are used as information sites, framing the issues, initiating events, but also as mobilizing and organizing global solidarity for the Free West Papua campaigns. This is typical and in accordance with previous research on ethnoreligious and sociopolitical conflicts (in this case a combination of both), as we have seen in the past with the anti-globalization, anti-corporate, anti-war movements and Chinese cyberdissidents, the ethnoreligious cyberconflicts (and their exclusionary fixed identity discourses) between Israeli and Palestinians, Indian and Pakistanis, and the use of the web by terrorist groups to organize, mobilize and recruit, such as Al-Qaeda (Karatzogianni 2006). The Papuan independence movement is a case where sociopolitical grievances and tensions of the indigenous populations are converged with the ethnoreligious elements of difference and exclusion brought by the Indonesian regime. The discourses are in sociopolitical terms in the independent media solidarity with the Papuans (reminiscent somewhat to the solidarity for the Zapatistas), while domestically in the region some ethnoreligious issues are at play. There are different tribes in Papua and according to the 2000 consensus 78 per cent of the Papuan population identified themselves as Christian, with 54 per cent being Protestant and 24 per cent being Catholic. 21 per cent of the population was Muslim and less than 1 per cent were Buddhists, animists are not recognized according to Indonesian policy (http://en.wikipedia.org/wiki/Papua_(Indonesian_province)). Indonesia, with a population of more than 200 million, 300 distinct native ethnicities and 742 different languages and dialects has faced many bloody ethnoreligious conflicts, such as the massacre of hundreds of Madurese by a local Dayak community in West Kalimantanand and conflicts in Maluku, Central Sulawesi (http://en. wikipedia.org/wiki/Indonesia).

Exorcizing uncertainty – reactivating the geography of anger: the case of Lebanon

The case of Lebanon is a case of an established small state with many and diverse groups fighting for dominance, while at the same time Lebanon is fighting for its own survival as a democratic state, relying on the ideas of equal representation of these extremely diverse groups. Appadurai writes that

> the metastasis of war we call terrorism and the rapid-fire spread in the discourse of terrorism as a name for any variety of anti-state activity has decisively blurred the lines between wars of the nation and wars in the nation.

The nation itself, following Appadurai, is steadily reduced to the fiction of its ethnos as the last cultural resource over which it may exercise full dominion (2006: 23). Lebanon is a state that has been long caught between its efforts to appear sovereign and in control of its population and openness, projecting the image of the 'Switzerland of the Middle East', in order to gain Western approval, tourism and investment. It has also been caught between the minorities within its own borders, and its own marginalization and weakness in regional politics.

The Israeli–Hezbollah war in 2006 was an example of how under the condition of social uncertainty 'violence can create a macabre form of certainty and can become a brutal technique (or folk discovery-procedure) about "them" and, therefore, about "us"' (Appadurai 2006: 6). Violence becomes 'a means for establishing sharp lines between normally mixed identities' (ibid.: 89). In this last section, the idea is to test these theoretical insights against a sample of the coverage the 2006 Lebanon war and its related cyberconflict.

Sampling Lebanon's war: main areas of coverage June–July 2007

- Sample one: 4–24 June violence (Lebanese army attacks camps, Beirut bomb, UN peacekeepers killed, ceasefire talks, stories on combatants killed).
- Sample two: July (assaults against camps intensifies, descriptions of fighting).
- Sample three: 10–12 July; country profiles Lebanon on Year On (stories on 'political paralysis', reconstruction, etc.).
- Sample four: opinion pieces from/on the main protagonists and personalities (Fatah al-islam, Hezbollah, Israel, Lebanese government and army, politicians from different factions in Lebanon, Palestinians, Syrians and Saudis, US backing, the international community).
- Sample five: social aspects of the war and interviews with local populations by local and international media outlets.
- Sample six: Lebanon's cyberconflict July 2006 onwards – (IDF's intelligence unit hacks Hezbollah TV station, radio and sites).

The following elements of analysis were used to look at the above sample (Philo and Berry 2004)

- Main areas and prominence, explanations and causes of conflict.
- Who got to speak and circumstances.

- News headlines and interviews.
- Victims and casualties coverage to examine the language used to describe motives and rationale.
- Retaliation and response.
- Perspectives, censorship, restrictions and propaganda wars.

Most mainstream media, most of the time, run the same story, sometimes the same narrative, and even the same exact discursive palette, as if they are written by the same person. Few examples on discursive/ideological difference: CNN tends to refer to 'UN peacekeepers', while most else use 'UN soldiers', France 24 will use 'Islamist camp', will most other use 'Lebanese camp'. There is immense surrealism, metaphor and banal imagining of violence, in the choice of words to describe the situation there by the mainstream media: 'Lebanon political paralysis' (BBC, 10 July 2007); 'Escape is impossible' (*Guardian,* 12 June 2007); 'Political squabbling', 'A son awaits to join Hizbullah to avenge shattered family' (*Guardian*) 'Commando action in Lebanon camp' (Al-Jazeera, English 22 June 2007); 'Lebanon army starts camp "clean up"' (Al-Jazeera English, 12 June 2007). An interviewee for the BBC is quoted as saying: 'I saw an arm lying in the street … someone picked up the arm, despite the damaged flesh and pulled off the ring to steal it' (Asser, 9 July 2007).

'Abu Omar looks like an Arab version of the Scandinavian god Thor' is another example, where a *Guardian* journalist describes one of the new generation of Palestinian militants in Lebanese refugee camps (*Guardian*, 12 June 2007). This is an example of how Hezbollah proved far more media savvy than its enemies, giving controlled access to the world's media. Hezbollah's press officer, Hussein Nabulsi, took CNN's Nic Robertson on a tour of southern Beirut, while Charlie Moore described a Hezbollah press tour of a bombed-out area in southern Beirut on 23 July 2006 as a 'dog-and-pony show' due to perceived staging, misrepresentation of the nature of the destroyed areas, and strict directives about when and with whom interviews could take place. On top of that there were more scandals on staged photos with individuals appearing in multiple photos. Reuters withdrew over 900 photographs by Adnan Hajj, a Lebanese freelance photographer, after he admitted to digitally adding and darkening smoke spirals in photographs of an attack on Beirut (http://en.wikipedia. org/wiki/2006_Israel-Lebanon_conflict#Media_controversy).

Alarmingly, the sample shows that the most interesting debates and opinion pieces tend are to be found in online partisan and propaganda media. This realization prompted me to conduct an email interview with Dr Dany Badran, Assistant Professor in English and Critical Linguistics at the Lebanese American University. Badran, who follows both Lebanese and outside media, said that such misrepresentation characterizes the majority of media coverage about Lebanon. Yet while this is more or less (and unfortunately so) anticipated in Lebanese reports on Lebanese issues – Lebanese newspapers, radio stations and televisions are predominantly owned by the politically and ideologically affiliated – it comes more of a surprise when 'responsible' and highly credible international media sources follow similar lines. Badran especially mentions the case of the Al-Jazeera reporting of news during the July 2006 war in Lebanon as an instance where one man's political agenda dictates the views of an entire network, with a vast area of audience coverage and reach, while he finds himself constantly resorting to tabloids:

> The extreme pro-Hezbollah (and ultimately anti-government) stance adopted by the network particularly in the face of the international community is logically difficult to justify. The leader of the Progressive Socialist Party leader, Walid Jumblat, gives his interpretation of the situation in a television interview, where he argues that that position reflects the Prince of Qatar's power struggle with the Kingdom of Saudi Arabia. The Prince's opposition to KSA is highlighted through his support of all what KSA opposes (Hezbollah) and opposition to what the kingdom supports (the Lebanese government – and by extension the international community). This fairly serious outcome of a personal political agenda has, unfortunately, influenced and swayed many of the Al-Jazeera news audience, confusing many by making biased emotional appeals. It, however, posed less of a serious threat to the serious/critical news follower who already knows that Al-Jazeera is a personally owned TV station which sensationalises news, possibly in the interest of ratings and/or personal political agendas. The main problem with such media representations, or misrepresentations for that matter, is that their effects can be disastrous for the silent followers (who mainly watch sensational TV), the self-proclaimed intellectuals (who predominantly read the arguments of flashy reporters but rarely the counter-arguments) and the highly critical readers (who have faith in the academic integrity of colleagues). Such distortion only encourages readers and news followers to consolidate existing biases and reinforce existing ideologies without seeking out a logical explanation to events and probable causes. Comments from readers on news websites are clear examples of just those points.
>
> As for us, the silent majority of the Lebanese, we are generally finding it harder and harder to listen to these extremely biased, contradictory and confusing views. Here's another example. While following a live coverage of the last day of fighting in the Nahr Al Bared Palestinian camp in the south of Lebanon, I intentionally flipped through all the Lebanese television channels, both pro government and opposition. The first thing that struck me (being a linguist) is the use of descriptive words. While all the pro-government reports referred to the Fateh Al Islam group as 'the terrorist group', 'the gang of Shaker Al Absi', the pro-Hezbollah channel referred to them as 'the fighters of Shaker Al Absi'. This not only struck me as odd, but rather dangerous. The attempt at 'neutrality' in portraying a group which has started its 'activity' by killing (so I avoid the more loaded word 'murdering') Lebanese army soldiers sleeping in their tents is, well, not neutral to say the least. Being in the opposition (yet effectively part of the government) should not put to question the status of a group which endangers the safety of soldiers and citizens alike. These views are very confusing to say

the least. And so, ironically, I find myself consciously resorting to tabloids. How absurd!

Thanks to the Internet and live 24/7 coverage, directly uploaded by journalists and bloggers onto cyberspace, the media had an unprecedented tactical and representational effect on policy. As Marvin Kalb (February 2007: 5) writes in his report 'The Israeli-Hezbollah War of 2006: The Media as a Weapon in Asymmetrical Conflict':

> For any journalist worth his or her salt, this should spark a respectful moment of reflection. Not only this new and awesome technology enable journalists to bring the ugly reality of war to both belligerents (and others around the world), serving as a powerful influence on public opinion and governmental attitudes and actions; it also became an extremely valuable intelligence asset for both Israel and Hezbollah, and Hezbollah especially exploited it.
>
> (February 2007: 5)

> Hezbollah whenever possible, pointed reporters to civilian deaths among the Lebanese, a helpful gesture with heavy propaganda implications. Early in the war, reporters routinely noted that Hezbollah started the war, and its casualties were a logical consequence of war. But after the first week such references were either dropped or downplayed, leaving the widespread impression that Israel was a loose canon shooting at anything that moved. 'Disporportionality' became the war's mantra.
>
> (ibid.: 9)

An example Kalb gives is that of BBC's 117 stories on the war, 38 per cent fingered Israel as the aggressor and only 4 per cent fingered Hezbollah. A YouGov poll of British viewers showed 63 per cent believing that Israel's response had been 'disproportionate'. Fox News favoured Israel, CNN tried to be balanced, and ABC, CBS and NBC were more critical of Israel than Hezbollah (Kalb 2007: 14).

The effect of the Internet on the coverage of the war and related cyberattacks

There were three major developments in relation to the Internet in this war:

1   the Internet causing leaks in military intelligence;
2   millions of bloggers taking sides and influencing public opinion;
3   hacking of the signal of the Hezbollah TV station, hacking for Lebanon, hacking for Israel.

First, during the war UNIFIL (the United Nations Interim Force in Lebanon) was accused of release information on its websites which would be regarded as 'actionable intelligence', as

> It was part of UNIFIL's responsibility to report violations of the ceasefire ...
> but presumably this information was to be conveyed through confidential
> channels, not on the internet. ... These postings, similar to others during the
> war, coincided with hevey fighting in the region.
>
> (Kalb 2007: 17)

Second, blogging became a ferocious tool for the different groups engaged in
the conflict, pro-Israeli and pro-Hezbollah bloggers (Kalb quotes a source for
sixty-three million as of January 2007):

> The effect was nonstop pressure on journalists to look over their shoulders –
> to conform either to extremes on both sides or to stick to the middle of
> public opinion. If 'proportionality' was the theme of the day, most reporters
> would try supporting or rejecting the theme but always keeping it at play. It
> was easier and safe to be in step with the public than to be walking into the
> wind.
>
> (Kalb 2007: 24)

This pressure on bloggers to either conform with extremes or stick to the middle
of public opinion perhaps explains the impression the sample gives of a very
uniform approach from mainstream media.

Third, there are the conflict-related cyberattacks. According to the report
from Eli Lake, in the middle of newscast and programming from Hezbollah's Al
Manar station, Israeli technicians hacked the signal and replaced it with a
ninety-second spot with a gun site superimposed on a crude drawing of Hezbollah's leader, Sheil Hassan Nasrallah, looking at the ground. The image was
punctuated by the sound of three gunshots and framed on the top with the words,
'Your day is coming, coming, coming'. On the bottom of the image of Sheik
Nasrallah were the words: 'The state of Israel.' For the next ninety seconds, the
message is clear: 'Give up. Resistance is futile.' The station managed to stay on
the air through broadcasting from alternate studios. One former Defense Force
official familiar with the operation said that 'the aim of psychological warfare is
to get the Lebanese to see terrorists are actually terrorists who are endangering
you, to understand that Nasrallah is masquerading as the liberator of Lebanon'.
Israel also hacked Lebanese phone lines with recorded messages urging listeners
to turn in Hezbollah fighters and operatives (*New York Sun*, 2 August 2006).

The Lebanon conflict and its media coverage raises many questions in terms
of the extraordinary influence of global public opinion through blogging on the
mainstream media. It is also the first time cyberwar is not only used by a state,
but it is freely admitted as a legitimate weapon of warfare and recognized as a
threat to the monopoly of military intelligence. Lastly, it proves that in asymmetric warfare the weaker party wins, if they play the media game right.

Conclusion

This research involves a large amount of data about the countries mentioned here. Some are more developed than others, however the purpose of this is to understand better how the Internet and cyberconflict affect small states in war, wannabe states and minorities. Presently I am undertaking similar research in respect to conflicts in Kosovo, Abkhazia, Baluchistan, Fuji, Solomon Islands, the Hmong in Laos and the Caprivi strip in Namibia, Ivory Coast in an effort to compare different regions and small countries experiencing similar issues and find patterns on how these are represented, or perhaps more accurately, simulated in an era of fast virtual communications depending on their position in the global system.

It is likely that minorities and small numbers benefit from ICTs far more their powerful enemies. In all these places, the mainstream media tended either to represent them as 'trouble in paradise', sided with the status quo state in cases of secession, or failed to engage seriously with the deeper roots of the conflict. In the advocacy or action websites, what is called currently by the popular press in France 'the 5th power of the Internet', has enabled players to punch above their weight and at least enter the competition for the battle for the ears of the global public opinion.

I have argued elsewhere that states need to become more networked to deal with the current networked resistances be they sociopolitical or ethnoreligious and that these resistances need to become more conscious of their hosting environment if they are to be attempting conflict transformations in today's global politics in the an era of fast virtual communications (Karatzogianni 2006). Further, I have placed myself in favour of the potential contained in network forms of social organization as a basis for constructing resistances to repressive apparatuses and to the world system as a system of global control (Karatzogianni and Robinson 2004). Appadurai, recognizes that we still live in a vertebrate world, albeit one in which the state is not the only game in town. He argues that

> alongside this exists the cellular world, whose parts multiply by association and opportunity rather than by legislation or by design. It is also a product of globalization – of the new information technologies, of the speed of finance and the velocity of the news, of the movement of capital and the circulation of refugees.
>
> (Appadurai 2006: 129)

And more importantly: 'We need to watch them, for the coming crisis of the nation-state may lie not in the dark cellularities of terror but in the utopian cellularities of these new transnational organizational forms' (ibid.: 137).

10 Rivalry in cyberspace and virtual contours of a new conflict zone

The Sri Lankan case

Harinda Vidanage

> When the computer screen becomes the surface of contact between two machinic species, people and computers, it also became a potential trap for individuals: software hacking, as was discovered early on, is powerfully addictive. Computer screens can become 'narcotic mirrors', trapping users by feeding them amplified images of their narcissistic selves. The same interface that allows users to control the machine, can give them a false and intoxicating sense of their power.
>
> (Manuel De Landa 1991: 230)

> The present epoch will perhaps be above all the epoch of space. We are in the epoch of simultaneity: we are in the epoch of juxtaposition, the epoch of the near and far, of the side by side, of the dispersed.
>
> (Michel Foucault 1986: 23)

This chapter traces the emergence of a new conflict zone, concurrent to one of the world's bloodiest secessionist conflicts, through the Sri Lankan Tamil diasporic political engagements in cyberspace. The battle is waged between the Sri Lankan state and the ethnic Tamil separatist rebel organization the Liberation Tigers of Tamil Eelam (LTTE), more commonly known as the Tamil Tigers. The objective of this chapter is to look at the diasporic political engagement in cyberspace and the new spatial dimension of the Sri Lankan conflict waged in cyberspace. This political conflict zone emerged with cyberspace providing the spatial attributes required for the becoming of a political space, especially for the Sri Lankan Tamil diaspora in the context of the Sri Lankan conflict. This has significantly shifted the ideological foundations of the ongoing conflict and remains an alternative but critical space for the actors of the conflict.

The comprehension of the importance of this space by both key actors in the conflict saw the Sri Lankan state attempting to striate and dominate it and the LTTE following suit. This reflects the classical attempts of waging war for the domination of spaces from antiquity to the modern age. The classic example is the ocean, identified as a smooth space, constantly viewed as needing to be subjected to state control or domination by vast fleets assembled by colonial pioneers. As Deleuze and Guattari note, 'one of the reasons for the hegemony of the west was the power in its state apparatus to striate by combining the technologies of the North and the Mediterranean and by annexing the Atlantic' (2004: 427).

Cyberspace has provided a smooth space to nomadic political forces leading to a radical alteration of the balance of power in this domain. This is an interesting observation, that in the evolution of this conflict, while simultaneously creating a conflict zone, the spatial conditions of cyberspace have radically altered the dynamics of the conflicts and strategies of the parties. It symbolizes the transformation of the war machine, as it organizes space in subtle ways, not just fortifications or battlefields. It often links together structures and places, which seem to us to belong to different orders.

The chapter traces the radical rupture in the development of political engagements in cyberspace in the context of the Sri Lankan conflict as the pattern of the cyberconflict has undergone significant transformation. This is introduced in two phases throughout this chapter. Where in the early phase the spatiality of land or state-based discourse dictated the cyber-political engagements and strategies, as illuminated above, the unique spatiality of cyberspace has dislocated this centrality and developed a radically new conflict zone, where the state-based strategic manoeuvres are constantly challenged, and where rethinking of such strategies has become a necessity. The analysis will run through the beginning of the Sri Lankan ethnic conflict, the formation of the ethnic Tamil diaspora, the theoretical framework which locates political spaces and relations of power and the actual cyberconflict which is taking place.

The ethnic conflict in Sri Lanka: contesting space

Multitudes of scholars, journalists and military analysts have provided interpretations and historical analyses of the ongoing conflict in Sri Lanka. In the light of the core context of the chapter, I will provide a spatial analysis to the conflict and the importance of certain hegemonic spatial attributes mutually perceived as vital for the conflicting parties to dominate each other.

The Sri Lankan conflict is also essentially a spatial one. In general, a conflict, as a struggle to ascertain political identity and acquire political landscapes to control, both internally and externally or intra or inter-state, is basically a struggle for the control of space. The spatial analysis of the Sri Lankan ethnic conflict is to develop the pattern of the conflict and to understand the emergence or transmutation of the conflict dynamic in cyberspace.

The conflict grew out of the demands to the state made by Tamils to alleviate their grievances and the consequent Sinhala-dominated central government's failure to remedy the discontents of the Tamil people. These demands turned radical with the declaration of Tamil homeland comprising of the northern and eastern provinces of Sri Lanka and the emergence of militant Tamil groups challenging the state authority in these provinces. These provinces, especially the northern, are mostly inhabited by Tamils and this made it a natural heartland of resistance. The Liberation Tigers of Tamil Eelam (LTTE/Tigers) emerged as the most dominant rebel outfit after a bloody campaign to wipe out opposition among other Tamil militant groups (Hoole *et al.* 1992) and ever since have resorted to battle the Sri Lankan state for the formation of a separate Tamil homeland.

The history of the militancy can be traced to its origins in the late 1970s. The militancy gained momentum in the aftermath of the pogrom unleashed against the minority ethnic Tamils by majority Sinhalese in 1983. That year has always been a significant historical conjuncture in the context of the conflict or a temporal marker. In a spatial analysis, the riots signified the final phase in the delinking of ethnic Tamil people from the political place of the Sri Lankan state, or severing of the umbilical cord of citizenship and the liberal rights of a citizen from the state. This was the climax to a process of making majority Sinhala state policies that led to the uprooting of Tamils and their claim for their rights of a political space or the space of the nation-state. The riots demonstrated that there was no safe space for the Tamils and created the conditions for an unprecedented shift into a massive militarism of the Tamil people's struggle.

The final political uprooting of the Tamil claims was the sixth amendment to the constitution (introduced in the aftermath of the riots), which basically demanded an oath of allegiance to a unitary state from all members of parliament if they were to continue with their elected post as MPs. This successfully ejected the largest Tamil composition of MPs in the history of Sri Lankan democracy from the legislature. This eviction dislocated the Sri Lankan Tamils' political ambitions of self-determination, self-rule and Tamil voice from the pivotal political power structure, which governed spatial relations of the Sri Lankan state.

The riots and the sixth amendment had a synergistic effect on the plight of Tamil people in Sri Lanka. Their right to inherit a political space was taken away, both through social violence and the sheer brute force upheld through a constitutional sanction. This led to the radical departure from democratic politics by certain Tamil organizations to claim their own state within Sri Lanka. Although the notion of self-rule and homeland was accepted by Tamil politicians in the early 1970s, military struggle was not on the cards. These two incidents sealed the need for a military struggle and establishment of a Tamil nation-state independent from Sri Lanka, which was termed as 'Tamil Eelam' or 'Tamil homeland'.

The military component of the ethnic conflict in Sri Lanka is analysed in certain stages or phases, defined in military terms as a series of military campaigns fought between the Sri Lankan government forces and the LTTE. The phases of these conflicts are named as Eelam wars. Eelam will give nearly a million hits on Google and this demonstrates the global spatial pollination of the term. Throughout the four phases of the conflict, the objective was clear from both the LTTE and the state, the LTTE wanted to become the sole powerbroker in Tamil politics and the key military might and they wanted the Sri Lankan state to realize from 1983 onwards.

The LTTE was one such outfit where its leadership understood the importance of spatial dominance in militarism and sustenance of military hegemony, and soon began taking on the Sinhala state with low-scale assassinations to ambushing and killing thirteen soldiers. This ambush signified the first virtual attack on the Sri Lankan state space and announced the beginning of the end of the traditional Sri Lankan space and the affirmation of a struggle to create a new political space independent of the political space of Sri Lanka. Ever since this incident, during the four phases, the struggle has been to hegemonize and control space. Each stage symbolized a certain political space from ideological, land, sea and air. In this struggle of hegemonizing of the political spaces and maintaining state control over them, the existence of a massive diaspora population has transferred to cyberspace. This has become the next space which the LTTE and the state later on realized to be an important political space for the continuation of the struggle.

Summed up above, the conflict has been the struggle between the Tamil Tiger rebels who have always challenged the striated, marked, territorialized Sri Lankan space and have successfully remapped certain territories of the state as under the control of the rebels. The rebels have engaged the Sri Lankan state simultaneously as a conventional army and in the form of a nomadic war machine, which has always challenged the state apparatus militarily. As De Landa (1991: 11) identifies, the tactics of the nomads were based on a combination of psychological shock and physical speed. The LTTE military strategies were mainly based on creating the above effect similar to that of the nomadic war strategies, while the Tigers integrated highly mobile guerrilla units and extensive mobile firepower to advance and take over Sri Lankan state territory. Most of their major military campaigns have been codenamed 'Unceasing Waves', adopted mainly from Vietcong type attack patterns. This also is similar to Deleuze's view of the nomadic war machine:

> If nomads formed the war machine, it was by inventing absolute speed, by being synonymous with speed, and each time there is an operation against the state – insurbodination, rioting, guerrilla warfare or revolution as act – it can be said that the war machine has revived.
>
> (Deleuze 2004: 426)

To respond to these movements of nomadic warriors, the state has responded with intense striations of space with the objective of appropriating the war machine, its speed and movement by establishing garrisons, checkpoints and High Security Zones. The LTTE in its operational tactics did use the power of shock and awe and the speed tactics to start hegemonizing the political space that was emerging with the political participation of the diaspora. They started proliferation of websites, and LTTE maintained a shock and awe tactic of military tactics in cyberspace. By 1997, they successfully used email bombing tactics on Sri Lankan embassies in Washington and Toronto.

The phases of war included long and bloody wars of attrition with both the state and the LTTE making no clear gains and political peace processes mediated by India and Norway in 1987 and 2002. Currently, it is said that Sri Lanka is experiencing an undeclared war of attrition, the fourth in its timeline. The state gained military victories in the eastern province, while the rebels responded with air strikes demonstrating their newly acquired military might. The LTTE has become the world's first terrorist organization to use air attacks without the support of any international state-entity. The organization's main sources of funding comes from a well established black market, operating shipping lines, providing logistics and smuggling support to the drug networks. A significant chunk of the funding comes from the internationally dispersed Tamil diaspora networks which the Tigers (LTTE) had absolute control of until recently. They are listed as the world's first terror outfit to use cyberterrorism techniques against the Sri Lankan state (Denning 1999; Vatis 2001).

The Sri Lankan Tamil diaspora

The Sri Lankan diaspora, more than being a product of the conflict, originated under the conditions of which the ethnic conflict in Sri Lanka was militarily triggered. Moreover, the Sri Lankan Tamil diaspora was the result of the historical uprooting of Tamil citizens from legitimate spaces of occupation. As the same conditions of the conflict created the Tamil diaspora, it has become an integral stakeholder in the conflict itself, since out of the nearly two million Tamils of Sri Lankan origin, nearly one-third come form the diaspora. The statistics and figures are mostly estimates, as no host country possesses exact number of Sri Lankan Tamils living in them.

Cyberspace enabled the diasporas to reterritorialize their inherently deterritorialized community action. As Deleuze and Guattari point out

> reteritorrialization must not be confused with a return to a primitive or older territoriality; it necessarily serves as a new territoriality by which one element, itself deterritorialized serves as a new territoriality for another, which has lost its territoriality as well.
>
> (Deleuze and Guattari 2004: 174)

This spatial folding enabled this diasporic space to facilitate an aggregated multitude.[1] This is alluding to the concept introduced by Hardt and Negri in their seminal *Empire* (2000). Thus, such websites facilitating unique political formations are not just providing information or issues of news values, they are holding them within a unique space that has been created in cyberspace.

Theoretical impetus

The theoretical analysis of this chapter is based on the notion of the formation of political spaces and the role of power in such contested spaces. Consequently, there is a strong allusion to post-structural and post-modern viewpoints of space in the theoretical basis of this chapter, as space is projected as being a product of a set of relations. The post-structural perspective is a clear shift from the sedentary thinking of space, which normally theorizes space as held in a container with the nation-state considered the primary container, and the notion of fixity or geographic congruence affiliated to such thinking. Cyberspace in the post-structural context is seen as an ideal site where open relations are possible and new spaces are created. As Foucault points out about these new relations 'we do not live inside a void that could be coloured with diverse shades of light, we live inside a set of relations that delineate sites which are irreducible to one another and absolutely not superimposed on one another' (1986: 23).

I have selected Massey and Deleuze as both theorists introduce space as the site of political engagement and power. The Deleuzian notion of space is linked to the notion of nomad. Massey's work has been central to transforming human geography into a disciplinary domain dedicated to the social theory project, while encouraging social sciences to take on complexities of space within their formulations. The significance of Massey's work arises from her insistence on conceptualizing space and place. For Massey, space is a social production, a sphere of possibility of multiplicity, space is always under construction. This type of theorizing really helps to critically understand the spatial formations in the form of cyberspace, as relations are seen as not just spatial, but also as political. In effect we are thinking of the spatial in a political way (Massey 2005: 9).

The concept of space is critical to the study of diaspora (Karim 2003: 6) and it is quintessential in understanding diasporan politics online. This is vital at the point of the diasporans' departure from physical political arenas to virtual sites of engagement and the forms that the engagements take, once they have been established in cyberspace. Doreen Massey views space as 'the simultaneous co-existence of social interrelations at all geographical scales, from the intimacy of the household to the wide spaces of transglobal connections' (Massey 1994).

In her recent studies Massey points out that her hope is to contribute to a process of liberating space from its odd chains of meaning and associating it with different ones which might have, in particular, a political potential. She criticizes the studies of space as immobile and closed instead of understanding it as dynamic with an ongoing process. Time and space are reducible to each other but they are both co-implicated (Massey 2005: 59). This is crucial for examining the emergence of distinct spatial properties in cyberspace, which induces political participation. As Hirst (2005: 3) points out, space is a resource for power, and the spaces of power are complex and qualitatively distinct. In this context, spaces do develop characteristics that affect the conditions in which power can be exercised, conflicts pursued and social control attempted. Thus, it is a space in which power projects take shape and hegemonic interests are unleashed.

Cyberspace is transformed through constant human engagement in it, thus these interactions continuously transform and shape properties in it. This shaping of cyberspace provides the space to be facilitating political practices. In the context of Tamil nationalist struggle, the differential placing of local struggles within the complex power geometry of spatial relations is a key element in the formation of their political identities and politics. In turn, political activity reshapes both identities and spatial relations. Thus, the notion of multiplicity, which both Massey and Deleuze elucidate, is a critical factor for theorizing cyberspace and its political formations. In the case of Tamil nationalist politics, the recent past witnessed the emergence of a dissident movement from the LTTE, which began its own political activation among the diasporans. These political activities have shaped their movement and emerged as an alternative political force, with major emphasis on cyberspace as a political place or location of operation for the dissidents. This represents complex power geometry of space/cyberspace as relational and as the sphere of multiplicity. This is an essential part of the character in constant power reconfiguration through political engagement.

Finally, in theorizing space Gilles Deleuze and Felix Guattari (2004) introduce the notion of a nomad space and its power, which can challenge the state structure. This theorization can be further explored in the case of virtual diasporans and the way they utilize cyberspace and how they evolve during the whole process. Their political engagement has made them some sort of nomads of cyberspace, challenging the Sri Lankan state. Deleuze and Guattari see this space as, 'not as a space with intrinsic properties that then determine relations, but as a space with extrinsic properties; the space is produced from the movements that then give that space its peculiar quality' (Deleuze and Guattari 2004: 401). Deleuze and Guattari's notion of nomadology and space is a classic analysis of the power of the nomad and the challenges faced by a state.

In the complex theoretical analyses of both Massey and Deleuze (Massey 1994a 2005; Deleuze and Guattari 2004) the notion of space for political engagement and the engagements reproducing the properties of the space are critical factors to be explored. In my research project, the notion of cyberspace as a site of political engagement and the interaction of diasporan agents within cyberspace are a major focus. This again can be linked to the manner in which the agency is reproduced in cyberspace, as well as spatial properties, when diasporan agents integrate with technology for political activities, which recursively reproduce new spatial properties.

Virtual conflict zone

Research into the shifting of political engagement into cyberspace, in the context of the Sri Lankan conflict, had very similar parallels to the ongoing conflict. But the shifting of the political engagements to cyberspace was mainly because of the significant diaspora population. The cyber engagements started off in the mid-1990s and the most significant porta was the launch of pro-LTTE or pro-Tamil nationalist website, www.tamilnet.com, in 1997.

The entrance into cyber engagements, through political activists from the diaspora, was limited mostly to the pro-LTTE operations network, which was established prior to the cyber networks. The cyber engagements started parallel to the third stage of the Eelam war, which also was significant in the technological advancement of the warfare as the third Eelam war phase was the most technologically advanced campaign from both the Sri Lankan government and the LTTE.

The LTTE unveiled two military tactics heralding the use of advanced technology in warfare. To begin with, they used Soviet-made, shoulder-launched surface-to-air missiles to down aircrafts belonging to the Sri Lankan Air Force. Second, Tigers used modified speedboats, designed parallel to the F 117 stealth fighter in body architecture, to ram naval gunboats and approach them evading radar (because of its unique design the boat was able to achieve speed similar to a wave piercer and stealth) (Davies 2001).

The mid-1990s saw the Sri Lankan government spend millions of dollars on obtaining heavy weapons, main battle tanks, APCs, UAVs, supersonic fighter aircrafts, advanced helicopter gunships, Super Dvora gunboats and electronic surveillance equipment. All these signified a technological leap in the context of the war. These developments were coinciding with the emergence of political engagements in cyberspace parallel to the escalating conflict in Sri Lanka.

During research, an interesting pattern emerged regarding the cyber-political engagements of the Sri Lankan Tamil diaspora. It revealed that the developments in the cyberconflict of the Sri Lankan case could be understood temporally in two phases. It became evident that in order to understand the distinct rupture in the paradigm of political engagements in cyberspace from 1994–2006, one should analyse the spatial context of the engagements.

Phase I 1994–2001

This phase is significantly parallel to the sedentary attempts of striation of geographic spaces for political and military engagement in Sri Lanka. The Sri Lankan state became involved in massive militarization of places where the LTTE threat was large, while the LTTE, using nomadic warfare to challenge the striation, simultaneously attempted to striate the geographic spaces, which were under their control, in order to establish the claim for a Tamil state. The same conflict and political engagements parallel to the ground condition transferred to cyberspace. In this context, the key feature from 1994–2001 in cyber engagements was that both the LTTE and the Sri Lankan state were competing for control of the web sphere being formed. One can see the coordinated and controlled websites, of both the LTTE and the state, emerging and creating a political space in cyber realms. Nevertheless, this smooth space underwent rapid attempts of territorialization and the same time hegemonizing and challenging rival ideology and political actions. Domination, hegemony and resistance are the key power dimensions that were created in this space. The LTTE wanted to maintain its fundamental ideology that it had as an organization. Their simple theory was to dominate and control any structure, institution or ideology. They used the same strategy of speed and shock and awe effects on taking over political spaces in cyberspace as well. In response, the state had one primary objective to maintain its presence, championing its discourse of a unitary, undivided Sri Lanka forced to eradicate terrorism.

The LTTE cyberattacks are mostly carried out from international locations. Mainly, groups from the mainstream Tamil diaspora are directly involved and others who are sympathetic to the cause. The actions of the sympathy groups will be analysed under the propaganda warfare. The attacks were mainly directed against government sites, which were of strategic importance to the LTTE and were a psychological advantage, especially hacking into the heart of Colombo-based government institutions and military installations. One incident is the launch of the Sri Lanka army website on 1 January 2001 followed by a pro-LTTE website, www.eelamnation.com, which on the very next day launched a homepage text,

> In an attempt to vie with Tamil websites all over the world depicting the local warring scene, Sri Lankan Army personnel are in the process of launching an army website to provide updated news from the battlefield, but not with much success though, admitted their commander-in-chief.

On the same day the army website suffered several blackouts, which officials said was a server initiation error, but research revealed officials knew that it was a greeting from the Internet Tigers, welcoming the army to a new battlefront. In 2002 the army website homepage was hacked into and a skull replaced the normal interface.

More than the official army website (www.slarmy.org, later www.army.lk), the cyberattacks were and are still being directed at the www.realityinsrilanka. com site which was manned by the Psyops (Psychological Operations Unit) division of the Sri Lanka army.[2] The army never admits the website is hosted by them, nor claims any responsibility for its content. From the year of hosting in 1997, simultaneous to the launch of www.tamilnet.com, the website has been targeted several times by hack attacks, mail bombs and sometimes virtual shutdown of the server. Nevertheless, the website still survives and is made an important link in many other websites hosted by Sinhala diaspora globally.

PRIU, the Policy Research and Information Unit website, the official website of the Sri Lankan government, which was hosted purely for government information services was also been targeted in 2004. The hack attack was considered to be of non lethal effect, however the point of concern for the government was the ability of the attackers to penetrate state-of-the-art counter-measures that were online.[3] PRIU is one of the few websites in Sri Lanka which is very concerned about security and constantly upgrades, using the services of professionals. The site also has experienced constant mail bombings in the form of hate mails directed towards the President of Sri Lanka. The PRIU officials said that they are now not taking chances and gearing up to face cyber-terrorist threats by installing state-of-the-art security measures.

Moreover, the Sri Lankan government has waged an underground cyber warfare campaign against prominent LTTE front office websites and on sympathy sites. The Sinhala diaspora also waged a similar campaign. The Sri Lankan policy makers on military and defence affairs saw, in the late 1990s, www.Tamilnet.com as a hostile site which had global reach and was a mouthpiece of the LTTE. This website, which started with a budget of US$400 with four people in the United States and one front office in Norway, became a priority target on the Sri Lankan government hitlist. Because the government lacked expertise to carry out a hack attack on the site, it sent a covert team to United States to hire hackers to attack the Tamilnet. Though initially this was a success, the Tamilnet recovered and through the advanced security measures provided by the web host Tamilnet was secured. The late Sivaram Darmeratnam, alias Taraki, who was the chief editor of the Tamilnet revealed this information (interview with the author). He traced the two-pronged strategy of the state to containing the operations of Tamilnet and using technological expertise to wage cyber warfare. The first strategy was the physical intimidation of the staff operating in Sri Lanka. The military made several raids on the house of Taraki. They began monitoring his telephone calls and blocking his dial-up connection making it impossible for Taraki to work. Second, Taraki revealed an interesting plot where the military was advising the government security officials on hiring hackers from USA to attack the website. Taraki claimed that his email accounts were hijacked and through phone-line tapping, email intercepts were carried out by DMI (Directorate of Military Intelligence) Sri Lanka.[4]

In early June 2007, the Tamilnet became totally inaccessible in Sri Lanka, with speculation rife that the military intelligence was behind the blocking of the servers. On 20 June 2007, in a weekly government press conference, government defence spokesperson Minister Keheliya Rambukwella was questioned by a journalist on the alleged state involvement in denying access to Tamilnet. The minister refuted the allegation, but went on to say on record 'I would love to hire hackers to disable TamilNet'. What the minister didn't know was that what he wished for was actually put into practice by previous governments with foresight on the future threat from Tamilnet to the Sri Lankan state. It appears, as revealed to this researcher, that the minister was not aware of earlier attempts to take out Tamilnet. Two years ago the chief editor of the website, Sivaram Darmeratnam, was abducted and killed and his murder trial has never been concluded.

Tamilnet itself has been the focus of many researches. Whitaker subtly brings out the intentions of the creators of Tamilnet. According to Whitaker,

> Their cyber-insurgency worked by sneaking their own perspective – through what stories they chose to report – into considerations of geopolitical and Sri Lankan elite, and thus shifting how the war was reported in the western press and debated by the various governments involved in the struggle between Sri Lankans dueling nationalist hegemonies.
>
> (2006: 266)

This certainly goes beyond the role of information provider to the Tamil world. It is the first site which came up in cyberspace with the Tamil diasporic political engagements, it is not just the pioneer of a Sri Lankan Tamil news service provider, but it also triggered the process of Tamil diasporic space being mapped in cyberspace.

Phase II 2001–6

Phase two traces the radical rupture in the strategy of holding and controlling cyber-political spaces, both by the Sri Lankan state and the LTTE as practiced and contested in mid-1990s. This paradigm change demonstrated the dislocation of the central axis of the political space, which was well connected to the conflict zone in Sri Lanka. It also took away the notion that this space can be striated or structured. These enclosure efforts were mainly the superimposing of intrinsic properties of state-centric discourse in cyber political space, such as the LTTE-dominated Eelamist web sphere or the Sri Lankan state-dominated web sphere. Cyberspace, in the context of the Sri Lankan political space, has been created more by movements, which then condition the spatial attributes that define the political space. This constant reshaping of the political space, both by involvement of traditional Tamil activists, and also attracting new political agents seeking an enabling political space, has resulted in significant constant transformations in this diasporic political space. This space is now evolving with an assemblage of a multiplicity of political actors. The ground conditions are still playing a major role, but the political spaces, which have opened up in cyberspace, are in the process of creating conditions which affect changes on the ground, or in a more geographic and place-based context. This is the reverse of what has been dominating cyberspace in the mid-1990s in the context of the Sri Lankan conflict. The conflict zone was a mirror image of the ground and centred on terms dictated by ground conditions that makes a unique contribution to the analysis of a new virtual conflict zone independent and yet more political. These findings do question and do reiterate the need to rethink previous literature and notions of network power in cyberspace, online political mobilization and cyber-terrorism.

The end of the millennium saw the phase one cyberwar reaching its peak and it was the beginning of the end, with this phase coinciding with certain key developments in the political realm. These included the rifts emerging within the organization, which culminated in a split in the LTTE in 2004, and the emerging of a powerful dissident Tamil political activism among the diaspora. These new political activists identify themselves as the dissidents or dissenting voice of the Tamil people, purely because they oppose the LTTE as the sole representative of the Tamil people. The LTTE never compromised on its role of being the single representative of the Tamil people and it used any means possible to maintain this, even resorting to extreme violence by eliminating its own people or any other party that challenged it. There would be no compromise of this core spatial attribute of the Tamil political space for the LTTE. The dissidents have managed to break through this well fortified political space and challenge the core hegemonic spatial principle of the LTTE.

This implosion in the Tamil political space, which emerged from the Tamil diasporic political space, has taken the cyberconflict away from the traditional Sri Lankan state versus LTTE struggle, adding a whole new dimension to it and radically altering the spatial configuration of political engagements in cyberspace. The dissident dimension in cyberspace heralded the rise of a nomadic type of resistance to sedentary hegemonies of both the Sri Lankan state and the LTTE. In an interview, Nallu, a leader of the dissident movement, proclaimed 'we rose through the Internet, if cyberspace was not there we could not be in politics'.[5] Whilst the dissidents are numerically still a minority, the effect they have had on altering the political landscape on the Internet is very significant and radical.

A key dissident political activist, Jeya, explained how he felt about being deprived of a political space (interview with the author). Jeya was a journalist by profession, but could not publish in any newspaper, unless it was supportive of the LTTE. He said the political space he needed to do his work was found through cyberspace and currently he publishes two newspapers and a monthly magazine, which is circulated throughout European Tamil diaspora communities.

The research revealed that the notion of online networks and the power of political mobilization using cyber-networks are not always straightforward, as cyberspace does provide political actors access to massive mobilization that can be affected by minimalist groups or individuals. The LTTE belief of holding its international network was to take over every Tamil organization, such as welfare, charities, media centres, local business societies and control. For this purpose, they established an extensive network of international cadres and sympathizers. The LTTE dominance is quite apparent if one visits East Ham high street or Wembley high street in London, as they are dominated by Sri Lankan Tamil businesses and every business has a significant poster of the LTTE leader Vellupillai Prabhakaran. This does not signify total allegiance of the community to the LTTE, but it does signify the control the LTTE extracted over them. The LTTE also organized massive demonstrations in London, Paris, Geneva and Toronto using their extensive organizational networks.

Thus, in the recent years with the rise of the dissidents many of these political mobilization tactics of the LTTE seems to be under threat. The dissidents, unlike the LTTE, are not all in one political organization, they do have different political ideologies and their versions of Tamil nationalism are not coherent. They do not operate as a single unit; they mainly operate in very small units. The dissidents have been able to use cyber-political engagements including cyber campaigns, e-lobbying and academic arguments. These efforts have had an immense effect on the LTTE front organizations and their mobilization strategies. These targeted campaigns have deterred the LTTE, while exposing most of its international operations and breaking the secrecy, and it has resulted drastic international condemnation and pressure exerted on the LTTE. The dissidents have taken on the Sri Lankan state as well, exposing human rights violations. These factors demonstrate that the politics of cyberspace do not just facilitate networks of power built on globalized forces, but also challenge them severely. The nomadic strategies of warfare demonstrate a resurgent potential in this new space, which is significantly harder to striate or dominate for any state-based entity.

The LTTE has resorted to using new web strategies to counter this emerging political threat on their domination. The LTTE counter-strategy was spearheaded by their unofficial website, www.Nitharsanam.com, which radically altered the way the web affects political activists and their day-to-day lives. Nitharsanam, run by an LTTE sympathizer on their payroll, started a campaign of using direct threats against dissident politicians and their families using photographs of dissident politicians, their residences and children.

This use of graphic images was an insidious way of threatening dissenting political activists. This tactic was identified as cyber-terrorism by many political activists (interviews with the author). Nallu, the dissident political activist, went on to say, 'If my name was Nitharsanam, I would be watching my back for three months, and would be extra careful about my security' and 'I know people who have changed door locks, installed alarm systems because of Nitharsanam'. CB, a Tamil journalist attached to a London-based international news agency, said 'Nitharsanam is carrying out acts of cyber terrorism and it has targeted us as well and it is scary'.

In response to this growing threat, dissident websites have resorted to similar counter-measures. They have identified key pro-LTTE political figures within the diaspora and have maintained a sustained personal attack on them. They were even successful in making the London police arrests these leaders, under the new anti-terror regulations. A dissident political activist, Raja, said in an interview, 'They attacked me, my family, they made pornography doctoring my photos, but now we have attacked them in return and now some of then even can't come out in the open'. The dissident website, www.tamilaffairs.com, has maintained this counter-attack. Their strategy was to isolate LTTE leadership from the Tamil community and project them as terrorists in Britain and this has successfully made some of them drop their political activities in fear of being arrested.

Pro-LTTE, dissidents and moderate political activists, respondents from different political ideologies, spoke about this new dimension in web-based politics. It was an interesting revelation. These individuals are not well read on cyber-theory or theories pertaining to cyber-security and cyber-terrorism, but the impact it has had on their lives has made them understand this phenomenon as terrorism. Dorothy Denning (2006), a leading academic and researcher in the field, has defined cyber-terrorism as

> generally understood to refer to highly damaging computer-based attacks or threats of attack by non-state actors against information systems when conducted to intimidate or coerce governments or societies in pursuit of goals that are political or social. It is the convergence of terrorism with cyberspace, where cyberspace becomes the means of conducting the terrorist act. Rather than committing acts of violence against persons or physical property, the cyber-terrorist commits acts of destruction and disruption against digital property.

This definition is more technologically based and is still aligned with the macro thinking of protecting critical infrastructure, which is the main focus of all cyber-terrorism studies. The notion of cyber-terrorism in the current context is mostly on identifying potential threats to a set of identified targets, which are linked to massive information systems hardware.

Denning further goes on to identify the qualities of such a terrorist act, 'To fall in the domain of cyber-terror, a cyber attack should be sufficiently destructive or disruptive to generate fear comparable to that from physical acts of terrorism, and it must be conducted for political and social reasons' (Denning 2006). In this context of the qualification of a cyber terror attack, the ongoing engagements on cyberspace in this second phase can be understood as acts of cyber-terrorism, thus there is definitely a need to rethink and recast the definition of cyber-terrorism and its application to micro political engagements.

The Sri Lankan cyberconflict did have its fair share of website defacements, Denial of Service attacks (DOS) on websites and servers. The other trend is the duplication of websites from all sides. The LTTE would immediately duplicate a rival website with a slight change only in the domain identity. The duplicate website would have the same template as the rival website. The duplicated website content would be used to attack the main website and the political activists who are operating the site. This has also been a successful tactic as visitors can be deceived into reading the duplicate site. The lobbying and political action methods also have drastically changed from street-based activism to mass mailing campaigns. Today, the rational space of the street has no political effect and both the LTTE and the dissidents have realized it. VK, a pro-Tamil nationalist activist who runs a major lobbying network sympathetic to the LTTE, said 'our emails reach each and everyone in the international community who has an interest and is capable of influencing in the Sri Lankan conflict, and this has proved more influential in pressurizing the state'.

Cyberconflict and cyber-terrorism have always been an aspect of the Sri Lankan ethnic conflict. Since the 1997 cyber-terrorist attacks by the Tigers, various aspects of online engagements have been discussed. In my interviews with political activists what emerged was a radical new dimension to the understanding of cyberconflict and cyber-terrorism. Existing literature has analysed the cyberconflict and terrorism dimension according to definitions of cyber-terrorism mainly developed on the levels of threats and mostly based around aspects of global scale terrorism and mobilization of terrorist organizations. These also depended on websites as the objects of studies, but what emerged in this research is that we need to look at cyberspace as a political space, and when political actors occupy such spaces, new forms of terrorism and conflict take place. The current definitions of cyberspace are still based on the notion of the 'Internet as communication medium, or conduit'. Spatial relationships or spaces in cyberspace should be theorized beyond hack attacks, web defacements or propaganda warfare. The political space itself has become the battleground. In the Sri Lankan ethnic conflict, this is quite a new phenomenon, therefore, it is a significant different type of cyberconflict or cyber-terrorism as it has moved beyond the state-centric struggle.

The Sri Lankan case demonstrates the shifting political landscapes in cyberspace, which facilitates a multitude of political engagements. Cyberspace is theoretically providing significant evidence of looking at the way new political spaces are being formed and the role of power in such conditions. These political spaces also question our understanding of politics, political space and the state-centric viewpoint of political spaces. The interesting emerging factor is how a political engagement online, which was more captured in the state-centric discourse and the spaces it created in the nexus of the state, has evolved into a unique political space. This chapter traces the political conflict which has emerged within this space. These alternative political spaces also have significant power relationships and power struggles that become their inherent dynamics, thus the geographic fixity or place dependence does not count in these unique conditions. Thus, these changes also make us question theories which looked at macro changes in the global changes, similar to Castells's spaces of flows, network theory analysis and superimposition of such models on developments in cyberspace. Activism and hacktivism is not just similar to that of the ground anymore. The power of so-called networks is challenged by individual agents and people organized in very loose formations and cyberspace has been a force multiplier in this context. Cyberspace is not a complete smooth space in Deleuzian context, it is always subject to territorialization by state-based entities or state structures itself. However, its inherent dynamic provides for the opening up of spaces and nomadic forces that can dominate and challenge spaces striated and hegemonized by state power and discourse and reshape political thinking of states in response to new political spaces and their assemblage.

Notes

1 Hardt and Negri introduced the concept in the context of rapid globalization and the new phases of capitalism as antidote or counteractive to this trend, which they termed 'rule of everyone by everyone, a democracy without qualifiers'. What are relevant from the point of the concept to this chapter are the new global cycle of struggles, and the mobilization of people which takes the form of an open, distributed network, in which no central control is possible.
2 The psychological operation was uncovered through series of discussions with senior army officials of the Sri Lanka Army. In military terms

> Psychological Operations are: Planned operations to convey selected information and indicators to foreign audiences to influence their emotions, motives, objective reasoning, and ultimately the behaviour of foreign governments, organizations, groups, and individuals. The purpose of psychological operations is to induce or reinforce foreign attitudes and behaviour favorable to the originator's objectives.
> (http://www.iwar.org.uk/psyops/)

3 The attacks on the PRIU were revealed through intensive research on the operations of the PRIU and in-depth interviews with PRIU web masters and senior officials in a series of interviews conducted in June 2003.
4 Tamil web operators provided these data and information in an interview on the potential attacks on their sites launched by the Sri Lankan government and Sinhala diaspora. The most important were the remarks made by the late Dharmeratna Sivaram, alias Taraki, who was the chief editor of www.Tamilnet.com.

5 All these names are pseudo names as the real identities of the respondents in my field-work have not been revealed as most of these activists are under threat from various stakeholders in the conflict. Most of them are ex-militants who have fled Sri Lanka and some are still operating as underground political activists while forming the leadership of different political organizations among the Tamil diaspora.

11 Feminist solidarity and the cyber crusade for women's activism

A case study of the Women in Black

Zinthiya Ganeshpanchan

Today a significant amount of creative energy and motivation in feminist activism is expressed in the form of networks of women's groups, gender institutes, politico-cultural performances, and feminist coalitions across the world. While many feel overwhelmed by the magnitude and scope of economic/social transformation, capitalist expansion, the squelching of human rights and political repression, women have joined hands to resist oppressive structures using a range of methods. Massive anti-war demonstrations and protests have been organised using cultural performances, art collectives and musical and theatrical performances, which have made inroads to the world of campaigning. The worldwide demonstrations in which activists gathered in capitals around the globe advocating a peaceful resolution to the conflict in Iraq is a result of this mass transnational mobilisation.

While more and more women are engaging in such protests in their own 'spaces' to make their voices heard, be it in the north or south through movements such as the Women in Black (WiB) and many other networks using the cyber space as a tool to reach out to their sisters, how far has their activism been able to encourage collaboration and build solidarity? Has this activism bridged, ignored or exacerbated the differences that exist between women when addressing intersecting issues connected to class, race, ethnicity, sexuality, (dis)ability, religion and nationality? How do they, alternatively, address questions of representation, engage and escape state/patriarchal power structures that shape women's political participation? In an attempt to uncover some of the issues, I will look at women's resistance to violent militarism and political repressions focusing on the Women in Black (WiB) where women have organised to protest against the war and human rights violence and defend human rights using the cyber space (read email and web) extensively to communicate. Relevant to this I will look at how the cyber space has provided opportunities and challenges to the women's movement.

Introduction

'The time for weeping has to stop; the time for confronting must begin' (Naomi Wolf posted to the WiB list, 16 October 2007). Globally women are engaging in activities to resist war and cultures of militarism. The anti-war demonstrations taking place in major cities around the world and 'Embrace the Base'[1] actions in Greenham Common (UK) are among the many campaigns organised by women. In this struggle women become active at a local as well as global level and are seeking to become more inclusive and representative of the diversity of women's experience. For example, the feminist response to the Iraq War witnessed protests appealing to local political process and global networks, which resulted in protests around the world. The La Ruta Pacifica de Las Mujeres[2] (Colombia), an alliance of more than 300 local women's groups in eight regions of the country, is another example of where women's grassroots activism has transformed to become a key force in the anti-violence and anti-militarism discourse in Colombia.

Through this activism and engagement, it could be argued that women today are experiencing a sense of belonging and connection and are seen to be creating an 'imagined community' (Anderson 1983). Such communities are not only limited to physical organisations, but are also a result of the rapid expansion of information technology and are becoming increasingly 'virtual'. It would be impossible to research the hundreds of thousands of websites that are devoted to women's anti-war activism. While these websites generally represent organisations in terms of mission, projects, history, membership and links to affiliated groups and contact information, the functions of these sites are to establish a kind of ongoing presence for organisations and other movement actors. It is also useful to note that in contexts of extreme repression, such websites may be the only way for organisations that operate entirely underground to have a persistent visible presence at all. The Revolutionary Association of the Women of Afghanistan (RAWA), is an example of how women's groups who come under extreme pressure use websites as 'virtual bases' from which they are able to create a space for the women to engage with other women's movements.

The WiB case

While it is difficult to capture the vast number of women's groups and sites that are using the cyber space as a means of activism as they are vast in numbers, and unevenly scattered, I will focus on the WiB: a worldwide anti-war movement, striving to work in solidarity and using the web as a tool for communication. The following posted on the Farmington WiB website can be seen as a comprehensive description of the WiB and its mission

> We stand in silence, because words alone cannot express the tragedy that wars and hatred bring.

> We stand in black, mourning lives broken or lost through violence in the United States, Iraq, Afghanistan, Palestine/Israel, and in all wars.

> We stand in witness to the suffering of victims of violence.

We stand in solidarity with those who struggle for justice and peace.

We stand convinced that the world's citizens can learn the difference between justice and vengeance and call world leaders to account to employ non-violent means to resolve conflicts.

We stand for justice.

We stand for peace.

We stand in solidarity with Women in Black around the world.

(cited on Farmington, Women in Black website)

The WiB has been selected as a case study for many reasons; first the WiB does not fall into a formal physical organisational structure, and therefore is fluid with no boundaries. This fluidity makes it possible for any person to enter and exit when they wish to do so. This means that any group of women anywhere in the world at any time may organise a WiB vigil against a manifestation of violence, militarisation or war. For example, when WiB in Israel/Palestine, as part of a coalition of Women for a Just Peace, called for vigils in June 2001 against the occupation of Palestinian lands, there were at least 150 groups across the world who responded from places such as Australia, Austria, Azerbaijan, Belgium, Canada, Denmark, England, France, Germany, India, Turkey, the USA and many other countries (WiB website). It is estimated that approximately 10,000 women may have joined in the demonstrations. This ability for participants to join voluntarily without any external pressure and leave when they want makes the WiB, not only an informal, but also a very democratic network. Through being involved voluntarily, it allows the participants to take ownership for the design of actions/vigils, which can make the process more meaningful, and a factor encouraging participation. Such voluntary participation without strings of an institutionalised loyalty can also work towards more collaborative work as one's loyalty (i.e. one of us or them) is not questioned.

Second, the WiB's strategy of silence as a mode of protest has become invaluable in a world where 'giving voice' to the other has become increasingly fashionable, especially in the north where many believe that 'we need to give voice' (Mohanty 1991; Spivak 1999; Naraynan 1997; Mani 1990). The WiB use 'silence' to capture the grief and sorrow of the women who have been affected by violence and conflict and use it to oppose the regimes that perpetrate such atrocities. Silence is used as a tool for reflection of the participant's own experiences of war/violence and to appeal for universal solidarity rather than 'giving voice or representing the other', a process which, Daphne Patai argues, can be exploitative and unethical, even if a feminist research methodology is adopted, because the exchange can never be what is considered equal (Patai 1994: 21–37)

Due to is dual strategy of 'silence' and 'active dialogue' along with its informal structure the WiB has transformed from a vigil that started in Gaza in 1988 to a unique worldwide network, which makes it suitable to research the primary questions of this chapter:

1   Have women's movements been able to bridge the existing gap between women's activism and build universal solidarity in the anti-war movement?
2   How far has the cyber crusade helped to promote inclusiveness among the women's movements?

Brief history and vision of the WiB

The WiB vigils started in Israel in 1988 by women protesting against Israel's occupation of the West Bank and Gaza (WiB website). The common elements of the movement are based on a shared mode of protest through silent public vigils where women dressed in black stand in silence mainly in public places carrying placards and at times handing out leaflets to the public. Today the network has spread its roots across many countries, mainly in the USA, UK, Italy, Spain and in Yugoslavia.

The networks are locally based but are connected globally and have been standing in solidarity with the women across the world. From its roots in the Middle East conflict as a group of Israeli women opposed to the occupation of Palestinian territory, WiB has grown to an international membership. Throughout this history the WiB groups around the world have been able to make an impact with their actions. WiB activists are generally women, nevertheless from time to time there have been a few men connected to different groups. Thus, the WiB can be classified as a transnational network of mainly women committed to peace and justice that actively oppose, war, militarism, militarist policies of governments and other forms of violence and work in solidarity supporting each other.

Mode of protest and the political use of silence

The symbolically powerful method of protest adopted by the WiB is turning the very act of silence to a public spectacle. The woman wearing black and standing in silence with placards of anti-war/violence messages held in public spaces, at times in adverse weather conditions have become a part of their grieving for the manifestations of violence. At the outset these images are likely to reinforce the role of women as passive, which denies them any form of political agency. However, during the long history of the WiB and with the responses to their activism, it has been proved that the use of silence has become visible, unavoidable and inescapably political. An example for this is when the 3,000 anti-war protestors assembled at the gates of the Mac Dill Air Base and the Gulf Coast and the WiB was invited to speak, they accepted – and used their time (five minutes) to maintain silence. Which spoke much more than words could.[3]

Through using women's traditional roles and mourning rights (i.e. the silence and wearing of black which is associated with mourning in many cultures and religions) as a method of political resistance, these women have used the strength of solidarity to enable their actions and reach out to others. They have been able to connect the private (read silence and mourning) with the political (protest).

Dialogue within/outside the movement

Jodi Dean (1996: 8) reflects on the necessity of difference to enable solidarity and the communication that adopts 'we' who express solidarity. Nina Ulasowski argues that such communication/dialogue is a vital for each person to own up, to position one's subject and recognise others (2007). The primary mode of communication is the vigils, which open up public discourse on the war and militarism. While this may seem as an inactive mode, the politicising of silence by using it to oppose war and militarism makes it the primary form of active communication/dialogue within and outside the network.

Second, the communication within the network takes place through emails. Exchange of information occurs regularly between the groups locally, nationally and globally. As a member of the lists since 2002,[4] I receive an average of four emails per day; either directly from the coordinator of the English list, or from other members or supporters from various parts of the world. These emails contain information of publicity on WiB vigils and activities, planning of new events, campaigns, sharing and exchange of information on political, military developments, political support to other groups/organisations and other actions of solidarity.

Third, there is a considerable web-based presence of WiB sites, which is used to communicate with the outside world. The growing facilities for increased access to information technology have created awareness on conflict, solidarity and activism and WiB has been successful in shaping the discourse of anti-violent/militarism struggle among its networks spread across the globe. This can be visible from the number of groups that emerge and the discussions that take place on the e-list. The many exchanges and personal reflections of women on the WiB list clearly demonstrate the transnational nature of the WiB. This ability of the WiB to reach women anywhere, without geographical limitations, has been an inspiration for many women whom I interviewed and also whom I met on the e-list to join the organisation and work towards a cause that they are not only passionate about, but a cause that has had an impact on many of their lives. For example, the women in the Israel–Palestine group whose lives are shattered with the daily experience of war, militarisation and violence, the women in Belgrade who have faced similar situations and myself, who have experienced the harsh realities of another prolonged conflict in Sri Lanka. The diversity and inclusiveness of the WiB can be witnessed by the international conferences where women gather to vigil/stand in solidarity from across the world. The WiB Conference in 2005 held in Jerusalem gathered women from diverse regions. The proceedings of the conference were made available to women around the world via an online audiovisual feed with linked space for comment and interaction.

Engaging with state/public

Political mobilisation can be seen as a process that goes beyond emotional rhetoric, a process that requires action by reasons combined with a moral obligation towards the other. Yet, when one's action becomes contested no matter what, how does one engage with the wider public/state discourse which by and large uses political/nationalistic rhetoric to justify its actions of impunity? Resistance to the wider women's movements in countries such as Afghanistan, Iran, Sri Lanka and Argentina, confirms that drawing from traditionalist images does not necessarily equate to public acceptance. Negative, and at times even violent responses from state/public become common when women are perceived as disloyal to the nation/political authority or the military regime that represent such authority. In the case of Sri Lanka, when the Mothers Front was formed to oppose state violence, the mothers came under tremendous pressure from the state and sections of the public, who had faced violence at the hands of the JVP, a Marxist-led political party mainly consisting of university students and youth of the south of Sri Lanka who took up to militarism (De Mel *et al.* 2004; De Alwis 1998; Ganeshpanchan 2007).[5] At the same time some members of the Mothers and Daughters of Sri Lanka, another women's group, had to go underground for proposing a political solution to the ethnic conflict rather than a military solution. They faced abuse from the JVP who were opposed to the Indo-Lanka accord.[6]

Similarly there have been many incidents of abuse and violence from the public and various groups against WiB members for taking a non-militarist stand. Many women have faced abuse from people from rival political groups within the communities they live in, often from people who had relatives in the armed forces. At times, these harassments have gone beyond normal verbal threats and have become physical.

A recent example for this was posted on the list server, of which I am a recipient.

On October 6, 2007 at 1:30 pm in Belgrade's Republic Square, at the Women's Nongovernmental Organizations Fair organized by The Incest Trauma Centre, in which Women in Black participated, a beam on which a PACE flag was hanging was broken. ('Pace' is peace in Italian.) Women in Black have used these peace flags in our protests since 1996. It is not only a symbol of peace, but also a symbol of respect for others and diversity. The wooden flagpole was placed in a flower stand. A man passed by, took the flag, broke the stick and threw the flag on the ground. Women in Black activist Milo Urošević reacted immediately, 'This gathering is registered with the police and you don't have the right to do that!' The man responded, 'Beat it, faggot, sicko! I will kill you, break your arms and legs!' Then, Women in Black activist Natalija Vušković interfered and Miloš went to the police. He approached the police and said that the gathering was attacked, that the flag was broken, and that they should come to the scene to identify the attacker. However, the police were completely passive; they did not pay attention to a violent act of vandalism. Miloš returned to the fair. Because the police didn't come, he again went to the police to look for them to react. Only then, after the second attempt, did the police officers go with Miloš to the table in Beoizlog Restaurant where the attacker was sitting. Miloš pointed to the attacker, who told the police officer in a 'brotherly' tone that he broke the flag. He said it as if his behaviour was normal, as if he can allow himself to commit an act of violence that endangers others and the different. The police did not react because they support a culture of impunity. The police officer told Miloš, 'You, bro, go over there!' Miloš left. Afterwards, the police came and told Miloš that the attacker told him that he broke the flag because it is a symbol of 'sick homosexuality that you promote.' Miloš said that that is an act of hates speech and that to use our sexuality in that way discredits all of us peace activists and defenders of human rights.

(email communication on the WiB English list, 2007)

This is only one incident of a series of attacks on the WiB and its members, for its stand on democratic political principals and the ethical principles of women's peace politics. This act of violence is a continuing phenomenon of the repression that women's groups experience from the public/state that support a social climate of impunity. However, despite this antagonism from a section of the community the public acceptance and support that the WiB receives today is becoming clear by the growing numbers of its activities and supporters. Even though there is no possibility to count the number of women who are directly part of the movement, there are many who admire the women's courage and effort. Despite the capacity of the membership, it is these methods adopted by the group that is challenging the regimes of violence today in their respective regions.

Intimidation and repression on women's groups such as the WiB and women activists also highlights an important point with regards to how patriarchy dictates women's political participation. A study of the Mothers Front in Sri Lanka and the Mayo de Plaza (Argentina), as well as the resistance to the WiB (example cited above), shows that in the context of militarised conflict/nationalist struggles, there is a tendency to restrict women's political/public participation, especially when they are deemed to be challenging the political/military institutions that are in power. This is largely due to patriarchal structures that govern women's lives at times of violent nation-building programmes. No sooner has the 'private become the public' and patriarchy adopts methods to curtail women's activism and political participation. Thus use of violence and intimidation becomes a tool in this controlling process.

Nevertheless, the strategies employed by the WiB show that they have identified the limitations women face in taking up public roles and collective resistance, and have worked around these limits. This is in line with similar movements such as the Mothers Front of Sri Lanka, that made use of women's traditional role of motherhood as a method of resistance. The WiB accesses the language of grief, that itself crosses many borders, which is associated with women's roles as weeping mothers or wives (Enloe 1993; Cockburn 2002) who grieve for their loved ones. The WiB's public spectacle of grief and emotion is capable of disrupting its association with the private and to move towards the public/political. This is made more potent by the extension of mourning for the 'other' (for the victims). These modes of political resistance, which can be less confronting and quite distinct from standard protests, have the ability to put more pressure on the 'enemy'. In a similar manner the Mothers Front (Sri Lanka) used traditional mourning and religious rituals to heap curses on a regime of violence. This had the ability to cause more distress to a president who was very superstitious[7] than any other actions taken by a women's group in the history of women's activism in Sri Lanka and as a result the president himself came out to openly sympathise with the mothers who had lost their sons to state violence.

Has the WiB been able to bridge the gaps and build solidarity?

As evident throughout the communications and the experience of the various groups, the notions of womanhood and the claims of solidarity and to be non-political do not come without difficulties and tensions. First, from the email evidence gathered, my observations are that a larger proportion of the emails focus on the Middle East and the Balkans. For example out of fifty emails received over a period of three months (August to October 2007) approximately twenty were on these two regions, around eight on WiB activities and conferences, four on India, four on Africa, three on Iran and the rest general emails exchanging information on various activities. The numerous instances where large-scale violence on women, such as in Darfur and recent military activities in Pakistan for example, have gone without much notice with only flying references (even on the Monday after which Pakistan declared emergency regulation and opposition groups were taken under house arrest). On a daily basis many women's groups, especially in the south, have to struggle on their own to bring the military exploitation and human rights violence they undergo to the public agenda. They not only struggle in isolation but also face multiple vulnerabilities in these efforts. Thus, paying limited attention to such countless actions and focusing more on a few regions can jeopardise the credibility of being a group committed to solidarity.

Second, the mode of protest adopted by the groups does not come without its problems, while some women I interviewed see silence as essential, others see the need to speak up at times and resort to other forms of non-violent actions. At the same time the use of silence, as opposed to women weeping, can also be interpreted as a class act. As suggested by De Mel *et al.* (2004) weeping is associated with the working class and women standing in silence maintaining dignity rather than weeping in public can be seen as more middle-class women's behaviour. This is also combined with the fact that the amount of time that women can devote to attend vigils, for example a young working-class mother will have more restrictions than a woman who is retired, unmarried or does not have children. This interpretation can project the WiB as a more class-based network rather than a group that cuts across the boundaries of class, nationality, ethnicity, age and motherhood.

In the same way, the individual identities formed among some groups have become a barrier to connect with the 'other' and to strengthen its positioning. For example, many of the WiB members identify themselves as 'lesbians' (Cockburn 2007). Such identity, along with the tensions mentioned earlier, can be a barrier for the inclusion of diverse range of women and can lead to problems between solidarity and difference in feminist practice.

These types of tensions are a common factor that can be seen within the wider women's movement. The global women's movement today is largely divided not only on ideology, but also geographically. There is a tendency to identify women's groups based on geographical patterns rather than the cause of grievance. While it can be argued that this type of identity formation is essential to understand the diverse experience of women, I would suggest that this has the potential to further exacerbate the gap between the north and south, mainly in terms of resources as well as ideology, feminist practice and forming a bond.

On the other hand, with these identities, the reasons for solidarity itself can be a fact that creates tension. For the south solidarity can be a way of survival, in the sense that, if they are to fight the social, economical and political exploitation and oppressions that women face on a daily basis, they need to work together in solidarity. While for the north it is more a political issue and a way of expressing political commitment or giving voice to the women in the south. This different stand can undermine the level of cooperation and create a sense of hierarchy that can be detrimental to the wider women's movement.

However, this is not to suggest that WiB has completely failed in its aim of building solidarity across women's movements. It has, within its limited resources, taken steps to accommodate other women's groups and call for actions not only on a regular basis on manifestations of war and violence. It also works towards increasing the number of women in the annual gatherings and increasing the number of languages that translate the proceedings. The very reason for that to look like paying more attention on a few geographical locations might be that the women in these regions are more formally organised and have more resources (in terms of conflict awareness, time, members and more importantly commitment) compared to the wider network. Or that the response to the WiB call for other parts of the world where many women had faced the same experiences of conflict to join them have not being received well not only due to a shortfall on the part of the WiB, but due to many other reasons that needs an in-depth analysis. Therefore, it can be suggested that even though there are difficulties and tensions, the WiB is translating knowledge into practice and is building a sense of collectiveness and working in solidarity rather than focusing on giving voice to the other and is becoming more inclusive and spreading its wings across borders.

Cyberspace as a space for solidarity and activism

Women's activism as described is not only limited to the organisations and networks that they form but, as described in the introduction, has become increasingly virtual. While the WiB is an example there are a number of other movements where the cyberspace has supported the advancement of the women's/social movement and helped these groups build coalitions. Today cyberspace is used not only as a tool for communication, but also as a political space within social movements. The one-million face campaign by Oxfam to make poverty history and the one-million signature campaign by Code pink again the war in Iraq are examples. Apart from these worldwide campaigns many groups adopt their own campaigning tools such as signatures, petitions and messages on issues they work around. The cyber revolution has helped more and more networks/organisations to be connected and build this imagined community for social justice.

The unlimited access to educational material that not only enhances one's knowledge but also builds awareness and creates public discourse on war and militarism and other individual campaigns, can be useful when organising campaigns. Access to funding resources, guidelines and at times online education have worked towards the advantage of groups/networks who would otherwise be limited geographically and spend large amounts of time and resources, which could add little value to their activities. Apart from some of these advantages the ability for online education is also a very important tool for women to gain informal education in the comfort of their homes/organisations, which enable these networks to build capacity with very little overheads and help women's empowerment. Through these advantages and numerous other opportunities today cyberspace has created a space for women's groups to build solidarity and fight injustice and violence as never before in history.

Cyberspace as a challenge to women's movements

Even though cyberspace can present a world of unlimited opportunities, not all movements and individual women benefit in the same way. While the Internet has facilitated the information flow, capacity building and organisational development of women's groups/social networks, it simultaneously presents some challenges that need understanding and addressing. First, grassroots movements, especially those located in rural areas, who do not have the comforts of Internet due to poor infrastructure and economic reasons, do not get the opportunity to reap the benefits of the Internet and other communication technology. As a result, the majority of women in underdeveloped countries and conflict regions such as Iraq, Afghanistan and Nepal, which is one of the poorest countries in the world, become excluded and sometimes invisible. At the same time women who are much more privileged and living in areas in these same countries where the infrastructure is developed get the opportunity to access these services. This is an example where cyber technology can work towards increasing the gap between the economically privileged and marginalised, leading to further divisions. For example a documentary telecasted by the BBC in the latter part of 2007 celebrating the independence of India, largely emphasised the development that is taking place in the urban landscape and paid very little attention to the poor marginalised areas of the country (i.e. rural and slums). Such partial representation of facts can create major challenges for women who are struggling to make their voice heard by a wider audience.

Second, language barriers and the lack of technical skills to use a computer/website is another factor that excludes women from the information-sharing process. It is true that many groups such as the WiB do provide translation services in other languages, and other women's groups in the north could afford to have versions in English as well as the other commonly used languages. The WiB conference report in Valencia 2007 was circulated in nine other languages and made available e-lists in English as well as Spanish. However, this is not so for many other women/groups who are illiterate due to various economical and cultural reasons and lack resources (read literacy, technical and financial) to manage a translation services. As such these women get left out and seriously lack the ability to connect with the developments of the wider women's movement as well as find it impossible to make their voices heard.

On the other hand, even when communication is developed and women have access to technology, oppressive/anti-democratic policies adopted by states/non-state actors deny women the freedom of using these technologies and sharing/accessing information. For example, the military state in Myanmar where all access is denied, China where information flow is monitored and Afghanistan where women activists/groups have to operate under strict secrecy. In such situations, it becomes impossible and seriously dangerous for women to become included in the wider women's movement.

Apart of these economical/political barriers to accessing communication, in certain cultures where patriarchal control and fundamentalism govern women's lives access to technology has also worked towards the oppression of women. A young Muslim girl, whom I came into contact with regularly, gave her mobile phone to her friend to take home, as she said she was prohibited from using a phone and if her parents came to know she would have to face serious consequences. Research in the area also suggests that the use of technology such as email and mobile phones can lead to an increase in domestic violence against women, as male partners feel insecure of women having their own mobiles, email accounts and become suspicious of them or put restrictions on their use. Many women (eight out of fifteen) whom I interviewed for my wider research,[8] confirmed that that their partners regularly checked their emails and telephones to find evidence of adultery, which has led to some women totally giving up using a phone to avoid verbal or physical violence.

In addition to the external barriers one's own physical/mental disability can be a major reason for many women to be excluded from accessing and using information technology. For example if a person is visually impaired or disabled, especially in countries where technology has not developed, it will be difficult for women to access these sites and communicate effectively. It is also true that today there is growing number of women who have been made disabled due to the consequences of conflict, many of these women have become victims of violence and have had their body parts amputated, become victims of landmines and the use of other weapons and at times have also been made disabled as a result of engaging in direct combat by joining armed groups such as in Sri Lanka,[9] Chechnya, Nepal and many other parts of the African continent (Save the Children 2005).

More directly the Internet also works towards the increase of violence against women through complex forms of pornography and trafficking. Today increasing levels of cross-border pornography and trafficking of women takes place via the Internet. Even when there are strict anti-trafficking laws in place, the ability to download/transmit pictures and information outside borders have made trafficking a lucrative business to gangs operating across the world and women, especially young girls, become victims.

The free access to information technology especially the Internet chatrooms and sites such as YouTube have also meant an increase in the number of sites that promote militarism and violence, the very evils that the women's movements are battling against. These sites have been able to promote violent alternatives to oppressions, such as the culture of suicide, martyrdom and destruction of the enemy that at times can be more attractive to young radicalised women who feel that the traditional women's movement is not offering a space for younger women to participate and be active (AWID 2007). There is also the increase of arms proliferation on the Internet that leads to more violence, not only at a global level but also at a local level.

These are only a few ways in which cyberspace has worked towards the exploitation of women. However, with research that enables us to gain a true understanding of the exploitative structures, and through developing systems that can minimise these risks, there is real opportunity for women's groups to harvest the benefit from cyberspace.

Conclusion

It is not untrue to say that women's organising to put into effect feminist ideals for participatory, democratic, non-hierarchical and autonomous engagement (Ferguson 1984) is often not without its difficulties and tensions. This work argues that feminist solidarity in the anti-war/militarist discourse is possible, and information technology has created a discursive space for progressive women's movements around the world. Nevertheless, it is essential to bear in mind that there is no movement that can be totally representative and there is a need to be aware of the 'difference', especially across the boundaries of factors such as political agency, class, ethnicity and religion. On the whole these differences should be translated to possibilities to build an indigenous movement that respects and celebrate differences rather than striving to impose a sense of 'assimilation'. Thus, the feminist discourse of solidarity is not without its differences and the development of technology has equally posed some real difficulties for women who still suffer from the consequences of poverty and patriarchal structures. However, with real commitment it is possible to translate the challenges to benefits that will enable women to continue with the crusade for a just and equal society that respects human lives rather than military might.

Notes

1 On 12 December 1982, around 3,500 women assembled at the Royal Air Force Base at Greenham Common in protest against the siting of US cruise and Pershing missiles. In an action called 'Embrace The Earth' they joined hands round its nine-mile fence lighting candles and singing songs (interview with an activist who participated).
2 www.rutapacifica.org.co.
3 See Cockburn (2007).
4 There is also a Spanish list.
5 For a detailed account of the JVP see Chandraprema (1991).
6 See more details in Rupasinghe K. Institute of Ethnic Studies, Sri Lanka. He has published widely on Sri Lanka and on conflict resolution.
7 For more details see de Mel (2000), De Alwis (1998), cited in the reference.
8 During the period 2004 to 2007 in the UK.
9 Doctoral research: Women and Conflict: A Case Study of Sri Lanka.

Part IV

Socio/politico/economic cyberconflicts

12 Electronic civil disobedience and symbolic power

Graham Meikle

Introduction

In May 2005, a small group of online activists called the Electronic Disturbance Theater staged a virtual sit-in. Their target was the website of the Minutemen Project, a vigilante organization which opposes immigration to the US, particularly from Mexico and Latin America. From 27 to 29 May, a claimed 78,500 people joined an online swarm that aimed to disrupt access to the Minutemen's website as a symbolic gesture of opposition, analogous to a physical sit-in at the organization's premises (Dominguez 2005; Kartenberg 2005; Jordan 2007). Such actions illustrate the practice of 'electronic civil disobedience' (ECD). The practice of ECD has been established since the mid-1990s and certain key characteristics have emerged – actions are publicized in advance in order to draw as many participants as possible; actions do not cause damage to the targeted site, but merely simulate a sit-in; actors are open about their goals and identities.

ECD is a key example of the Internet's capacity to enable users to exercise what Castells terms 'counter-power' – 'the capacity by social actors to challenge and eventually change the power relations institutionalized in society' (2007: 248). However, the discourse of ECD is contested, and where its proponents seek to align it with the civil disobedience tradition of Thoreau, Gandhi and Martin Luther King, it is frequently implicated in other discourses: in the concept of 'hacktivism' (e.g. Jordan 2002, 2007; Vegh 2003; Jordan and Taylor 2004); in the concept of 'netwar' (e.g. Arquilla and Ronfeldt 1997, 2001a, 2001b, 2001c; Arquilla 1998; Arquilla *et al.* 1998); and in debates about terrorism (e.g. Denning 2000, 2001a, 2001b; Manion and Goodrum 2000; Margolis and Resnick 2000; Hoffman 2006a).

In an information society, suggests Melucci, 'the power of information is essentially the *power of naming*' (Melucci 1996: 228, emphasis in original). The contested term 'electronic civil disobedience' and its imbrication with other discourses of hacking and hacktivism, of netwar and terrorism, is, in Melucci's terms,

> a *conflict of nomination*, conflict over the meaning of words and things in a society in which the name to an increasing degree supplants reality [...] in

today's information society, the manner in which we nominate things at
once decides their very existence.

(Melucci 1996: 161, emphasis in original)

This chapter suggests that ECD can be better understood and distinguished from
competing discourses by viewing it in terms of symbolic power (Bourdieu 1991;
Thompson 1995; Couldry 2000, 2003). The chapter first expands upon the concept
of symbolic power, before sketching the history of ECD. It then discusses, in turn,
the distinctions between ECD and hacktivism, netwar and terrorism.

Symbolic power

The mediascape is, as Castells argues, 'the social space where power is decided'
(2007: 238). The media enable an arena for the defining of reality. James Carey
once argued that reality is 'a scarce resource' (1989: 87). In this, the ability to
define reality is also, as Carey puts it, a 'fundamental form of power' (p. 87).
This 'fundamental form of power' is what Bourdieu calls 'symbolic power' –
'Symbolic power is a power of constructing reality' (1991: 166). This is the
ability 'to intervene in the course of events, to influence the actions of others and
indeed to create events, by means of the production and transmission of symbolic forms' (Thompson 1995: 17). Thompson distinguishes symbolic power
from other dimensions of power – the coercive power of the military or the law,
the political power of governments, and the economic power of corporations.
Coercive power works through the use or threat of force; political power through
the coordination and regulation of individuals and groups; economic power
through productive activity, the creation of raw material, services and goods,
and financial capital (1995: 12–18).

Symbolic power grows out of 'the activity of producing, transmitting and
receiving meaningful symbolic forms' (Thompson 1995: 16). Such symbolic
forms would include ideas and images, stories and songs, information and entertainment. They would also, of course, include activist communications, media
interventions, and online campaigning. Symbolic power, as Bourdieu put it in
defining the concept that Thompson develops, is the power of 'making people
see and believe' (1991: 170). It is the power to name, to define, to endorse, to
persuade. Institutions such as the media, universities, schools, government and
religious organizations are all in the symbolic power business – they are, as
Hartley has it, 'sites of knowledge-production and meaning-exchange' (1999:
6). New media activism such as a virtual sit-in campaign involves the exercise
of symbolic power – the creation and distribution of symbolic content; the
exchange of shaped information; the expression of cultural skills and values;
advocacy, rhetoric, appeal and persuasion.

Symbolic power is not separate from other forms of power, but bound up
with them – political power generates resources of symbolic power; economic
power can be expressed as symbolic power; coercive power can be demonstrated through the exercise of symbolic power. Not everyone is able to exercise this

power in the same kinds of way or with the same kinds of success. Certain types of institution, and certain individuals, have greater resources than others – schools and universities; churches, temples and mosques; and media organizations. These are the main centres of symbolic power – and each, as Hartley argues (1998, 1999), is built around *teaching*, a positive activity. ECD is one set of practices in which media, politics and pedagogy can be seen to converge.

But all kinds of teaching are messy – and the difference between what gets taught and what gets learned can be a big one. The exercise of symbolic power is not a simple, one-way transaction – like all forms of power, it is expressed within relationships, and so is not entirely predictable; it is, as Foucault has it, 'exercised from innumerable points, in the interplay of nonegalitarian and mobile relations' (1978: 94). Communicative acts can be interpreted in different ways. In the contemporary mediascape, communication is a dynamic process – even, in some accounts, a chaotic one (McNair 2006).

ECD is not implicated in economic power (it does not produce or exploit transformative capacity). It is not implicated in political power (there is no exercise of legal authority or legislative capacity, no coordination or regulation of populations). And above all it is not implicated in coercive power (there is no exercise of force, legitimate or otherwise). ECD is instead within the domain of symbolic power. What is at stake here is a persistent re-framing of ECD as coercive, whether as hacking, netwar or terrorism. Each of these misrecognizes the practice of ECD and so works to delegitimize its practitioners.

Electronic civil disobedience

Electronic civil disobedience was first proposed in 1994 by Critical Art Ensemble (CAE) a small group of digital theorists and artists (http://www.critical-art.net). In their definition, electronic civil disobedience was 'hacking that is done primarily as a form of political resistance rather than as an idiosyncratic activity or as a profit- or prestige-generating process' (CAE interviewed in Little 1999: 194). The group's involvement with the AIDS activism of ACT UP in the 1980s had suggested to them that the established repertoire of protest gestures had lost their efficacy. Their response was to call for new alliances between hackers and activists, and for hacker actions against the cyberspace presence of institutions (CAE 1994, 1995).

In naming this proposed practice, CAE aligned the concept of electronic civil disobedience with the widely-understood principles of traditional civil disobedience, in a conscious attempt to draw legitimacy from the legacy of such figures as Thoreau (2000), Gandhi (2000) and Martin Luther King (2000). There were certain continuities with the established traditions of civil disobedience, such as the use of trespass and blockades as central tactics. However, there were also certain discontinuities, such as the de-emphasizing of mass participation in favour of decentralized, cell-based organization, using small groups of from four to ten activists, and in particular the argument that electronic civil disobedience should be surreptitious, in the hacker tradition. Where practitioners of civil disobedience have been transparent about their opposition to the laws they break (Gandhi 2000: 410), CAE argued for a clandestine approach, proposing electronic civil disobedience as 'an underground activity that should be kept out of the public/popular sphere (as in the hacker tradition) and the eye of the media' (CAE 2001: 14).

The concept of electronic civil disobedience was developed further by the Electronic Disturbance Theater (EDT; http://www.thing.net/~rdom/ecd/ecd. html), a four-person group founded by one-time CAE member Ricardo Dominguez. (There was friction between CAE and Dominguez, which seemed to centre around ownership of the concept of electronic civil disobedience and its history. See, for example, CAE 1998.) The EDT moved away from CAE's emphasis on the clandestine exercise of elite hacker skills towards a more transparent public spectacle which aimed to draw as many participants together as possible (Wray 1998; Electrohippies Collective 2000). Denning (2001b: 72) suggests the first action of this kind was undertaken in protest at the French government's nuclear test policies in December 1995 by a group called the Strano Network. In this kind of prototype virtual sit-in, the 'flooding' effect was to be obtained simply by mobilizing large numbers of people to visit the target site simultaneously and repeatedly reload/refresh the page (see also Jordan 2002: 123).

The EDT developed a piece of software called FloodNet, which both simplifies and automates such actions, which the EDT now labelled virtual sit-ins. Where CAE envisaged a small number of hackers with elite computer expertise, the EDT created a situation in which the more participants the better, and in which being able to click on a hyperlink was sufficient technical ability. The virtual sit-in enacts a simulation of a real-life physical gathering. As the Electrohippies, who organized a virtual sit-in as part of the Seattle WTO demonstrations in November 1999, put it, such actions: 'require the efforts of real people, taking part in their thousands simultaneously, to make the action effective. If there are not enough people supporting then the action doesn't work' (Electrohippies Collective 2000: unpaginated). Any legitimacy the action might have derives from the number of people it gathers. These actions, as Dominguez puts it, are about 'creating the unbearable weight of human beings in a digital way' (interviewed in Meikle 2002: 142).

The EDT initially developed the tactic to use in support of the Mexican Zapatistas, although FloodNet has been used in actions for a large number of other causes. In 2001, the Electrohippies staged an online action to coincide with the WTO meeting in Qatar (Jordan and Taylor 2004: 41). On 20 June of the same year, activists targeted Lufthansa's Annual General Meeting, to protest about the airline's involvement in the forcible deportation of asylum seekers. As well as physical protests at the meeting itself, a virtual sit-in of the Lufthansa website was organized. While demonstrators in Cologne crowded the meeting venue, others around the world crowded the company's website in a what one observer terms: 'a hybrid of immaterial sabotage and digital demonstration' (Schneider 2002: 178). Other uses of the virtual sit-in tactic have targeted the US Republican National Committee, Dow Chemical, the Michigan State Legislature, and the infamous website of the Westboro Baptist Church of Topeka, Kansas at http://www.godhatesfags.com.

The highest-profile use of the tactic to date was one in which the EDT were also key participants: the 1999 Toywar, in which an online toy retailer with the domain name etoys.com, registered in 1997, disputed the right of the pre-existing European art group etoy to use their own domain name etoy.com, registered in 1995. Legal action by the retailer was met with a sophisticated suite of tactical media responses, including a virtual sit-in of the toy store's website. The retailer capitulated in January 2000, two months before filing for bankruptcy (agent.NASDAQ 2001; Meikle 2002; Wishart and Bochsler 2002; Wark 2003a; Jordan and Taylor 2004).

The central discourse here is that of tactical media (Bey 1991; Garcia and Lovink 1997, 1999; CAE 2001; Lovink 2002; Boler 2008). While this, as one of its main proponents notes, is 'a deliberately slippery term' (Lovink 2002: 271), it emphasizes the technological, the transitory and the collaborative. Tactical media mix subversive creativity and creative subversion. Tactical media projects are characterized by mobility and flexibility, by novelty and reinvention, and by a certain transient and temporary dimension – 'hit and run, draw and withdraw, code and delete', as Lovink and Schneider put it (2001: unpaginated).

While the virtual sit-in and the wider discourse of tactical media both emphasize novelty and re-invention, it is important to note that there are continuities here as well as transformations. On the one hand, the sit-in is a tactic with a long history. Sharp traces its uses as far back as 1838, and emphasizes its association with the US Civil Rights movement and, before that, with Abolitionist campaigns (Sharp 1973: 371–4); Ackerman and Du Vall document a successful use of the tactic against the Nazis in 1943 (2000: 237). Such history can offer pedagogical possibilities for Internet activists introducing virtual versions of familiar tactics. Yet at the same time, the virtual sit-in is significant in that it takes cyberspace as the actual site of action. In this sense, the virtual sit-in also represents a move towards using the technical properties of new media to formulate new tactics for effecting social change.

Such actions can be seen as vehicles for capturing the attention of the established news media, in order to force a cause onto the news agenda: activists can exploit the appetite for sensationalism (Vegh 2003: 92). However, there is a dilemma here for activists, in that while the news media are drawn to novelty and disruption, their coverage is also more likely to focus on that very novelty and disruption than on the underlying issues or causes involved, which may in fact work against the activist cause (Scalmer 2002: 41). This dilemma is especially pertinent in relation to the example of the virtual sit-in and its discourse of electronic civil disobedience.

Electronic civil disobedience and hacktivism

The practices of ECD are frequently subsumed under the discourse of 'hacktivism' (Denning 2001a; Jordan 2002; Vegh 2003; Jordan and Taylor 2004;

Gunkel 2005; Taylor 2005). For Denning: 'Hacktivism is the convergence of hacking with activism [...] Hacktivism includes electronic civil disobedience' (2001a: 263). 'Hacktivism', suggest Jordan and Taylor, 'is activism gone electronic' (2004: 1); it is 'a combination of grassroots political protest with computer hacking' and 'the emergence of popular political action [...] in cyberspace' (2004: 1).

In part, the discourse of hacktivism is an attempt to link ECD to the original discourse of the 'hacker ethic' (Levy 1984: 26–36). Taylor (2005) suggests that hacking had become the pursuit of technological mastery as an end in itself, whereas hacktivism introduced a new kind of political objective. If the EDT are hackers at all, it is in Levy's sense, which he applied to the innovators and designers of the early computer industry. Hacking, in Levy's description, was: 'a philosophy of sharing, openness, decentralization, and getting your hands on machines at any cost – to improve the machines, and to improve the world' (Levy 1984: ix). A 'hack' was an elegant solution to a technological problem; more than that, it had to be, as Levy says, 'imbued with innovation, style, and technical virtuosity' (1984: 10). In Levy's usage, hacking was about improving systems rather than crashing them; about sharing information rather than stealing or changing it. The early hackers made computer breakthroughs, not break-ins. 'The hacker', as Turkle put it, 'is a person outside the system who is never excluded by its rules' (1984: 208). The early hacker ethic, in Paul Taylor's analysis, had at its core three features: 'the ingenious use of any technology; the tendency to reverse engineer technology to do the opposite of its intended design; and the desire to explore systems' (Taylor 2005: 628). Or as cyberpunk science-fiction novelist William Gibson observed, 'the street finds its own uses for things' (1986: 215). The hacker ethic persists in the open source software movement, and in related movements inspired by it, such as the open publishing models of the global Indymedia movement, and there have also been important restatements of this hacker ethic discourse (Himanen 2001; Wark 2004).

However, the discourse of 'hacking' has shifted radically in the more than two decades since Levy popularized the hacker ethic. Hackers have become, in Stanley Cohen's term, 'folk devils' (1972). The roots of this shift can be traced to the 1990 coordinated arrests and show trials in the US, Operation Sundevil (Sterling 1992; Jordan 1999). Sterling sees the real struggle in this and the early hacker show trials that followed as one over control of *language*: 'The real struggle was over the control of telco language, the control of telco knowledge. It was a struggle to defend the social "membrane of differentiation" that forms the wall of the telco community's ivory tower' (1992: 274). A struggle, in other words, over inclusion and exclusion, and over naming and control; a struggle expressed through and for symbolic power.

In this context, it becomes important to ask whether FloodNet is in fact hacking in any meaningful sense. EDT member Carmin Karasic points out that: 'FloodNet never accessed or destroyed any data, nor tampered with security, nor changed websites, nor crashed servers' (http://www.pixelyze.com/scrapbook/index.htm). If FloodNet does not make sense as hacking, therefore, is there anything at stake for the EDT in their implication within the hacktivism discourse? Hacking, after all, is something that many people would consider frightening, unfamiliar, criminal behaviour – the precise opposite of the connotations that the EDT see as advantages of using the term electronic civil disobedience. One conclusion to be drawn from this argument is that promoting an emergent cyberspatial politics as 'hacktivism' means dealing with the baggage of the 'hack' component of the term. This term may make it all too easy for electronic civil disobedience to be marginalized and demonized in turn. One challenge for activists, then, is not just to formulate new strategies and tactics appropriate to a shifting mediascape, but to recognize the ongoing need to create a careful vocabulary for discussing those tactics and strategies.

Electronic civil disobedience and netwar

On 31 October 1998, the *New York Times* declared on its front page that the Electronic Disturbance Theater had declared 'netwar' on the Mexican government. From some angles, this would appear to be a good result for the group in publicity terms. Vegh, for example, contends that 'While the U.S. mainstream media are in the hands of the corporate world, the sensationalist nature of hacktivism works to the activists' advantage' (2003: 92). However, the *New York Times* example, with its media declaration of 'netwar', points to how the practices of ECD can be framed within military discourses. Central to this is the discourse of netwar (Arquilla and Ronfeldt 1997, 2001a, 2001b, 2001c; Arquilla 1998; Arquilla *et al.* 1998):

> Netwar refers to information-related conflict at a grand level between nations or societies. It means trying to disrupt, damage, or modify what a target population 'knows' or thinks it knows about itself and the world around it. A netwar may focus on public or elite opinion, or both. It may involve public diplomacy measures, propaganda and psychological campaigns, political and cultural subversion, deception of or interference with local media, infiltration of computer networks and databases, and efforts to promote a dissident or opposition movements [*sic*] across computer networks.
>
> (Arquilla and Ronfeldt 1997: 28)

Arquilla and Ronfeldt's emphasis in this definition on information, opinion, diplomacy and propaganda identifies the concept as one within the domain of symbolic power relations. However, their choice of 'war' as the key term and discursive framework implies a coercive dimension which is in fact absent from the practice of ECD.

An essential component of the netwar concept is the use of network forms of organization:

> The [information] revolution is favoring and strengthening network forms of organization, often giving them an advantage of hierarchical forms. The

rise of networks means that power is migrating to nonstate actors, because they are able to organize into sprawling multiorganizational networks [...] more readily than can traditional, hierarchical, state actors. This means that conflicts may increasingly be waged by 'networks', perhaps more than by 'hierarchies'. It also means that whoever masters the network form stands to gain the advantage.

(Arquilla and Ronfeldt 2001a: 1)

A key tactic of such netwar practice is swarming: 'a seemingly amorphous, but deliberately structured, co-ordinated, strategic way to strike from all directions at a particular point or points' (Arquilla and Ronfeldt 2001a: 12). This is the principle underlying the tactic of the virtual sit-in. Swarming is a concept which has to some extent been popularized in Howard Rheingold's analogous concept of 'smart mobs'. Smart mobs, writes Rheingold, 'consist of people who are able to act in concert even if they don't know each other' (2002: xii). The role of mobile communications in connecting and coordinating the crowds that forced the ouster of Philippines President Joseph Estrada in January 2001 is one example (Goggin 2006; Rafael 2006). Others would include the various so-called anti-globalization protests in Seattle, Prague, Melbourne, Genoa and elsewhere (Electrohippies Collective 2000; de Armond 2001; Meikle 2002; Jordan and Taylor 2004; Kahn and Kellner 2004), or the monthly 'organized coincidence' that is Critical Mass, with its regular coordinated bike rides by transport activists in cities around the world.

Arquilla has described the virtual sit-in as a harbinger of more widespread and effective tactics, framing it explicitly in terms of military discourse:

FloodNet is the info age equivalent of the first sticks of bombs dropped from slow-moving Zeppelins in the Great War [...] The implication, of course, is that netwar will evolve, as air war did, growing greatly in effect over time.

(Arquilla interviewed in Meikle 2002: 157)

A central question, however, is whether such events are best described using terms built around the vocabulary of warfare. The RAND analysts have acknowledged, for instance, that what they term 'social netwars' may in fact have 'some positive consequences, especially for spurring social and political reforms' (Arquilla *et al.* 1998: 120). Given this point, and the participation of such groups as the Red Cross and the Catholic Church in the Zapatista support campaigns, it can be contended that there is something problematic about the 'war' component of the term 'netwar'. Why not, for example, 'netpeace'? It is important to emphasize that ECD was framed from the beginning by its theorists as a nonviolent concept. For example, ECD, wrote CAE, is 'a nonviolent activity by its very nature, since the oppositional forces never physically confront one another' (1995: 18). There is something problematic about this militarization of humanitarian actions: specifically, the connotations of netwar tend to demonize non-state actors while legitimizing state actors and actions. It is a vivid illustration of a struggle expressed over and through the exercise of symbolic power.

Electronic civil disobedience and terrorism

The third discourse under which ECD is often subsumed is that of terrorism. For example, one survey of Internet politics includes a brief account of the EDT and FloodNet in a chapter on 'criminal activity in cyberspace', which concludes that cyberspace 'needs to be safeguarded against terrorist attacks' (Margolis and Resnick 2000: 202). Terrorism analyst Bruce Hoffman also discusses ECD in a terrorism frame, quoting a human rights activist from an established NGO under the sub-heading 'Terrorist and Insurgent Use of the Internet' (2006: 201), and implying a link between electronic civil disobedience in support of the Zapatistas and the use of the Internet by terrorist groups (2006: 204). One content analysis of US newspaper articles about hacking suggested that the discourse about hacking was increasingly blurred with that of cyberterrorism, with online protest activity represented as disruption, vandalism or worse (Vegh 2005).

In one of the most important examples of this linkage, the writings of computer security analyst Dorothy Denning repeatedly place activists, hacktivists and 'cyberterrorists' within the same analytical frame, suggesting that 'the boundaries between them are somewhat fuzzy' (2001a: 241) and that 'an individual can play all three roles' (2001a: 242). This is a problematic analysis, which yokes together disparate behaviours and practices in a hypothetical frame (Denning's discussion of cyberterrorism is entirely future-oriented). Denning's use of terms such as 'hacker warriors' and 'cyber warriors' blurs the line between non-violent symbolic protest, and coercive action. One essay (2001b) conflates activism and terrorism, writing of 'hacker warriors' who 'often initiate the use of aggression and needlessly attack civilian systems' (2001b: 70). In this discussion of cyberspace as 'digital battleground' (2001b: 75), the very real distinctions between symbolic political protest and coercive violence are elided. The potential consequences of all this for political activists are contained in a line from Denning's own work: 'the threat of cyberterrorism, *combined with hacking threats in general*, is influencing policy decisions related to cyber-defence at both a national and international level' (2001a: 288, emphasis added).

It should be acknowledged that elsewhere Denning has emphasized the distinction between civil disobedience and terrorism: 'Both EDT and the Electro-hippies view their operations as acts of civil disobedience, analogous to street protests and physical sit-ins, not as acts of violence or terrorism. This is an important distinction. Most activists [...] are not terrorists' (2000: unpaginated). It is indeed an important distinction, and Ricardo Dominguez has quoted this more than once in support of his own organization (Dominguez 2005; Kartenberg 2005). But by placing activists and non-violent protests within the same frame as terrorism, Denning undermines the distinction.

In September 1999, EDT member Stefan Wray made a presentation to the US National Security Agency. Wray pointed out that the event's programme had renamed his group 'the Electronic *Disruption* Theater' and described the Zap-atistas as a 'sect'. While these could, of course, have been the result of simple errors, Wray argued that they might have also represented what he termed 'an attempt to recategorize who we are into a framework that is understandable to the national security minds' (1999). This is not a trivial issue: the ways in which actions are framed and described, the motives attributed, meanings sought and implied, are a fundamental symbolic power struggle. For example, as Schlesinger *et al.* have argued in relation to definitions of terrorism: 'Contests over definitions are not just word games. Real political outcomes are at stake [...] Language matters, and how the media use language matters' (Schlesinger *et al.* 1983: 1).

The most sobering relevant example of the dangers of allowing symbolic protest to be conflated with terrorism is the case of Steve Kurtz of Critical Art Ensemble, the group who initiated the discourse of electronic civil disobedience. In May 2004, Kurtz was detained by FBI agents on suspicion of 'bioterrorism'. Agents seized lab material used in CAE's artworks about genetic modification, as well as their writings, and initially sought to bring charges relating to biologi-cal weaponry. Although it became clear that the materials were harmless and readily obtainable by anyone, and moreover had been used in legitimate art-works at public galleries, the investigation was not dropped and the charges were changed to allegations of 'mail fraud' and 'wire fraud', revolving around technical details of how Kurtz obtained some of the material, worth $256, from his co-accused Professor Robert Ferrell. At the time of writing in January 2008, Kurtz and Ferrell face potential prison sentences of twenty years, in a precedent-setting conflation of art criticism and 'terrorist' scare-mongering (http://caede-fensefund.org).

ECD can be distinguished from terrorism insofar as the practice of terrorism is coercive (although its discourse may also be symbolic). In the case of ECD, both practice and discourse are symbolic. This point is developed below in the final section of this chapter.

Conclusion

In what ways is electronic civil disobedience implicated in symbolic power? We can distinguish between the practice of ECD and the discourse of ECD. The practice of ECD involves publicizing and promoting actions, such as virtual sit-ins. This usually involves distributing information through email lists and web-sites, although it has also involved participation in art events, academic conferences, and gatherings of hackers or security personnel, as well as giving frequent interviews to journalists, academics, other writers, broadcasters and film-makers. The practice of ECD involves the carrying out of actions, which are on one level simulations and are partly rhetorical. FloodNet does not crash or immobilize servers: it enables a simulation of a physical gathering in order to draw attention to a cause. Furthermore, the practice of ECD involves exploiting this attention – particularly the attention of the established media, and any subsequent discussion of the action or, more rarely, the cause in support of which the action was held. The discourse of ECD involves the invoking of high-value historical antecedents from the civil disobedience tradition, such as Gandhi or Thoreau. Nevertheless, it also involves problematic involvements with the discourses of hacktivism, netwar and terrorism, as well as a dispute over 'ownership' of the concept between CAE and EDT. In both the practice and the discourse of ECD, all of these key aspects revolve around claim and counter-claim, around rhetoric and persuasion, within the arena of symbolic power relations. If legitimate forms of non-violent online protest are to continue, they need to be recognized as manifestations not of coercive violence or force, but of symbolic power.

13 The Internet and decentralized architectures

Email lists and the organizing process of the European Social Forum

Anastasia Kavada

Introduction

Social movements are generally thought to be organized as 'networks of networks' (van de Donk *et al.* 2004: 3), as decentralized coalitions of distinct clusters that are connected through informal non-hierarchical relationships. This claim was first put forward by Gerlach and Hine, as early as 1970, emerging as a conclusion of their seminal ethnographic study of the Pentecostal movement and the Black Panthers. Gerlach and Hine argued that this decentralized architecture is suitable for social movements since it allows them to evade repression by the authorities, enabling them to 'penetrate into a variety of social niches through factionalism and schism, adapt to circumstances, and promote innovation' (Baldassari and Diani 2007: 8).

The SPIN model continues to be one of the main points of reference for writings on the organizing structure of social movements, with various studies adopting it as a theoretical basis or setting out to prove empirically some of its main tenets (see for instance Baldassari and Diani 2007). The rise of new communication technologies, as well as the increasing popularity of 'network theories' have further ensured the enduring relevance of the model to current modes of conflict. For Ronfeldt and Arquilla (2001: 322), the SPIN model 'remains relevant for understanding the theory and practice of netwar', a type of network-based conflict that they predict will be a major phenomenon in the years ahead. Such networks are thought to be established and sustained through the use of the Internet, whose role is considered instrumental for decentralized organizing. However, empirical evidence is still scarce in this field of enquiry, which is also lacking a more in-depth understanding of new communication technologies. This chapter aims to address this gap by focusing on the role of the Internet in the organizing structure of the 'movement for alternative globalization'.

The SPIN model

According to Gerlach and Hine (1970), decentralized architectures exhibit three main characteristics: they are segmented, polycentric and integrated. The polycentric aspect refers to the lack of a centralized command. Instead, the leadership of social movements tends to be temporary and fragmented, with leaders arising in response to particular challenges but commanding only a limited following (Gerlach and Hine cited in della Porta and Diani 1999: 140). This also stems from the inability to track and document the membership of the movement as processes of affiliation are often flexible and informal (Gerlach and Hine 1970: 37). Indeed, the distinction between a 'participant' and a 'member' is rarely made, as there are no 'card-carrying' members (Gerlach and Hine: 1970: 292). In addition, leaders in such movements cannot 'make decisions binding on all of the participants in the movement, and none can speak for the movement as a whole' (Gerlach and Hine 1970: 36).

Decentralized structures are also segmentary, 'with numerous different groups or cells in continual rise and decline' (della Porta and Diani 1999: 140). These diverse segments and organizational units 'overlap and intertwine complexly, so that many people are members of several segments at the same time' (Gerlach 2001: 290). New segments constantly arise through splits in existing ones and the addition of organizing units and functions. Segments tend to divide as a result of differences over ideologies and tactics, often following 'Preexisting cleavages derived from socioeconomic differences, factionalism, and personal conflicts' (Gerlach 2001: 292). Divisions may also arise through the competition between movement members for access to rewards of a political, social, economic or psychological nature.

However, movement segments are not isolated from each other but 'form an integrated network or reticulate structure through nonhierarchical social linkages among their participants and through the understandings, identities, and opponents these participants share' (Gerlach 2001: 295). This process of networking allows movement participants to exchange information, coordinate actions, recruit supporters and gain access to resources (Gerlach 2001: 295–6). Such linkages are, first of all, created through personal relationships among members that unify the movement in the absence of a central authority. Movements also integrate through visitors and travelling evangelists who carry information from segment to segment, establishing personal relationships with the visited groups (Gerlach 2001). In addition, large gatherings, conferences, workshops and conventions provide the opportunity for movement participants to create new bonds, to re-affirm their commitment to the movement and to become better acquainted with its goals and ideologies (Gerlach 2001).

Gerlach (2001) later updated the SPIN model to fit more closely with contemporary social movements. He changed the term polycephalous to polycentric, 'indicating that, like earlier SPIN movements, global activist networks have many centres or hubs, but unlike their predecessors, those hubs are less likely to be defined around prominent leaders' (Bennett 2004: 127). In addition, he noted that movement integration is currently produced less through ideology and more through personal relationships among activists (ibid.).

In the revised version of the SPIN model, Gerlach also added communication technologies in the factors aiding the integration of movements. This is because digital communication allows 'individuals to extend their reach far beyond their own group' (Gerlach 2001: 297) permitting the coordination of activities over much larger geographical distances. However, viewing communication technologies solely as an integrative factor seems to over-simplify their role within the process of organizing. Instead, this chapter will demonstrate that online communication is also related to the segmentary and polycentric aspects of social movements. This analysis is based on a case study of the 'movement for alternative globalization', one of the most prominent social movements of recent times.

The 'movement for alternative globalization', the Internet and decentralization

The 'movement for alternative globalization' made its first impact on public consciousness during the Seattle meeting of trade ministers in late 1999. The 'Battle of Seattle', as it was later named, was followed by demonstrations at almost every summit of a transnational economic organization or major political power, including the International Monetary Fund (IMF), the World Bank, the FTAA, the EU or the G8. However, mass protests have been later eclipsed by another type of event, the World Social Forum and a number of regional and local social forums. Such events have become 'the primary vehicles where diverse movement networks converge across urban space to make themselves visible, generate affective attachments, and communicate alternatives and critiques' (Juris 2005: 255).

The World Social Forum (WSF) was founded in Brazil in 2001 as an alternative to the World Economic Forum (WEF).[1] According to its Chapter of Principles, the WSF constitutes 'an open meeting place for reflective thinking, democratic debate of ideas, formulation of proposals, free exchange of experiences, and interlinking for effective action' (WSF Charter of Principles, 20 May 2006). The concept of the 'open space' is crucial here, since it emphasizes the role of the WSF as a 'public square' rather than a social movement (Whitaker 2004: 113).

The WSF idea was met with such success that since its inception regional or even national and local 'social forums' have swiftly started to crop up around the world, in Asia, Europe and the Americas. The first European Social Forum (ESF) took place in Florence in 2002 and attracted around 60,000 participants (Juris 2005: 265). Its meetings were instrumental for setting the date of 15 February 2003 as a Global Day of Action against the war in Iraq, leading to a globally coordinated collective action that was the largest to have ever occurred (Chesters 2004: 332). The second ESF was held in Paris in 2003 and was attended by around 40,000 participants, while the third ESF in London in 2004 attracted 20,000 people. However, attendance numbers have risen in the latest ESF, which took place in Athens in 2006, whereby 35,000 registered participants attended over 500 seminars and workshops.

The adoption of decentralized organizing methods is considered as a defining aspect of the ESF process and every event or gathering organized by the 'movement for alternative globalization'. As Castells argues,

The anti-globalization movement does not have a permanent, professional organization, does not have a center, a command structure, or a common program. There are hundreds, thousands of organizations and individuals, around the world, converging in some symbolic protests, then dispersing to focus on their own specific issues – or just vanishing, to be replaced by new contingents of newly born activists.

(2001: 142)

However, this loose and flexible structure becomes even more apparent in the social forum process, where it is combined with the rhetoric of the 'open space' and a belief in participatory and consensual decision-making. In a study of the Genoa Social Forum, della Porta (2005a: 89) has shown that forum activists privilege consensus rules versus majority ones and emphasize direct participation over representative mechanisms. They also attempt to prevent power from becoming centralized or consolidated through, for instance, the rotation of chairs of meetings, as well as the replacement of leaders by short-term spokespersons with a limited public mandate. Della Porta further suggests that the internal plurality of social forums leads to a continuous search for 'forms of participation that respect individual subjectivity and avoid exclusive commitments and vertical control' (ibid.: 81). Thus, decentralized organizing becomes indispensable for the coordination of diverse groups and individuals, since it allows them to collaborate without having to subsume their goals or identity to those of the movement.

In fact, the value of decentralized organizing has such strong ideological connotations that organization seems to have become something of a 'meta-ideology' (Bennett 2005: 216–17). As Juris (2005: 257) puts it:

Beyond social morphology, networks have more generally emerged as a broader cultural ideal, a model of and model for new forms of directly democratic politics at local, regional, and global scales. Moreover, such values are increasingly inscribed directly into emerging organizational architectures. [...] Indeed, activists increasingly express utopian political imaginaries directly through concrete political, organizational, and technological practice.

It is worth noting however that the vision of the social forums as spaces free from power play and manipulation is rarely realized in practice. Instead, the forums seem to suffer from some of the well-known problems of decentralized architectures, such as informality, hidden leadership and opaque structures (della Porta 2005: 82).

This flexible structure is thought to be influenced and afforded by the use of new communication technologies. In that respect, the Internet is believed to drive the 'alter-globalization' movement towards looser and less hierarchical modes of organization, which reflect its own loose and non-hierarchical structure. According to Klein (2002: 17), for instance, 'What emerged on the streets of Seattle and Washington was an activist model that mirrors the organic, decentralized, interlinked pathways of the Internet'. This can be attributed to the low cost of the medium 'which simplifies mobilization and favors highly flexible, loose organizational structures' (della Porta and Mosca 2005: 168). In addition, contrary to the more conventional means of communication which are relatively expensive and tend 'to foster just a few centres of communication (and often related to this, of power and decision making)', the Internet does not 'demonstrate an inherent tendency to be concentrated and controlled in the hands of a few movement entrepreneurs' (van de Donk *et al.* 2004: 9). Instead, the Internet facilitates horizontal, bi-directional and interactive communication, allowing for the same message to be sent to many recipients scattered in distant geographical locations. In addition, by easing the affiliation of activists to the movement and allowing information about targets, protests and campaigns to be diffused in interpersonal and inter-organizational networks the Internet allows the movement to expand in an organic way.

In fact, current literature tends to consider the Internet not only as a new form of communication, but also as an organizational process in itself (Tarrow 2002: 15). Bennett brings the example of the transnational protest network that coordinated the 'Battle of Seattle', noting that it lacked the conventional characteristics of an organization. Instead, 'It was more a meta-organization, or, better, a *hyper-organization* that existed mainly in the form of the website, e-mail traffic, and linked sites' (2005: 218, emphasis in original). In that respect, the organization did not 'exist apart from the technology', but was constituted by it in conjunction with the other modes of communication through which activists interacted (Bennett 2005: 219).

However, empirical evidence connecting the movement's decentralized architecture with its use of the Internet is relatively scarce. This gap is compounded by a more general lack of research in the internal processes of social movements. As Klandermans argues, 'leadership and decision making are aspects of social movement organizations which are more often debated than studied empirically' (1997: 133). He attributes this gap to the fluid character of social movement organizations that complicates the research of such practices: 'How can one study leadership and decision making in organizations that have no clear boundaries, that have distributed, rotating or multiple leadership or that claim they have no leadership at all?' (Klandermans 1997: 133).

This chapter will address these issues by focusing on the case study of the London 2004 European Social Forum. Taking the SPIN model as its theoretical framework, it will highlight the links between new communication technologies and the three aspects of decentralized architectures proposed by the model. The data derives from in-depth interviews with twenty-four activists involved in the organizing process of the London ESF. Two-thirds of the sample were activists based in Britain since they were responsible for the day-to-day organizing of the ESF. The interviewees also originated from different political backgrounds and ideological positions reflecting the plurality of actors participating in the ESF. The sample varied in age but two-thirds of it was male.[2] Data from the interviews was complemented by participant observation of all the major organizing meetings, as well as the main email lists devoted to the organizing of the ESF. Further, the minutes and official reports of important meetings, as well as the proposals and position papers circulated either online or offline, were archived and analysed.

Email lists, working groups and polycentric leadership

Within the organizing process of the London ESF, email lists played an instrumental role in the definition of new organizing units and their informal leaders. The main decision-making body of the process was the European Preparatory Assembly (EPA), essentially an open face-to-face meeting attended by delegates and representatives of the groups, networks and organizations interested in the ESF. The EPAs took place every two to three months in different locations across Europe. However, the day-to-day preparation for the ESF was undertaken by smaller working groups, each one responsible for a specific area of organizing. The London process was ran by three major working groups: Programme, Practicalities, Culture, while other groups were added later on to the structure (Office, Outreach, Memory). The email lists of these working groups were intimately connected to the polycentric aspect of the ESF process, allowing flexible forms of affiliation and the establishment of new units.

Affiliation and the definition of new organizing units

According to the minutes of meetings and my own participant observation, working groups tended to emerge in the offline organizing meetings, either the EPAs or meetings of the British movement. In the overwhelming majority of cases, the establishment of a working group at an offline meeting was accompanied by the setting up of an email list devoted to the group. Activists interested in participating could thus provide their email address in order to become subscribed to the email list of the group. The minutes of the first meeting of the Practicalities working group illustrate this point: 'We collected everybody's email which is to be put on a practicalities mailing list which was set up by the Paris group last year. [...] The list will be open and public, and only to discuss practicalities' (13 December 2003).

The email list of the working group serves a twofold function. First, it defines a space where the working group can exist independently of the physical meetings. Second, it identifies, at any point in time, the membership of the group. Therefore, email lists provide working groups with a constant or permanent space where all of their members, active or inactive, are potentially present since they are subscribed to the list and receive the relevant information. They thus allow the movement a degree of continuity and coherence in-between meetings and across large geographical distances.

The ease of setting up an email list renders the process of dividing labour and allocating responsibilities much more flexible. This means that the organizing structure of the movement is free to sprawl into different directions, spawning new task-related working groups easily and at no extra cost when the need arises. As one of my interviewees put it, 'it's like creating this space where things get discussed and then this space keeps shifting and moving and getting divided in different rooms' (Interviewee 7, 10 June 2004). This further encourages the segmentary nature of the movement, as working groups, each one responsible for specific tasks, tend to proliferate.

Furthermore, the email list serves to define the membership of the group, as subscription to the list ensures automatic affiliation. This eliminates the need for a more formal and hierarchical process of allocating tasks and responsibilities, as activists can voluntarily become part of a working group without the need for a central authority overseeing this process. In addition, since the email list defines the membership of the working group at any point in time, the organizing process can do without official lists of participants. Again, this allows working groups a degree of flexibility as their membership is not written in stone, but can shift and change as activists subscribe and unsubscribe from the list.

Furthermore, email lists enable activists to manage their degree of involvement to the group according to their own time or needs. Also, this means that commitment to the activities of the movement is not a prerequisite for admitting an activist to the group, since anyone can become a member by subscribing to the email list. Instead, commitment is built through direct participation in the offline meetings of the group, whereby activists assume more responsibilities and become more intimately related with the rest of the members.

It is worth noting however, that even though admission to the email lists was not formally regulated, informal restrictions to participation were always in operation. Apart from the obvious barriers concerning the time and technological skills required for participating in the email lists, additional barriers to entry referred to the difficulty of learning about the existence of these lists. First of all, since the groups and their email lists are mainly set up in the offline meetings, activists unable to attend the meetings were inevitably left out from this process. They could of course join the list later on, provided that they had the requisite information about how and where to subscribe. In the case of the London ESF organizing process, this information was not available on the official website meaning that newcomers would have to obtain it from their own networks of personal contacts. Therefore, activists unable to attend the meetings or not involved in the necessary networks faced greater restrictions in participating in the working groups.

While this inevitably puts a question mark on the openness and accessibility of the ESF process, it is not an altogether negative point. This is because email lists devoted to organizing tend to function efficiently when they have a small number of members who also meet regularly face-to-face (Interviewee 21, 11 November 2004). Thus, these barriers to entry seem to make sense in terms of the effectiveness of organizing since they constitute an informal screening of suitable participants. This becomes more apparent if we consider again the characteristics of the activists who found it easier to subscribe to the lists. First, they were either activists attending the meetings or, in other words, activists that could more easily become part of the physical structure of the group. Second, they were activists already involved in some of the ESF networks which provided some guarantee of their trustworthiness.

Email lists as a source of power and leadership

While the 'movement for alternative globalization' does not embrace the idea of spokespersons, as there is no central leadership and no one can claim to speak for the movement, spokespersons for specific issues or working groups tended to emerge spontaneously from the email lists. For working groups in particular, the activists assigned to answer the emails on behalf of the group often ascended in leadership positions since they assumed the responsibility of speaking for the group. This responsibility often extended from online to offline activities, with the 'email spokespersons' becoming the general spokespersons of the working group. One of my interviewees who acted as a contact person for the Programme Working Group explained how this process unfolded:

> Anyway I got dragged into the Programme group, partly, I went to a few meetings and then, I mean the way these things happen is kind of instructive, cause I've followed the process previously I kind of knew the way it would go which was the, I mean there was a meeting and we were talking about the structure, the working structure of the programme and initially, I mean someone suggested, I can't believe it, how about [name], [name] and myself be the email, people who answer the emails for the programme group [...] and so I sort of said 'yes, I would like to be involved in that' [...] and I knew it would pan out the way it did because from that initial 'yes, we're going to temporarily just answer the emails', you know, it then became the people who answer the emails, it then became contacts for the programme group, we then, I mean as it escalated, it became 'well, who's gonna do the timetabling?', 'well how about the three of us take responsibility for the timetabling [...]' which was basically how it developed, I mean out of that initial three people volunteering answering some emails.
>
> (Interviewee 21, 11 November 2004)

Activists could also install themselves in positions of leadership through speaking not only for the group but also to the group. In other words, they could attempt to control the communication on the email list, turning it from a space of interaction, where information and ideas are exchanged laterally among the participants, to a broadcasting space, where information is transmitted from a centre to the rest of the group with limited scope for feedback or response. The email list of the British Programme Working Group constitutes an example of this practice. According to members of the group (Interviewee 21, 11 November 2004; Interviewee 16, 15 July 2004), the list was used in a very formal, one-sided way, mainly for disseminating announcements or the minutes of meetings. These tended to be circulated by specific activists who had thus seized control of the email space. As another interviewee noted, 'the programme working group, you know, started a list, which started unofficially almost ... there were all these discussions, one person holding control of all the emails and communicating you know like a broadcast from one email address' (Interviewee 7, 10 June 2004).

It is also worth noting that the person responsible for collecting the email addresses and setting up the list also has the power to control it, albeit temporarily. This is because the email register constitutes the only 'membership list' of the group. Hence, the activists who collect the email addresses have access to privileged information in relation to the other members as they are the only ones with a complete roster of the group's participants. This provides the opportunity for the collectors of the email addresses to become 'broadcasters' and to attempt, either formally or informally, to regulate admission to the list. Nevertheless, a point for consideration here is whether and to what extent 'broadcasters' can maintain control of the communication process in an application that is more suitable to lateral rather than hierarchical communication.

Therefore, the email lists can constitute sources of power for activists who serve as the email contacts of the group or for those who are responsible for setting up the list. They are thus an integral component of a process of bottom-up leadership through which individuals ascend, temporarily and informally, to positions of power. Yet, the power derived from these positions refers to the particular list or working group and not to the whole movement. This is because with new email lists cropping up easily and at very low cost it is very difficult to keep a tag on every working group and to compile a definitive list of their members and participants. Instead, and as it was mentioned earlier, email lists tend to enhance the flexibility and adaptability of the movement by enabling the organizing structure to grow and shift towards new directions in response to emerging needs. This makes it almost impossible to establish a central control of this process and to concentrate power in the hands of the few. Email lists thus tend to facilitate the polycentric character of the movement as they do not support long-term, unitary and centralized leadership.

Email lists, segmentation and integration

Founded as a space for the effective networking of diverse activist groups, the ESF seems to fulfil its role as a space for convergence and integration. According to most of my interviewees, the establishment of new relationships constituted the main benefit of participating in the ESF process. Furthermore, as many of them noted, such bonds were predominantly built through common work. In a movement with diverse participants, where the lack of common values and beliefs can make cooperation difficult, the imperative of co-organizing an event can form some sort of, albeit temporary, unity. In the words of one of my interviewees:

If you've got an event or something to organize around which forces that unity because let's face it if it wasn't for the European social forum happening in October or November or whenever it is gonna be those people at the European Social Forum would not get together.

(Interviewee 4, 15 March 2004)

My interviews further suggested that relationships across ideological divides tended to be built on the interpersonal rather than the inter-organizational level. As one of my interviewees noted:

It's highly personalized trust relationships, it's basically through [...] the process you learn that whatever people's political backgrounds are, there are certain people who, yeah, they've got a certain philosophy in politics but also they're personally trustworthy.

(Interviewee 19, 21 July 2004)

On this interpersonal level espousing the same ideology is not necessarily a solid basis of trustworthiness. As another interviewee put it:

I never trusted anybody for the state of their belief [...] it's a question of what is the, how, what is the link? That's the reason: what is the link between the political belief and the relations here, what is the link, what is the gap, what is the articulation between their belief, you know, and how they act upon, that's, that relation is very important, so you build trust on the basis of that.

(Interviewee 6, 31 March 2004)

Therefore, my interview data seem to concur with Gerlach's updated SPIN model that placed more emphasis on the integrative effect of interpersonal relationships rather than that of common ideologies.

Evidence from my interviews further suggests that email indeed helps the 'movement for alternative globalization' to shift in scale by allowing interpersonal communication across large geographical distances. However, for email lists in particular the integrative role of the Internet needs to be qualified. As I will show in the following sections, the information overload of email lists often makes them unsuitable for establishing connections among diverse participants. Email lists are also limited in their capacity to deepen those bonds and to create relationships of trust. Email list communication may also lead to segmentation as it is prone to much harsher conflicts than the ones arising within a face-to-face context.

Integration and geographical scale

When asked whether the 'alter-globalization movement' would be the same without the Internet, most of my interviewees referred to issues of scale, noting that new communication technologies enable efficient coordination on a regional or global level. In that respect, the Internet has brought an explosion of the activists' own interpersonal networks by allowing them to communicate with their distant counterparts at a low cost. In the words of one of my interviewees:

> The international relationships now you can very easily create by yourself as an individual, it's an enormous revolution in the kind of relationship that you are building through the Internet and it is changing radically your way of doing things.
>
> (Interviewee 8, 19 June 2004)

Relationships that had to be developed within the confines of formal organizational channels, simply because communicating with others on such a scale was too expensive to be done individually, can now flourish within channels of informal, personal communication.

Evidence from my interviews further suggests that for such relationships of cooperation, common work or even friendship, email tends to reconfigure the sense of distance and proximity by rendering geographical location almost irrelevant. Since it costs the same to send an email to someone sitting next to us as to someone on the other side of the world, the recipient's location is no longer an issue. It is also no longer noticeable. This is something that became very evident in my in-depth interviews. When asked whether they send more emails to people they see face-to-face or those living far away, my interviewees had trouble answering. Most of them had to think about it for a couple of minutes, while others had to look through their email outbox to provide an estimate. The general consensus was that they were sending more emails to the people with whom they were working most closely with irrespective of their geographical location. This often meant that the bulk of email communication was directed to people they were seeing regularly face-to-face. As one of my interviewees put it:

> It depends on the context of the work that I'm doing, I think, which is to say in other words that it's not, it's not technology [...] I don't think the answer lies in the email form, I think it lies in the nature of the work I'm doing basically.
>
> (Interviewee 21, 11 November 2004)

Therefore, when physical distance is no longer an issue, it is rather the closeness of the relationship or the nature of the work that needs to be done that dictates the amount and pace of email interaction.

Information overload

The ESF email lists, particularly the ones operating on a European or national level, have a considerably diverse subscription base. They thus constitute spaces where one can encounter different ideas and engage with a wide range of authors. However, evidence from my interviews suggests that the potential of email lists to aid integration is tempered by their information overload.[3] In that respect, most of my interviewees complained about the number of emails they received:

> I keep meaning to count approximately how many ESF emails I get every day but I know that it's a lot and it's, I think email also for me adds to the, I've got this constant feeling about the ESF that I'm not keeping up with it.
>
> (Interviewee 16, 15 July 2004)

Indeed, during the organizing year of the ESF nearly 1,600 messages were posted on the European-level email list, while the national list of the British coordination counted more than 1,000 messages.

Taking into account that activists are subscribed to many lists at once, coping with this information overload becomes an absolute necessity. Activists thus employ a series of criteria in order to judge whether a message is worth reading. These criteria include the subject of the message, its author, the country that the message comes from or refers to, as well as its relevance to the ESF process. For instance, according to one of my interviewees:

> The subject is really important, if you put a proper subject line you know and then, then it's, it evolves from that, and sometimes it's who posted it, if I know the person writes interesting things then I read it sometimes.
>
> (Interviewee 18, 19 July 2004)

Having a preference for certain authors, most often people that someone already knows, is another major criterion. In the words of one of my interviewees:

> If on the European list there's an email from the Belgian trade unions about something that's happening in Congo I delete that because I can't help anyone in Congo [...] but if it's an email that's coming from people that I now know in the process to always send good emails or very relevant to the process, then I read them.
>
> (Interviewee 19, 21 July 2004)

For others, particular authors can be a deterrent from reading the email: 'I judge them from the titles and there are some people for example who send emails, I don't open the email' (Interviewee 14, 7 July 2004). Relevance to the ESF process and specifically to practical and organizational issues is also crucial as 'you start with the things you're most directly involved in' (Interviewee 17, 15 July 2004). Finally, one of my interviewees adopted a far more radical strategy for coping with information overload: she did not subscribe to any of the email lists, opting instead to use email on a one-to-one basis (Interviewee 20, 29 October 2004).

Therefore, the fact that email lists are open to a variety of subscribers posting messages about diverse issues does not necessarily mean that all of these voices are heard. Instead, activists seem to prefer messages coming from authors that they are already familiar with or concerning issues that they are already involved in. Thus, rather than bridging ideological divides or bringing activists in contact with completely new people or ideas, email lists may actually reinforce pre-existing ideological and social cleavages.

We can compare this with the experience of attending an ESF preparatory meeting, where the nature of the occasion does not provide its participants with such freedom to decide who they are going to listen to. In the ESF meetings everyone has a right to speak and, when they do, they are heard by everyone in the room. The norms of politeness governing synchronous embodied communication limit freedom of choice when it comes to listening. These obligations seem to loosen or simply vanish within the context of email interaction where the mere fact that a message is posted on an email list constitutes no guarantee that it is going to be read by everyone.

Interpersonal trust

Evidence from the interviews further suggests that email lists are limited in their potential to deepen the bonds between individuals and to develop relationships of trust. In that respect, most of my interviewees consider face-to-face communication indispensable for trust-building, even with people that they already know online. Reasons for this relate both to the cognitive and affective bases of trust.[4] In terms of cognitive-based trust, the key question concerns the believability of evidence of trustworthiness. According to my interviews, this believability seems to increase within a context of co-presence. As one of my interviewees put it:

> You need to meet people, it's so fundamental, it changes your entire thing, the entire thing about trust and the way you can count on people, the feeling you can count on people that gives your self-assurance and all that, that's to do with face-to-face, there's no way out, you, you don't trust an electronic text.
>
> (Interviewee 6, 31 March 2004)

This is because an electronic text does not provide concrete evidence of the identity of its author. People can easily lie on email and not only in conditions of anonymity. In addition, it is difficult to be entirely certain whether one has correctly understood what is meant. The absence of physical cues makes this knowledge precarious. Instead, being able to 'look each other in the eyes' constitutes the most solid basis of believability. For instance, according to the same activist:

> I met people on the Internet but then learned about them in the face-to-face, it's different, so you meet them on the Internet, 'wo that's a good position' but still you do not build trust on the Internet, that's the point, you do not, you have to see people in the eyes when you talk to them on a particular issue in order to trust them.

This theme of 'looking each other in the eyes' came up in other interviews as well. An activist from Hungary mentioned it as a prerequisite for true political discussion (Interviewee 23, 26 February 2005), while an organizer from Globalize Resistance considered face-to-face communication as more reliable in assessing the political climate and understanding whether mobilization efforts have been successful (Interviewee 4, 15 March 2004).

Therefore, even when there is common work online, activists still need to 'authenticate' these relationships offline. Also, in case of a disparity between online and offline behaviour, face-to-face contact can damage the foundations of trust built online if someone shows a negative side in a face-to-face meeting. One of my interviewees recounted such an incident:

> I think that people got quite a shock when this guy who was contributing kind of didn't behave that well in a meeting and [...] I've spoken to people since and quite a few people feel that they could be variously sabotaged. That's a problem.
>
> (Interviewee 15, 8 July 2004)

In other words, face-to-face contact seems to have a much higher position in the hierarchy of truth and authenticity than email communication.

Furthermore, face-to-face contact is considered indispensable for affect-based trust. This is because it is more effective in transmitting emotive content as it appeals more fully to the senses. As an interviewee put it:

> There's a whole series of, a whole range of human expression that is not captured by, by email basically and the people. I mean even if you do show emotion, people haven't found ways of, of gathering those non-verbal forms of communication in email form.
>
> (Interviewee 21, 11 November 2004)

However, the ability of people to judge the others' trustworthiness or to convey emotive content online may also depend on their aptitude with the technology. Activists who are more technologically adept may be more skilled in expressing their emotions via email by using the full range of available tools, such as emoticons. In addition, activists with more experience in collaborating with others online may have more confidence in their ability to judge the others' trustworthiness through email contact.

Arguments and segmentation

The tendency for conflicts to escalate when carried out online further reduces the suitability of email lists for establishing new relationships. According to many of my interviewees, it is very easy for people to get the tone wrong on email, resulting in more frequent, and at times ferocious, misunderstandings. This tendency is heightened by language barriers which tend to be more pronounced in written communication, thus increasing the possibility for people to misread the tone (Interviewee 14, 7 July 2004).

Furthermore, it seems that people are prone to be harsher towards others when they are not in physical proximity. As the same interviewee noted,

> you let yourself, I know that myself I do it, you can be more, much more rude [...] when you don't have a human being in front of you and you don't see how, for example, upset you're making these people by saying or writing these things.

Some located the problem to specific individuals who do not dare to instigate conflict face-to-face and instead hide behind emails (Interviewee 4, 15 March 2004). According to another interviewee, this is even the case 'when people know who you are, there is still anonymity there that still makes you feel you have the license to be quite rude' (Interviewee 15, 8 July 2004). What is more, conflict on email can become more generalized as 'it's something that happens with emailing and if you see one person getting a kind of b******t about something, it can actually spur other people on to do the same' (ibid.). This can be very damaging to the atmosphere of the list, as well as to the activists' morale, since, according to an Italian interviewee, email tends to give the impression that conflict is much more widespread than it actually is (Interviewee 10, 19 June 2004).

In that respect, face-to-face contact serves as an antidote to email conflict, since online disputes tend to be settled when activists meet face-to-face. In the words of one of my interviewees, 'after a very hostile spout of emailing, I've noticed that when we do meet up again, it blows over [...] people don't necessarily want to carry on that hostility into everyday life' (Interviewee 15, 8 July 2004). Thus, face-to-face meetings tend to repair the fabric of personal relations that frays with email conflict and restore the sense of unity and belonging; where email segments, face-to-face integrates.

However, considering that such internal conflicts are almost unavoidable, online clashes can in fact be beneficial to the process. This is because they constitute a way of letting off some steam, which may prevent conflict from developing face-to-face where it is much more hurtful. As one of my interviewees noted, 'email does have the effect of making conflicts less intense because it's all, you know, it's all virtual that however rude people are it's less kind of intense or confrontational' (Interviewee 24, 14 March 2005). Therefore, when viewed in relation to offline communication, arguments on email lists may not be as destructive since they serve to air feelings that would be more damaging to express in a face-to-face context.

Conclusion

Adopting the SPIN model as its theoretical framework and focusing on the case study of the European Social Forum, this chapter attempted to provide a more nuanced empirical account of the relationship between new communication technologies and decentralized architectures. Literature on the subject tends to focus on the integrative effects of the Internet, noting its potential to bring together activists who are located in different parts of the world. Evidence from the interviews concurred with this analysis. It suggested that email increases the scale of current movements by allowing individuals to establish and maintain relationships on an international scale without relying on formal organizational channels. What is more, in the context of such relationships of trust and collaboration email renders geographical location hardly noticeable.

Yet, what also became apparent is that for email lists in particular the claims concerning integration need to be better qualified. This is because the information overload of email lists often prevents activists from coming in contact with ideas or people that are distant, unfamiliar or simply different. In addition, many of the interviewed activists found it difficult to establish relationships of trust based solely on email. Instead, face-to-face contact and the ability to 'look each other in the eyes' was thought to accelerate the process of trust-building for reasons relating both to cognition and affect. Communication on email lists is also more prone to misunderstandings, often resulting in ferocious arguments that are destructive to an atmosphere of trust and unity. Thus, email lists may actually enhance the fissiparous tendencies of the movement, leading to segmentation rather than integration.

Segmentation is further afforded by the facility with which new organizational units can be created and defined through the use of email lists. As the section on working groups demonstrated, email lists allow the movement's structure to adapt to emergent needs by facilitating the flexible addition of new units and functions. Enabling activists to regulate their involvement in the movement and inhibiting the establishment of more formal processes of affiliation, email lists prevent leaders from wielding control over individual activists. And even though on the level of the working group they may aid activists in ascending to positions of informal and temporary leadership, email lists tend to inhibit the centralization of control, leading to a polycentric model of power.

Thus, a more detailed empirical investigation of the ESF email lists revealed them to be an integral part of the decentralized structure of the 'movement for alternative globalization'. And while the usefulness of the SPIN model remains undisputed, the theory can benefit from a more in-depth understanding of new communication technologies, whose role is increasingly important in current modes of conflict.

Notes

1 The World Economic Forum is an independent organization consisting of the 1,000 leading businesses in the world, meeting every year in Davos to discuss the global state of affairs.

2 As is often the case in open-ended interviews, my sample was chosen in a deliberate rather than random way (Blee and Taylor 2002: 100). My criteria of sample selection involved my interviewees' positions within factions of the movement, their political

background, their roles in the ESF organizing process, as well as their country of residence, age and gender. My sampling was initially guided by the principle of diversity, aiming to garner the opinions of as diverse participants as possible. However, after the first interviews my sampling choices started to be influenced by the emergent patterns and understandings of the study. This led me to place particular emphasis on the criteria of factional belonging and role in the ESF process.

3 This information overload is partly a result of unsophisticated use of the Internet with activists circulating the same message in every list they are subscribed to. Indeed, being careful not to cram the list with irrelevant messages was considered by many of my interviewees as a mark of politeness and an indication of people's experience with the technology. This is also reflected in current norms of email lists where activists regularly offer their 'apologies for cross-posting' when the same message is posted on many lists.

4 According to Mayer *et al.* (1995: 717–19), trust derives both from cognition and affect. Assessing another's ability, integrity and benevolence, the main elements of trustworthiness, can be based both on good reasons or evidence and on the emotional bonds between individuals.

14 Some notes on the social antagonism in netarchical capitalism

Michel Bauwens

An analysis of the new logic of the Web 2.0 sharing platforms and Linux-type commons-based peer production discovers two distinct logics with two different underlying social contracts, and their accompanying lines of tension and struggle. Sharing communities face off with platform owners, and commons communities face off with their business ecosystem. Netarchical capitalism is a concept, which can explain a new type of strategy by capital to both enable and profit from the direct social creation of value. If our views are correct, new ways of thinking are required that are not just a repeat of traditional arguments against capitalist exploitation, but require the continued strengthening of sharing and commons communities as the key agents of social change.

Different models of the common have different social contracts

The social web facilitates an unprecedented level of social sharing, but it does so mostly through the vehicle of proprietary platforms. The issue therefore is to clearly distinguish the invisible architecture, i.e. the 'protocol' of the facilitating technology, which needs to be separated from the ownership issue as such. By protocol we mean, following Alexander Galloway's definition, the totality of visible and invisible technical rules which constrain choice and behaviour in online environments (Galloway 2004).

This protocol needs to be sufficiently open to allow for the process of sharing to occur, but at the same time, it has to be 'sufficiently closed' to create scarcities that can be exploited by the platform owners, and this is a clear line of tension between the user community and the corporate hierarchy. Indeed, openness creates value, but enclosure allows capturing and monetizing that value. Total openness does not allow any corporation to capture that value in any exclusive way, and by destroying scarcity, and therefore the tension between supply and demand, it undermines market logics.

For platform owners, openness will always be a double-edged sword. On the one hand, it is beneficial to open up and create a stronger and wider commons, from which more value will be derived, on the other hand, total openness also means total loss of control, and therefore difficulties in capturing value for one's own shareholders. This means that tension between the community of users and the platform owners is structural, as well as the competitive antagonism between the different platforms competing for user adherence.

We therefore believe that the social web obeys to an underlying, but unstable social contract. This social contract basically says, from the point of view of the users:

> we appreciate the facilitation of the sharing processes, and we understand that operating such platforms comes with a cost, and with an expectation of profitability. We therefore allow our attention to be monetized through advertising, as long as it does not interfere to with our sharing. If the interference crosses a certain line of acceptability, we will either revolt, or go elsewhere.

Note that the social web has as basic orientation the convergence of individual and collective interests, that it is geared around the sharing of individual expression, and that it therefore is based on weak ties in the user community. Such weak ties are the very reason that the user communities are not easily able to create their own platforms, and why they need third parties.

The social web and its sharing economy should not be confused with the commons economy, which has its own infrastructure. The commons economy exists when the communities are geared towards the production of common artefacts, and not just towards the sharing of individual expressions. Real common production, because it requires a qualitatively higher level of coordination and engagement, therefore creates stronger ties between participating individuals. These different logics of participation are also reflected in different forms of open licenses that are used for sharing versus a commons, i.e. Creative Commons vs General Public License. Because of these stronger ties, we notice that commons-oriented projects, unlike the sharing oriented platforms, have their own infrastructures. Instead of a dual structure between user community and proprietary platform, the commons economy has a triune structure, combining the self-organized produser[1] communities (Bruns 2007), democratically governed for-benefit institutions[2] (Eaves 2006) which insure the necessary infrastructures, and an ecology of businesses which create marketable scarcities around the commons.

Different social contracts have different business models

The former point is very important. Though they are intertwined, and hybrid forms may exist, generally for sharing platforms, it is crucial to distinguish between the logic of sharing, and the logic of selling attention. The former is the precondition of the latter, but the former cannot be reduced to the latter. The platform is the precondition for the sharing, and the sharing a precondition for the attention economy that will benefit the platform owners. The overwhelming majority of sharers are not in the game for personal monetary gain, but rather to exchange creative expression, for which they obtain various non-monetary benefits, such as reputational gains. The notion of crowding out means that the logic of sharing, or the logic of commons production for that matter, cannot be contaminated by the competing logic of monetary gain. Introducing monetary gain actually destroys the logic of sharing. The latter only works if voluntary engagement is combined with universal accessibility, and there is no perceived inequity between the volunteers. This is the reason why revenue-sharing schemes are generally counterproductive. The lack of revenue sharing cannot therefore be equated with a simple concept exploitation, and any calls for 'fair revenue sharing' are actually counterproductive, since they would not only reintroduce capitalist and monetary logics in the sharing community, but would actually also destroy and displace the post-capitalist sharing practices.

There is of course an extra issue. While the users create social wealth, and the platform owners monetize it, what kind of return can be created? Google and YouTube have shown to what extent monetary value can be extracted from such social processes, but the user communities generally do not receive a direct monetary return.

The proper way to create a return for the positive externalities of the sharing or of the commons, is not through revenue sharing but through benefit sharing. The latter is characterized by a generalized support for the infrastructure of sharing or commons production, by a sustenance of the user community, and in such a way that no crowding out or inequity occurs.

In the case of commons-oriented production, or assuming that some sharing communities might have their own platforms, the situation is quite different. The case of the Wikimedia Foundation, which manages the infrastructure of Wikipedia, but not its value-creation processes, shows that for-benefit institutions are not naturally geared to capital accumulation or profit maximization, as we see the Wikipedia refusing advertising (as does, for that matter, the strong community oriented logic of Craigslist), and the blog of the Mozilla Foundation has featured discussions about the difficulty to allocate financial revenue in the context of the crowding out effect. Given this alternative, we cannot simply wish, if we deem monetization to be exploitation, call for an expropriation of that revenue, that it would simply be returned to the sharing communities. As, indeed, doing so would destroy the sharing logic, by making the monetary logic dominant, causing the crowding out effect to occur.

There is only one exception to this rule. Some platforms are specifically geared towards the freelance or minipreneurial creation of exchange value (threadless.com etc.), and therefore, in such cases, the issue of revenue sharing and monetary exploitation can arise. These are cases of distributed labour, but not of peer production. In this mechanism, it is the producers who take the full risk for their market-oriented production, the platform being merely an enabling marketplace, which receives a fee for its brokerage function.

Now, if all the above is correct and properly understood, then it follows that certain types of leftist discourse, about the exploitation of free labour, and the alienation of the user communities, are misguided and politically counterproductive.

The fact that user communities, both in a sharing or commons context, seem to have no beef with their proprietary partners, is not that they are alienated, but on the contrary, that they have a correct interpretation of their vital interests in the preservation of sharing and the commons as fundamental social advances with clear immediate personal and collective benefits. In the case of sharing, they naturally rejoice in the empowerment of the sharing, and understand the necessity of a sustainable business model; in the case of the commons, they understand the non-reciprocal nature of peer production, from which it inevitably follows that commercial use is acceptable, as the universal availability implies free usage according to need. Some of these usages may indeed be commercial. It is not a coincidence that the radical commons-oriented licenses, such as the GPL, allow for commercial usage, while the most chosen amongst the more moderate sharing oriented Creative Commons license, are the ones prohibiting commercial usage. The reason is that the GPL creates a true commons with a full non-reciprocal logic, and the CC is merely a license to modulate intensities of sharing under the control of individual proprietors. A true commons does not require revenue sharing, but benefit sharing so that the commons can be sustained, which is also in the self-interest of participating companies.

The political stress on exploitation is counterproductive because it requires to convince the vast majority of happy sharers and peer producers, that their joy in sharing is misplaced and alienated; it is in fact often a call to introduce monetary and capitalist practices (revenue sharing) in the sharing and peer production process. No industrial worker needs to be convinced that he/she is exploited, this consciousness comes naturally, he/she can feel it in his bones. Similarly, the consciousness that the sharing and commons orientation are positive social developments comes equally naturally.

This is not to say that nothing can be done on the monetization side, in favour of institutional vehicles, which would increase equity. Both sharing and commons-oriented communities would benefit from forms of monetization that are increasingly ethical and in line with the values of sharing. Therefore, rather than have the monetization happen through purely for profit companies, there could be a push for different forms of capital. An example of this would be the creation of cooperatives, such as for example the OS Alliance in Austria.

The key is to remember that non-reciprocity is only possible in the sphere of non-rival immaterial production, but that the sphere of physical production, where monetization can occur, requires that investment capital needs to be returned for new cycles of production. This can happen through market exchange, or through renewed economic forms based on reciprocity.

Social conflict in peer production

What then is the true social configuration of antagonistic interests, and the lines of tension that are worth concentrating one's energy on?

Not just the knowledge workers, but in fact all producers, are reconfiguring at least part of their lives to the direct social production of use value through sharing or a commons approach. Peer production is not limited to highly educated knowledge workers but its principle of equipotentality[3] and the self-selection of granular tasks mean that it is accessible to all producers. Because knowledge is at the core of the networked information economy, such practices are at the very core of our society, as Benkler (2004) has convincingly explained. Because peer production is economically more productive, politically more participative, and more distributive as a form of ownership, it is also a post-capitalist mode of value creation that will inevitably move to centre stage.

But peer production also reconfigures the ownership class. The twin pillars of cognitive capitalism, namely the extraction of surplus rent through intellectual property monopolies, and the monopoly of the means of distribution, are being systematically undermined by the distributed networks. Marginal costs of reproducing informational artefacts, the copy-ability of the informational core of high value physical products, and the social web as a universal distribution platform for informational artefacts and for open design of physical products, are displacing such monopolies.

It is therefore logical that, out of self-interest, sections of the ownership class convert themselves to the position of netarchical capitalists, those who enable and empower the sharing communities and entertain benefit-sharing agreements with the commons-oriented production communities.

What is the relative position of produsing communities and the netarchical platform owners? The short answer is that they have both convergent and divergent interests.

To the degree that these platform owners enable sharing, they are allies of the peer producers and sharers. To the degree that such platform owners need enclosures and scarcities to enter a competitive market, the interests diverge. What is needed therefore is a literacy of participation, not geared towards the opposition against an abstract 'exploitation of free labour', but rather on the invisible architectures of sharing (which need to be truly open, participative and commons-oriented), and against the restrictions to freedom that proprietary capture requires.

On the macro-level, again the netarchical capitalists can be allies to the degree that they join the agenda for social policies geared to the promotion of sharing and commons production (see the stance of Google on the open spectrum as a positive example of policy convergence); but to the degree they may want to enclose openness the interests are divergent.

Conditions for a genuine circulation of the common

To flourish, the sharers and commonists need three things:

1   open and free raw material so that the sharing and common production can occur. Produser communities will naturally favour such approaches such as free software, open content, open access.

2   They need the lowest possible threshold of participation, so that any motivation, any granular contribution, can become possible and productive.
3   They need to protect the resulting commons from private appropriation, this require attention to the particular licensing requirements and vigilance against expropriation strategies, for example the a priori signing away of creative rights to platform owners.

All this requires a literacy of participation, an intelligent discourse of the relative convergent and divergent interests, not a knee-jerk opposition to platform owners.

The platform owners of the social web have a double logic. On the one hand, they need sufficient levels of openness for the sharing to occur, while they also attempt partial enclosures to dispose of marketable scarcities. This competing logic is a line of tension, and conscious user communities can ensure that openness is primary and not contaminated by proprietary logics.

The social web may well be a transitionary stage. It is the result of the relative weakness of the sharing communities, but as the stronger commons-oriented communities are multiplying, they may very well create new distributed and open architectures that could eventually displace proprietary platforms (though this is not a certainty). These commons-created platforms can/could then be used by the sharing communities.

The need for capital which these platforms represent, is not just an objective necessity, but results from policy choices in the realm of infrastructure, and the lack of alternatives. Centralized server parks, such as the ones used by Google, could be replaced by true distributed peer-to-peer systems, using user-generated capital, therefore undermining the exclusive need for owned platforms. The call for open social graphs, for open and interoperable infrastructures, will probably gradually diminish lock-ins. At this time, the platform owners may switch from a focus on the creation of artificial scarcities, to the creation of true added values, as is now the case around Linux and some other open source software projects. Again, the realization for the need of such distributed infrastructures is a matter of literacy.

Notes

1   Bruns (2006) writes:

> Produsage can be roughly defined as modes of production which are led by users or at least crucially involve users as producers – in other words, the user acts as a hybrid user/producer, or produser, virtually throughout the production process.

2   Eaves (2006):

> Companies or foundations that run open source project are not software firms, they are community management firms whose communities happen to make software. Consequently to survive and thrive these projects need to invest less in enhancing governance structures or employees who/that will improve their capacity to code. Instead, we should consider skills and structures that emphasize facili-

tation, mediation, and conflict management – tools, skills and structures that will enable the community to better collaborate.
(From David Eaves, http://eaves.ca/2006/12/17/community-management-as-open-sources-core-competency/)

3   This quote by Ferrer (undated) is a good illustration of the underlying value behind equipotentiality in peer production environments:

> equals in the sense of their being both superior and inferior to themselves in varying skills and areas of endeavor (intellectually, emotionally, artistically, mechanically, interpersonally, and so forth), but with none of those skills being absolutely higher or better than others. It is important to experience human equality from this perspective to avoid trivializing our encounter with others as being merely equal.

Bibliography

Ackerman, P. and Du Vall, J. (2000) *A Force More Powerful: A Century of Nonviolent Conflict*, Basingstoke: Palgrave Macmillan.

Adoni, H. and Mane, S. (1984) 'Media and the Social Construction of Reality', *Communication Research*, 11, pp. 323–40.

Advisory Opinion on the Legality of the Threat or Use of Nuclear Weapons (1996) International Court of Justice Reports, 226, 244.

agent.NASDAQ (aka Reinhold Grether) (2001) 'How The Etoy Campaign Was Won: an Agent's Report', in Peter Weibel and Timothy Druckrey (eds), *Net Condition: Art and Global Media*, Cambridge, MA: MIT Press, pp. 280–5.

Ago, R. Addendum to Eighth Report on State Responsibility [1980] II (1) International Law Commission Yearbook, 13, 69.

Ahrari, E. (1999) 'China Changes its Strategic Mindset – Part Two', *Jane's Intelligence Review*, December 1999.

Aksoy, A. (2006) 'Transnational Virtues and Cool Loyalties: Responses of Turkish-Speaking Migrants in London to September 11', *Journal of Ethnic and Migration Studies*, 32: 6, pp. 923–46.

Alagappa, M. (1998) *Asian Security Practice: Material and Ideational Influences*, Palo Alto, CA: Stanford University Press.

Al-Jazeera English (18 March 2006) 'Papua Clamp Down after Protests'. Online, available at: http://english.aljazeera.net/English/Archive/Archive?ArchiveID=21513 (accessed 5 May 2007).

Al-Jazeera English (9 April 2006) 'Australia to Review Refugee Process'. Online, available at: http://english.aljazeera.net/English/Archive/Archive?ArchiveID=21825 (accessed 5 May 2007).

Al-Jazeera English (20 September 2006) 'Trans-Dniestr Votes to Join Russia'. Online, available at: http://english.aljazeera.net/English/Archive/Archive?ArchiveID=36055 (accessed 5 May 2007).

Aljazeera.net (5 March 2007) 'Vanuatu under State of Emergency' [source AFP] (accessed 5 May 2007).

Allan, S. (2006) *Online News*, Maidenhead: Open University Press.

Althaus, S. L. (2003) 'When News Norm Collide, Follow the Lead: New Evidence for Press Independence', *Political Communication*, 20, pp. 381–414.

Anderson, B. (1983) *Imagined Communities: Reflections on the Origin and Spread of Nationalism*, revised edition, London: Verso.

Anderson, R. H. and Hearn, A. C. (1 February 1997) *An Exploration of Cyberspace*

Security R&D Investment Strategies for DARPA, Santa Monica, CA: Rand Corporation. Online, available at: http://www.rand.org/publications/MR/MR 880.

Anderson, R. H., Feldman, P. M., Gerwehr, S., Houghton, B., Mesic, R., Pinder, J. D. and Chiesa, J. (1 April 1999) *Securing the US Defense Information Infrastructure: A Proposed Approach*, Santa Monica, CA: Rand Corporation. Online, available at: http://www.rand.org/publications/MR/MR 933.

Andrew, N., Yang, D. and Liao, W. C. (1999) 'PLA Rapid Reaction Forces: Concept, Training, and Preliminary Assessment', in J. C. Mulvenon and R. Yang (eds), *The People's Liberation Army in the Information Age*, Santa Monica, CA: RAND Corporation.

Appadurai, A. (1996) *Modernity at Large: Cultural Dimensions of Globalization*, Minneapolis, MN: University of Minnesota Press.

Appadurai, A. (2003) 'Disjunctive and Difference in the Global Cultural Economy', in L. Parks and S. Kumar (eds), *Planet TV: A Global Television Reader*, New York, NY: New York University Press, pp. 40–52.

Appadurai, A. (2006) *Fear of Small Numbers: An Essay on the Geography of Anger*, Durham, NC: Duke University Press.

Arena, M. P. and Arrigo, B. A. (2006) *The Terrorist Identity*, New York, NY and London: New York University Press.

Arend, A. C. and Beck, R. J. (1993) *International Law and the Use of Force: Beyond the UN Charter Paradigm*, London: Routledge.

Arquilla, J. (1998) 'The Great Cyberwar of 2002', *Wired*, 6.02, February. Online, available at: http://www.wired.com/wired/archive/6.02/cyberwar.html (accessed 10 January 2008).

Arquilla, J. and Ronfeldt, D. (1993) 'Cyberwar is Coming!', *Comparative Strategy*, 12.

Arquilla, J. and Ronfeldt, D. (1 March 1995) *Cyberwar and Netwar: New Modes, Old Conflict*, Santa Monica, CA: Rand Corporation. Online, available at: http://www.rand.org/publications/randreview/ issues/RRR.fal95.cyber/.

Arquilla, J. and Ronfeldt, D. (eds) (1997) *In Athena's Camp: Preparing for Conflict in the Information Age*, Santa Monica, CA: Rand Corporation. Online, available at: http://www.rand.org/publications/MR/MR 880.

Arquilla, J. and Ronfeldt, D. (1999) *The Emergence of Noopolitik: Toward an American Information Strategy*, Santa Monica, CA: Rand Corporation. Online, available at: http://www.rand.org/publications/MR/MR 1033.

Arquilla, J. and Ronfeldt, D. (eds) (2001a) 'The Advent of Netwar (Revisited)', in John Arquilla and David Ronfeldt (eds), *Networks and Netwars: The Future of Terror, Crime, and Militancy*, Santa Monica, CA: RAND Corporation, pp. 1–25. Online, available at: http://www.rand.org/pubs/monograph_reports/MR1382 (accessed 10 January 2008).

Arquilla, J. and Ronfeldt, D. (2001b) 'Fighting the Network War', *Wired*, 9.12, December. Online, available at: http://www.wired.com/wired/archive/9.12/netwar.html (accessed 10 January 2008).

Arquilla, J. and Ronfeldt, D. (eds) (2001c) *Networks and Netwars: The Future of Terror, Crime, and Militancy*, Santa Monica, CA: RAND Corporation. Online, available at: http://www.rand.org/pubs/monograph_reports/MR1382 (accessed 10 January 2008).

Arquilla, J., Ronfeldt, D., Fuller, Graham F. and Fuller, M. (1998) *The Zapatista 'Social Netwar' in Mexico*, Santa Monica, CA: RAND Corporation. Online, available at: http://www.rand.org/publications/MR/MR994 (accessed 10 January 2008).

Asarayala, A. (2002) 'College Questioning Site's Link', *Wired News* (28 September).

Online, available at: www.wired.com/news/politics/0,1283,55450,00.html (accessed 25 July 2003).

Ash, T. G. (19 May 2005) 'Exchange of Empires: Who will Dare to fill the Black Holes being left by Russia's Long Retreat?', *Guardian*. Online, available at: http://www.guardian.co.uk/Columnists/Column/0,1487266,00.html.

Asia Pacific Network Information Centre (16 August 1999), 'Taiwan Defense Ministry Sets up Information Warfare Committee'. Online, available at: http://www.apnic.net/-mailing-lists/s-asia-it/archive/1999/08/msg00 (accessed 13 July 2007).

Asser, M. (9 July 2007) 'Rumours and Violence Fuel Lebanon Anxiety', BBC News. Online, available at: http://news.bbc.co.uk/2/hi/middle_east/6283164.stm.

Associated Press (9 February 2007) 'Walter Cronkite: Media Profits Threaten Freedom', NewsMax. Online, available at: http://archive.newsmax.com/archives/ic/2007/2/9/112828.shtml (accessed 4 November 2007).

Association for Women in Development (November 2007) Friday File. *Making Movements Work*. Online, available at: http://www.awid.org/.

Aviation and Aerospace (10 September 2007) 'Chinese Military Hacked into US Defence Secretary's Office: Pentagon'. Online, available at: http://www.domain-b.com/aero/Sept/2007/20070910_defence.htm.

Awan, A. N. (2007a) 'Transitional Religiosity Experiences: Contextual Disjuncture and Islamic Political Radicalism', in T. Abbas (ed.), *Islamic Political Radicalism: A European Comparative Perspective*, Edinburgh: Edinburgh University Press.

Awan, A. N. (2007b) 'Virtual Jihadist Media and the Ummah as Transnational Audience: Function, Legitimacy, and Radicalising Efficacy', *European Journal of Cultural Studies*, 10: 3.

AWID (Association for Women's Right in Development) (2007) Online, available at: http://www.awid.org/.

Axel, B. (2002) 'The Diasporic Imaginary', *Public Culture*, 14, pp. 411–28.

Badie, B. (2000) *The Imported State: The Westernization of the Political Order*, Stanford, CA: Stanford University Press, trans. Claudia Royal.

Baldassari, D. and Diani, M. (2007) 'The Integrative Power of Civic Networks'. Online, available at: Baldassari_Diani_civic_networks_Ajs_02.2007.pdf (accessed 16 June 2007).

Barnett, C. (2003) *Culture and Democracy: Media, Space and Representation*, Edinburgh: Edinburgh University Press.

Bauman, Z. (2006) *Liquid Fear*, Cambridge: Polity Press.

BBC News (8 February 2006) 'Troops Face "Uneven Battlefield"'. Online, available at: http://news.bbc.co.uk/2/hi/uk_news/politics/4692572.stm.

Beer, D. and Burrows, R. (2007) 'Sociology and, of and in Web 2.0: Some Initial Considerations', *Sociological Research Online*. Online, available at: http://www.socresonline.org.uk/12/5/17.html.

Beetham, D. (1991) *The Legitimation of Power: Issues in Political Theory*, London: Macmillan.

Bello, W. (2005) *Dilemmas of Domination: The Unmaking of the American Empire*, London: Zed Books.

Bendrath, R. (2001) 'The Cyberwar Debate: Perception and Politics in US Critical Infrastructure Protection', *Information and Security*, 7.

Benjamin, W. (1977) 'The Work of Art in the Age of Mechanical Reproduction', in W. Benjamin, *Illuminations*, London: Fontana, pp. 219–53.

Benkler, Y. (2004) *The Wealth of Networks*, New Have, CT and London: Yale University Press.

Bennett, L. W. (2004) 'Communicating Global Activism: Strengths and Vulnerabilities of Networked Politics', in W. van de Donk, B. D. Loader, P. G. Nixon and D. Rucht (eds), *Cyberprotest: New Media, Citizens and Social Movements*, London and New York, NY: Routledge.

Bennett, L. W. (2005) 'Social Movements beyond Borders: Understanding Two Eras of Transnational Activism', in D. della Porta and S. Tarrow (eds), *Transnational Protest and Global Activism*, Lanham, Boulder, New York, Toronto, Oxford: Rowman & Littlefield.

Bennett, L. W., Lawrence, R. G. and Livingston, S. (2007) *When the Press Fails: Political Power and the News Media from Iraq to Katrina*, Chicago, IL and London: The University of Chicago Press.

Benschop, A. (2004) *Chronicle of a Political Murder Foretold*, Amsterdam: Sociosite. Online, available at: http://www.sociosite.org/jihad_nl_en.php.

Berger, P. L. and Luckmann, T. (1966) *The Social Construction of Reality: A Treatise in the Sociology of Knowledge*, Garden City, NY: Anchor Books.

Berkman Center for Internet & Society (24 September 2002) 'Replacement of Google with Alternative Search Systems in China Documentation and Screen Shots', Harvard Law School. Online, available at: http://cyber.law.harvard.edu/filtering/china/google-replacements/ (accessed 4 November 2007).

Bernstein, D. (4 March 1998) 'Infosecurity News Industry Survey', *Infosecurity News*, 8: 3, May 1997, pp. 20–7.

Bey, Hakim (1991) *T.A.Z.: the Temporary Autonomous Zone, Ontological Anarchy, Poetic Terrorism*, New York, NY: Autonomedia.

Birt, Y. (2007) 'Beyond Siddique', *Prospect*, 135, June. Online, available at: http://www.prospect-magazine.co.uk/article_details.php?id=9644.

Bitzinger, R. A. and Gill, B. (1996) *Gearing Up for High-Tech Warfare? Chinese and Taiwanese Defense Modernization and Implications for Military Conflict Across the Taiwan Strait, 1995–2005*, Washington, DC: Centre for Strategic and Budgetary Assessments.

Blair, T. (7 July 2005) 'Statement from the PM following COBR Meeting'. Online, available at: http://www.number-10.gov.uk/output/Page7858.asp.

Blee, K. M. and Taylor, V. (2002) 'Semi-Structured Interviewing in Social Movement Research', in B. Klandermans and S. Staggenborg (eds), *Methods of Social Movement Research*, Minneapolis, MN and London: University of Minnesota Press.

Boler, Megan (ed.) (2008) *Digital Media and Democracy: Tactics in Hard Times*, Cambridge, MA: MIT Press.

Boltanski, L. and Thévenot, L. (2006) [1991] *On Justification: Economies of Worth*, Princeton, NJ: Princeton University Press, trans. C. Porter.

Boot, Max (29 June 2006) 'Statement Before The House Armed Services Subcommittee on Terrorism, Unconventional Threats, and Capabilities' CFR. Online, available at: http://www.cfr.org/publication/11027/statement_before_the_house_armed_services_su bcommittee_on_terrorism_unconventional_threats_and_capabilitieshtml (accessed 4 November 2007).

Borowitz, A. (12 May 2006) 'Bush Demands That Iran Halt Production of Long Letters', truthdig. Online, available at: http://www.truthdig.com/report/item/20060512_andy_ borowitz_iran_letters/.

Bourdieu, P. (1991) *Language and Symbolic Power*, Cambridge: Polity.

Bowdish, Randall G. (2002) 'Global Terrorism, Strategy, and Naval Forces', in S. J. Tangredi (ed.), *Globalization and Maritime Power*, National Defense University. Online, available at: http://www.ndu.edu/inss/Books/Books_2002/Globalization_and_Maritime_Power_Dec_02/01_toc.htm (accessed 4 November 2007).

Brecht, B. (1977) 'The Radio as an Apparatus of Communication', in J. Willett (ed. and trans.), *Brecht on Theatre: The Development of an Aesthetic*, New York, NY: Hill and Wang.

Broad, William J. (3 November 2006) 'U.S. Web Archive Is Said to Reveal a Nuclear Primer', *New York Times*.

Brown, R. (2005) 'Getting to War: Communications and Mobilization in the 2002–2003 Iraq Crisis', in P. Seib (ed.), *Media and Conflict in the Twenty-First Century*, New York, NY: Palgrave MacMillan.

Bruns, A. (25 March 2006) 'Produsers and Produsage'. Online, available at: http://snurb.info/produsage (accessed 10 February 2008).

Bruns, A. (2007) 'Produsage, Generation C, and their Effects on the Democratic Process', Queensland University of Technology, Brisbane, Australia. Online, available at: web.mit.edu/comm-forum/mit5/papers/Bruns.pdf/

Burke, J. (2003) *Al-Qaeda: Casting a Shadow of Terror*, London: I.B. Tauris.

Burnett, P. and Marshall, O. (2003) *Web Theory*, London and New York, NY: Routledge.

Buruma, I. (2006) *Murder in Amsterdam: The Death of Theo Van Gogh and the Limits of Tolerance*, London: Atlantic Books.

Butsch, R. (2007) 'Introduction: How are Media Public Spheres', in R. Butsch (ed.), *Media and Public Spheres*, Basingstoke: Palgrave Macmillan.

Button, J. (31 December 2005) 'The Nowhere Generation', *The Age*, Melbourne.

Buxbaum, Peter (10 October 2007) 'U.S. Grapples with Cybersecurity', *ISN Security Watch*.

Carey, J. (1989) *Communication as Culture*, New York, NY: Routledge.

Carragee, K. M. and Roefs, W. (2004) 'The Neglect of Power in Recent Framing Research', *Journal of Communication*, 54, pp. 214–33.

Casarini, N. (6 November 2007) 'A New Space Order', *ISN Security Watch*.

Corfu Channel Case (merits) (1949) International Court of Justice Reports, 4, 31.

Case Concerning the Military and Paramilitary Activities in and against Nicaragua (merits) (1986) International Court of Justice Reports, 14.

Case Concerning United States Diplomatic and Consular Staff in Tehran (1980) International Court of Justice Reports, 3.

Casey, T. (18 September 2006) Deputy Spokesman Press Statement, Washington, DC. Online, available at: http://www.state.gov/r/pa/prs/ps/2006/72413.htm.

Castells, M. (2001) *The Internet Galaxy: Reflections on the Internet, Business and Society*, Oxford: Oxford University Press.

Castells, M. (2007) 'Communication, Power and Counter-Power in the Network Society', *International Journal of Communication*, 1: 1, pp. 238–66.

CBC News (18 October 2007). Online, available at: http://www.cbc.ca/money/story/2007/10/18/bbc-plan-cuts.html?ref=rss (accessed 4 November 2007).

Cebrowski, A. K. (V. ADM., US Navy Ret.), (4 April 1999) Sea, Space, Cyberspace: Borderless Domains. Online, available at: http://www.nwc.navy.mil/press/speeches/borderless.htm.

Center for Infrastructural Warfare Studies (5 February 2003) Information Operations: Information Warfare Tutorial. Online, available at: http://www.iwar.org.uk/iwar/resources/carlisle/iw-tutorial/ececsum.htm.

CERT (1 January 2004) CERT Coordination Center Annual Reports. Online, available at: http://www.cert.org.

CERT (1 January 2004) CERT/CC Statistics 1988–2003. Online, available at: http://www.cert.org.

Cetina, K. (2005) 'Complex Global Microstructures: The New Terrorist Societies', *Theory, Culture and Society*, 22, pp. 213–34.

Charter of the United Nations, The (ed. B. Simma) (2002) 2nd edn, Oxford: Oxford University Press.

Chase, M. and Mulvenon, J. (2002) *You've Got Dissent! Chinese Dissident use of the Internet and Beijing's Counter-strategies*, Santa Monica, CA: RAND Corporation.

Chen, H. (1997) 'The Third Military Revolution', in M. Pillsbury (ed.), *Chinese Views of Future Warfare*, Washington, DC: National Defense University.

Chereshekin, D., Tsygichko, V. and Smolyan, G. (5 March 1995) *A Weapon That May Be More Dangerous than A Nuclear Weapon: The Realities of Information Warfare.* Online, available at: http://www.iwar.org.uk/iwar/resources/parameters/iw-deterrence.htm.

Cherribi, S. (2006) 'From Baghdad to Paris: Al-Jazeera and the Veil', *Harvard International Journal of Press/Politics*, 11, pp. 121–38.

Chesters, G. (2004) 'Global Complexity and Global Civil Society', *Voluntas: International Journal of Voluntary and Nonprofit Organizations*, 15: 4, pp. 323–42.

Chouliaraki, L. (2006) *The Spectatorship of Suffering*, London: Sage.

CIWARS (2 June 2004) CIWARS Intelligence Report. Online, available at: http://www.iwar.org.

CJCSI Instruction 3121.01 (1994) *Standing Rules of Engagement for US Armed Forces*, Washington, DC: Joint Chiefs of Staff.

CJCSI S-3210 (1996) *Joint Information Warfare Policy*, Washington, DC: Joint Chiefs of Staff.

CJCSI 6510.01 (1996) *Defensive Information Warfare Implementation*, Washington, DC: Joint Chiefs of Staff.

CNN (23 February 2007) 'Australia Blocks Asylum Seekers', Online, available at: http://edition.cnn.com/2007/WORLD/asiapcf/02/23/australia.asylum.reut/index.html.

Cockburn, C. (2002) 'Bat Shalom: A Women's Group for Peace', *Feministcerceve*, 8 March 2002, Istanbul, Turkey.

Cockburn, C. (2007) *From Where We Stand: War Women's Activism and Feminist Analysis*, London: Zed Books.

Cockburn, C. and Zarkov, D. (2002) 'Women's Organization in the Rebuilding of Post-war Bosnia Herzegovina', in C. Cockburn, and O. Zarkov (eds) *The Post-war Moment: Militants, Masculinities and International Peace Keeping*, London: Lawrence and Wishart.

Cohen, Stanley (1972) *Folk Devils and Moral Panics: the Creation of the Mods and Rockers*, London: MacGibbon & Kee.

Coleman, S. (2005) 'Blogs and the New Politics of Listening', *Political Quarterly*, 76: 2, pp. 272–80.

Coll, Stephen and Glasser, Susan B. (7 August 2005) 'Terrorists Turn to the Web as Base of Operations', *Washington Post*. Online, available at: http://www.washingtonpost.com/wpdyn/content/article/2005/08/05/AR2005080501138_pf.html (accessed 4 November 2007).

Cooper, S. D. (2006) *Watching the Watchdog: Bloggers as the Fifth Estate*, Washington, DC: Marquette Books.

Cooperative Strategy (2007) 'A Cooperative Strategy for 21st Century Seapower Represents a Historical first'. Online, available at: www.navy.mil/maritime/MaritimeStrategy.pdf.

Corman, S. and Schiefelbein, J. (2006) 'Communication and Media Strategy in the Jihadist War of Ideas', White Paper #0601, Consortium for Strategic Communication. Online, available at: http://www.asu.edu/clas/communication/about/csc/publications/jihad_comm_media.pdf.

Cottle, S. (2006) *Mediatized Conflict: Developments in Media and Conflict Studies*, Maidenhead: Open University Press.

Couldry, N. (2000) *The Place of Media Power*, London: Routledge.

Couldry, N. (2003) *Media Rituals*, London: Routledge.

Couldry, N., Livingstone, S. and Markham, T. (2007) *Media Consumption and Public Engagement: Beyond the Presumption of Attention*, Basingstoke: Palgrave.

Critical Art Ensemble (1994) *The Electronic Disturbance*, New York, NY: Autonomedia.

Critical Art Ensemble (1995) *Electronic Civil Disobedience and Other Unpopular Ideas*, New York, NY: Autonomedia.

Critical Art Ensemble (28 September 1998) 'An Open Letter to Ricardo Dominguez', posted to the Nettime list. Online, available at: http://www.nettime.org/Lists-Archives/nettime-l-9809/msg00154.html (accessed 10 January 2008).

Critical Art Ensemble (2001) *Digital Resistance: Explorations in Tactical Media*, New York, NY: Autonomedia.

Crypt Newsletter (1 January 1998) 'Air Force Investigative Office Deemed Incompetent during Rome Labs "Info-War" Break in'. Online, available at: http://sun.soci.niu.edu/~crypt/other/crpt46.htm.

CSIS (1 March 1999) 'A Washington Think Tank Has Issued A Report'. Online, available at: http://www.Infowar.com/mil_C4I_122298A_jshmtl.

Dahlberg, L. (2007) 'The Internet, Deliberative Democracy, and Power: Radicalizing the Public Sphere', *International Journal of Media and Cultural Politics*, 3:1, pp. 47–64.

D'Amato, A. (2000) *International Law Cybernetics and Cyberspace, Naval War College Int'l Law Studies Blue Book* – Volume 7, Newport, RI: Naval War College Press.

DARPA Strategic Plan (2007) Online, available at: http://www.darpa.mil/body/news/2007/2007StrategicPlan.pdf (accessed 4 November 2007).

Dartnell, M. (1999) 'Insurgency Online: Elements for a Theory of Anti-government Internet Communication', *Small Wars and Insurgencies*, 10: 3, pp. 117–136, (Winter 1999).

Dartnell, M. (2001) 'Insurgency Online: http://burn.ucsd.edu/~ats/mrta.htm'. Online, available at: http://web2.uwindsor.ca/courses/ps/dartnell/mrta.html.

Dartnell, M. (2003) 'Information Technology and the Web Activism of the Revolutionary Association of the Women of Afghanistan (RAWA) – Electronic Politics and New Global Conflict', in R. Latham (ed.), *Bombs and Bandwidth: The Emerging Relationship Between IT and Security*, New York: New Press.

Dartnell, M. (2005) 'Communicative Practice and Transgressive Global Politics: The *d'ua* of Sheikh Muhammed Al-Mohaisany', *First Monday*, 10: 7 (July 2005), URL: http://firstmonday-org/issues/10_7/darnell/index.html

Davies, Roger (2001) 'Sea Tigers, Stealth Technology and the North Korean Connection', Janes Defence Review, 7 March 2001. Online, available at: http://www.janes.com/regional_news/asia_pacific/news/jir/jir010307_2_n.shtml (accessed 23 November 2005).

De Alwis, M. (2002) 'The Changing Role of Women in Sri Lankan Society', *Social Research*, 69: 3, fall 2002.

De Armond, P. (2001) 'Netwar in the Emerald City: WTO Protest Strategy and Tactics', in John Arquilla and David Ronfeldt (eds), *Networks and Netwars: The Future of Terror, Crime, and Militancy*, Santa Monica, CA: RAND Corporation, pp. 201–35.

Online, available at: http://www.rand.org/pubs/monograph_reports/MR1382 (accessed 10 January 2008).

Deane, J. (1996) *Solidarity of Strangers: Feminism after identity Politics*, Berkeley, CA: University of California Press.

Deane, J. (4 February 1999) Digital Dragnet: The Hacking Crackdown. Online, available at: http://www.zdnet.com/zdtv/thesite/0597w3/life/life550_051297.

Deibert, R. (1997) *Parchment, Printing, and Hypermedia: Communication in World Order Transformation*, New York, NY: Columbia University Press.

De Landa, Manuel (1991) *War in the Age of Intelligent Machines*, New York, NY: Zone Books.

Deleuze, G. and Guattari, F. (2004) *A Thousand Plateaus: Capitalism and Schizophrenia*, Minnesota, MN: University of Minnesota Press.

della Porta, D. (2005a) 'Making the Polis: Social Forums and Democracy in the Global Justice Movement', *Mobilization: An International Journal*, 10: 1, pp. 73–94.

della Porta, D. (2005b) 'Between the European Social Forum and the Local Social Fora', in D. della Porta and S. Tarrow (eds), *Transnational Protest and Global Activism*, Lanham, MD: Rowman & Littlefield.

della Porta, D. and Diani, M. (1999) *Social Movements: An Introduction*, London: Blackwell.

della Porta, D. and Mosca, L. (2005) 'Global-net for Global Movements? A Network of Networks for a Movement of Movements', *Journal of Public Policy*, 25: 1, pp. 165–90.

DeLong, J. B. and Summers, L. H. (2001) 'The "New Economy": Background, Historical Perspective, Questions, and Speculations', in Federal Reserve Bank of Kansas City (30 August – 1 September 2001) Economic Policy for the Information Economy, Jackson Hole, WY. Online, available at: http://www.kc.frb.org/publicat/sympos/2001/sym01prg.htm (accessed 4 November 2007).

De Mel (2001) *Women and the Nations Narrative: Gender and Nationalism in Twentieth Century Sri Lanka*, Sri Lanka: Social Scientists Association.

De Mel, S., Swarna, J. and Parakrama, S. (2004) 'A Subnational Analysis of Millennium Development Indicators (MDIs) for Sri Lanka, 1990–2000', unpublished manuscript.

de Mesquita, B. and Lalman, D. (1992) *War and Reason: Domestic and International Imperatives*, New Haven, CN: Yale University Press.

Denning, D. E. (1999) 'Activism, Hacktivism, and Cyber Terrorism: The Internet As a Tool for Influencing Foreign Policy'. Online, available at: www.nautilus.org/info-policy/workshop/papers/denning.html (accessed 8 November 2004).

Denning, D. (23 May 2000) 'Cyberterrorism: Testimony Before the Special Oversight Panel on Terrorism Committee on Armed Services, U.S. House of Representatives'. Online, available at: http://www.cs.georgetown.edu/~denning/infosec/cyberterror.html (accessed 10 January 2008).

Denning, D. (2001a) [1999] 'Activism, Hacktivism, and Cyberterrorism: The Internet as a Tool for Influencing Foreign Policy', in J. Arquilla and D. Ronfeldt (eds), *Networks and Netwars: The Future of Terror, Crime, and Militancy*, Santa Monica, CA: RAND Corporation. Online, available at: http://www.rand.org/pubs/monograph_reports/MR1382 (accessed 10 January 2008).

Denning, D. (2001b) 'Cyberwarriors: Activists and Terrorists Turn to Cyberspace', *Harvard International Review*, 23: 2, pp. 70–5.

Denning, E. D. (2002) *Information Warfare and Security*, New York, NY: ACM Press, pp. 28–30.

Denning, D. (2006) 'A View of Cyberterrorism Five Years Later', in K. Himma (ed.),

Readings in Internet Security: Hacking, Counterhacking, and Society, Boston, MA: Jones and Bartlett.

Dibb, P. (1997) 'The Revolution in Military Affairs and Asian Security', *Survival*, 39: 4.

DiCenso, D. J. (1 June 2003) 'Information Warfare Cyberlaw'. Online, available at: http://www.airpower.maxwell.af/mil/airchronicles/apj/apj99/sum99/dicenso.html.

Dinstein, Y. (1987) *The Right of Self-Defense against Armed Attacks*, Lund: Juristforlaget i Lund.

Dinstein, Y. (2001) *War Aggression and Self-Defense*, Cambridge: Cambridge University Press.

Dominguez, Ricardo (31 May 2005) 'SWARM the Minutemen – Post Action Update May 30th, 2005', posted to the Nettime list. Online, available at: http://www.nettime.org/Lists-Archives/nettime-l-0505/msg00071.html (accessed 10 January 2008).

Dourish, P. (2001) *Where the Action Is: The Foundations of Embedded Interaction*, Cambridge, MA: MIT Press.

DPP Policy Committee (23 November 1999) 'White Paper on National Defense'.

Drezner, D. W. and Farrell, H. (2004a) 'The Power and Politics of Blogs', paper presented at the Annual Conference of the American Political Science Association, July 2004.

Drezner, D. W. and Farrell, H. (2004b) 'Web of Influence', *Foreign Policy* Nov/Dec. Online, available at: http://www.foreignpolicy.com/story/cms.php?story_id=2707&popup_delayed=1 (accessed 18 November 2007).

Du, H. S. and Wagner, C. (2006) 'Weblog Success: Exploring the Role of Technology', *International Journal of Human-Computer Studies*, 64, pp. 789–98.

Dunnigan, J. F. (2002) *The Next War Zone: Confronting the Global Threat of Cyberterrorism*, New York, NY: Osborne/McGraw-Hill.

Dupont, A. (2001) *East Asia Imperilled: Transnational Challenges to Security*, Cambridge: Cambridge University Press.

Durodie, B. (22 September 2006) 'We are the Enemies Within', *Times Higher Education Supplement.* Online, available at: http://www.durodie.net/articles/THES/20060922 enemies.htm.

Eaves, David (2006) 'Community Management as Open Source's Core Competency'. Online, available at: http://eaves.ca/2006/12/17/community-management-as-open-sources-core-competency/ (accessed 9 February 2008).

Electrohippies Collective (2000) 'Client-side Distributed Denial-of-Service: Valid Campaign Tactic or Terrorist Act?', Electrohippies Occasional Paper No. 1. Online, available at: http://www.fraw.org.uk/download/ehippies/op-01.html (accessed 10 January 2008).

Eliasoph, N. (1998) *Avoiding Politics: How Americans Produce Apathy in Everyday Life*, Cambridge: Cambridge University Press.

Elliston, J. (9 January 1999) 'The CIA and Cyberwar'. Online, available at: http://www.Parascope.com/ds/cyber1.htm.

El-Nawawy, M. and Iskandar, A. (2002) *Al-Jazeera: How the Free Arab News Network Scooped the World and Changed the Middle East*, Cambridge, MA: Westview.

Embassy of Japan (10 April 2003) Japan Brief/FPC No. 0318. Online, available at: http://www.fr.emb-japan.go.jp/brief/03-JB318.html (accessed 4 November 2007).

Enloe, C. (1989) *Bananas, Beaches and Bases: Making Sense of International Politics*, London: Pandora.

Enloe, C. (1993) *The Morning After: Sexual Politics at the End of the Cold War*, Los Angeles, CA, London and Berkeley, CA: University of California Press.

Entman, R. M. (2003) 'Cascading Activation: Contesting the White House's Frame After 9/11', *Political Communication*, 20: 4, pp. 415–32.

Entman, R. M. (2004) *Projections of Power: Framing News, Public Opinion, and U.S. Foreign Policy*, Chicago, IL: University of Chicago Press.

Entman, R. and Page, B. (1994) 'The News before the Storm', in L. W. Bennett and D. L. Paletz (eds), *Taken by Storm: The Media, Public Opinion, and U.S. Foreign Policy in the Gulf War*, Chicago, IL and London: The University of Chicago Press.

Farris, K. (2001) 'Chinese Views of Information Warfare', *Defense Intelligence Journal*, 10: 1.

Fawcett, J. E. S. (1961) 'Intervention in International Law: A Study of Some Recent Cases', *Recueil des Cours de l'Academie-de Droit International*, 103.

Fearon, J. D. (1994) 'Domestic Political Audiences and the Escalation of International Disputes', *American Political Science Review*, 88: 3, pp. 577–92.

Ferguson, K. E. (1984) *The Feminist Case against Bureaucracy*, Philadelphia, PA: Temple University Press.

Ferrer, J. N., Albareda, R. V. and Romero, M. T. (undated) 'Embodied Participation in the Mystery: Implications for the Individual, Interpersonal Relationships, and Society'. Online, available at: http://www.estel.es/EmbodiedParticipationInTheMystery,%201espace.doc (6 February 2008).

Finkelstein, D. (1999) 'China's National Military Strategy', in J. C. Mulvenon and R. Yang (eds), *The People's Liberation Army in the Information Age*, Santa Monica, CA: RAND Corporation.

Foucault, M. (1978) *The Will to Knowledge: The History of Sexuality*, Volume 1, London: Penguin.

Foucault, M. (1986) 'Of Other Spaces', *Diacritis*, 16, pp. 22–7, trans. J. Miskowiec.

Fraser, N. (1992) 'Rethinking the Public Sphere: A Contribution to the Critique of Actually Existing Democracy', in C. Calhoun (ed.), *Habermas and the Public Sphere*, Cambridge, MA: MIT Press.

Frazer, E. and Hutchings, K. (2007) 'Argument and Rhetoric in the Justification of Political Violence', *European Journal of Political Theory*, 6: 2, pp. 180–99.

Freedman, L. (4 October 1996) 'Information Warfare: Will Battle ever be Joined?' Lecture given at the launch of the International Center for Security Analysis in London. Online, available at: http://www.kcl.ac.uk/orgs/icsa/larry.htm.

Freedman, L. (1998) 'The Revolution in Strategic Affairs', Adelphi Paper 318, Oxford: Oxford University Press.

Freeh, L. J. (4 March 1997) Director of the FBI speech at the 1997 International Computer Crime Conference. Online, available at: http://www.fbi.gov/dirspch/ compcrim.htm.

Fulghum, D. A. and Wall, R. (3 November 2001) 'US Shifts Cyberwar to Combat Commands'. Online, available at: http://www.dia.smil.mil/admin/EARLYBIRD/010226/e20010226usshifts.htm.

Galloway, A. (2004) *Protocol. How Control Exists after Decentral*ization, Boston, MA: MIT Press..

Gandhi, M. K. (2000) [1920] 'A Selection From His Writings', in P. Lauter (ed.), *Walden and Civil Disobedience*, Boston, MA: Houghton Mifflin.

Ganeshpanchan, Z. (2007) 'Mothering the Other', presented at the Civil Rights, Liberties and Disobedience: Alternatives to Governance in the 21st Century Conference, Loughborough University, 27–28 July 2007.

Garcia, D. and Lovink, G. (16 May 1997) 'The ABC of Tactical Media', posted to the Nettime list. Online, available at: http://www.nettime.org/Lists-Archives/nettime-l-9705/msg00096.html (accessed 10 January 2008).

Garcia, D. and Lovink, G. (22 February 1999) 'The DEF of Tactical Media', posted to the Nettime list. Online, available at: http://www.nettime.org/Lists-Archives/nettime-l-9902/msg00104.html (accessed 10 January 2008).

Gardner, H. (2005) *American Global Strategy and the War on Terrorism*, Aldershot: Ashgate.

Gardner, H. (2007) *Averting Global War: Regional Challenges, Overextension and Options for American Strategy*, New York, NY: Palgrave.

Gaudin, S. (26 November 2001a) 'The Terrorist Network', Network World. Online, available at: http://www.networkworld.com/research/2001/1126featside4.html (accessed 4 November 2007).

Gaudin, S. (26 November 2001b) 'The Lehman Network Survives', Network World. Online, available at: http://www.networkworld.com/research/2001/1126feat.html (accessed 4 November 2007).

General Assembly Resolution 3314 (XXIX) (1974) 29(1) Resolutions adopted by the General Assembly, 142 Articles 1, 3.

Gerlach, L. P. (2001) 'The Structure of Social Movements: Environmental Activism and Its Opponents', in J. Arquilla and D. Ronfeldt (eds), *Networks and Netwars: The Future of Terror, Crime, and Militancy*, Santa Monica, CA: RAND Corporation.

Gerlach, L. P. and Hine, V. H. (1970) *People, Power, Change: Movements of Social Transformation*, Indianapolis, IN and New York, NY: The Bobbs-Merrill Company.

Gibson, W. (1986) 'Burning Chrome', collected in (1995) *Burning Chrome and Other Stories*, London: HarperCollins.

Gill, B. (1997) 'Chinese Military Hardware and Technology Acquisitions of Concern to Taiwan', in J. R. Lilley and C. Downs (eds), *Crisis in the Taiwan Strait*, Washington, DC: National Defense University.

Gillespie, M. (2006a) 'Security, Media, Legitimacy: Multi-ethnic Media Publics and the Iraq War 2003', *International Relations*, 20: 1, pp. 467–86.

Gillespie, M. (2006b) *Journal of Ethnic and Migration Studies*, Guest Editor of Special Issue: After September 11: Television News and Transnational Audiences, 32: 6.

Gillespie, M. (2007) 'Media, Security and Multicultural Citizenship: Collaborative Ethnography and Integrated Research Design', Guest Editor of Special Issue, *European Journal of Cultural Studies*, 10: 3.

Gitlin, T. (1980) *The Whole World is Watching: Mass Media in the Making & Unmaking of the New Left*, Berkeley, CA and London: University of California Press.

Gitlin, T. (1989) 'Public Spheres or Public Sphericules?', in T. Liebes and J. Curran (eds), *Media, Ritual and Identity*, New York, NY: Routledge.

Global security.org 'Transdniester'. Online, available at: http://www.globalsecurity.org/military/world/war/transdniester.htm.

Goggin, Gerard (2006) *Cell Phone Culture*, London: Routledge.

Gordon, Robert J. (Fall 2000) 'Does the "New Economy" Measure up to the Great Inventions of the Past?', *Journal of Economic Perspectives*, 14: 4–5.

Gow, J. (with Michalsi, M.) (forthcoming, 2007) *War, Image, Legitimacy: Viewing Contemporary Conflict*, London: Routledge.

Gray, C. (2004) *International Law and the Use of Force*, Oxford: Oxford University Press.

Greenberg, L. T., Goodman, S. E. and Soo Hoo, K. J. (2 June 1988) *Information Warfare and International Law*, Washington, DC: National Defense University Press. Online, available at: http://www.dodccrp.org/.

Grindstaff, D. A. and DeLuca, K. M. (2004) 'The Corpus of Daniel Pearl', *Critical Studies in Media Communication*, 21: 4, pp. 305–24.

Guardian (28 April 2005) 'Welcome to Nowhere'. Online, available at: http://travel.guardian.co.uk/article/2005/apr/28/1 (accessed 5 May 2007).

Gunkel, D. J. (2005) 'Editorial: Introduction to Hacking and Hacktivism', *New Media & Society*, 7: 5, pp. 595–7.

Hamilton, A. (2003) 'Best of the War Blogs', *Time*, 161: 91.

Hamre, J. (23 March 1996) 'DoD is Very Interested – Statement by the Deputy Secretary of Defense in the US Senate's Subcommittee on Technology, Terrorism and Government Information'. Online, available at: http://www.fas.org/irp/congress/1988_hr/98–06–11.htm.

Hardt, M. and Negri, A. (2000) *Empire*, Boston, Ma: Harvard University Press.

Harknett, R. J. (1996) 'Information Warfare and Deterrence', *Parameters: US Army War College Quarterly*.

Harry, M. H. (1986) 'The Right of Self-Defense and the Use of Armed Force against States Aiding Insurgency', *Southern Illinois University Law Journal*, 11, pp. 1289, 1299.

Hartley, J. (1998) 'Juvenation: News, Girls and Power' in C. Carter, G. Branston and S. Allan (eds), *News, Gender and Power*, London: Routledge, pp. 47–70.

Hartley, J. (1999) *Uses Of Television*, London: Routledge.

Harshberger, E. and Ochmanek, D. (21 February 1999) *Information in Warfare: New Opportunities for US Military Forces*, Santa Monica, CA: Rand Corporation. Online, available at: http://www.rand.org/publications.MR/MR1016.

Hastings, D. (20 February 2003) 'Talk to the Federation of American Scientists', Space Panel Report 9: Appendix 1: Panel Biographies in Ensuring America's Space Security Federation of American Scientists. Online, available at: http://www.fas.org/main/content.jsp?formAction=297&contentId=311 (accessed 4 November 2007).

Hastings, M. (2003) 'Bloggers over Baghdad', *Newsweek*, 141, pp. 48–9.

Hawksley, H. (15 September 2007) 'Big Brother is watching us all' BBC News. Online, available at: http://news.bbc.co.uk/2/hi/programmes/from_our_own_ correspondent/6995061.stm (accessed 4 November 2007).

Held, D. (2001) 'Violence, Law and Justice in a Global Age', in SSRC after September 11

Held, D., McGrew, A., Goldblatt, D. and Perraton, J. (1999) *Global Transformations: Politics, Economics and Culture*, Stanford, CA: Stanford University Press.

Herman, E. S. and Chomsky, N. (1988) *Manufacturing Consent: The Political Economy of the Mass Media*, New York, NY: Pantheon.

Herring, S. C., Scheidt, L. A., Kouper, I. and Wright, E. (2007) 'Longitudinal Content Analysis of Blogs: 2003–2004', in M. Tremayne (ed.), *Blogging, Citizenship and the Future of Media*, New York, NY: Routledge.

Hey, J. (ed.) (2003) *Small States in World Politics: Explaining Foreign Policy Behaviour*, Boulder, CO and London: Lynne Reinner.

Himanen, P. (2001) *The Hacker Ethic*, New York, NY: Random House.

Hine, C. (ed.) (2005) *Virtual Methods: Issues in Social Research on the Internet*, Oxford and New York, NY: Berg.

Hirst, P. (2005) *Space and Power: Politics, War and Architecture*, London: Polity.

Hoffman, B. (2006a) *Inside Terrorism* (revised edition), New York, NY: Columbia University Press.

Hoffman, B. (2006b) 'The Use of the Internet by Islamic Extremists', Permanent Select Committee on Intelligence.

Homer-Dixon, Thomas (January/February 2002) 'The Rise of Complex Terrorism',

Foreign Policy. Online, available at: http://www.foreignpolicy.com/story/cms.php? Story_id=170 (accessed 4 November 2007).

Hoole, R., Somasundaram, D., Sritharan, K. and Thiranogama, R. (1992) *The Broken Palmyrah: The Tamil Crisis in Sri Lanka: An Inside Account*, Claremont, CA: The Sri Lanka Studies Institute.

Hoskins, A. (2004) *Televising War: From Vietnam to Iraq*, London: Continuum.

Hoskins, A. and O'Loughlin, B. (2007) *Television and Terror: Conflicting Times and the Crisis of News Discourse*, London: Palgrave.

Hoskins, A. and O'Loughlin, B. (forthcoming, 2008).*War and Media: Diffused War in the New Media Ecology*, Cambridge: Polity Press.

Hosmer, S. T. (1 November 1999) *The Information Revolution and Psychological Effects*, Santa Monica, CA: Rand Corporation. Online, available at: http://www.rand.org/ publications/MR/MR1016.

Hundley, R., Anderson, R. H., Arquilla, J. and Molander, R. C. (1 January 1996) *Security in Cyberspace: Challenges for Society*, Santa Monica, CA: Rand Corporation. Online, available at: http://www.rand.org/publications/MR/MR880/MR880.ch10.htm.

Hughes, P. (Lt. Gen. US Army) (28 January 1998) 'Global Threats and Challenges: the Decades Ahead', Statement for the Senate Select Committee on Intelligence. Online, available at: http://www.globalsecurity.org/intell/library/congress/1999_hr/99020208_tlt.htm.

Ifrah, Laurence (3 September 2007) 'Europe Confronted by Digital Crime', *European Issues*, 70, Foundation Robert Schuman. Online, available at: http://www.robert-schuman.eu/pdf.qe.php?num=qe-70 (accessed 4 November 2007).

Innis, H. (1999) *The Bias of Communication*, Toronto: University of Toronto Press.

Iranian Oil Platforms Case (merits) (2003) International Court of Justice Reports, paras 51, 64.

IWAR (7 March 2003) Information Warfare Tutorial. Online, available at: http://www.iwar.org.uk/iwar/resources/carlisle/iw-tutorial/execsum.htm.

James, E. (2001) 'Learning to Bridge the Digital Divide: Computers Alone are not Enough to Join the E-economy. Digital Literacy is Essential Too,' *OECD Observer* (14 January), and at http://www.oecdobserver.org/ (accessed 21 June 2005).

Jane's Geopolitical Intelligence Foreign Report (various issues). Online, available at: http://www.janes.com/janes.html.

Jencks, H. W. (1997) 'Wild Speculations on the Military Balance in the Taiwan Strait', in J. R. Lilley and C. Downs (eds), *Crisis in the Taiwan Strait*, Washington, DC: National Defense University.

Jiefangjun bao (25 June 1996) 'Army Paper on Information Warfare', in Foreign Broadcast Information Service – China (Internet version), 20 November 1996.

Johnson, L. S. (1997) 'Toward a Functional Model of Information Warfare', *Studies in Intelligence*, 1: 1.

Johnson, P. A. (1999) *An Assessment of International Legal Issues in Information Operations 2–3*, Washington, DC: Department of Defense.

Johnson, T. and Kaye, B. K. (2007) 'Blog Readers: Predictors of Reliance on War Blogs', in M. Tremayne (ed.), *Blogging, Citizenship and the Future of Media*, New York, NY: Routledge.

Johnston, A. I. (1995) 'Thinking about Strategic Culture', *International Security*, 19: 4.

Johnston, T. (23 March 2003) 'Mine Hits Deep Seam of Papua Unrest', Online, available at: http://news.bbc.co.uk/go/pr/fr/-/2/hi/asia-pacific/4837360.stm (accessed 5 May 2007).

Joint Chiefs of Staff (2003) *Joint Vision 2020*, 3, Washington, DC: Department of Defense.

Joint Command Control (2003) Joint IO Planning Handbook [3.9MB], Joint Command, Control and Information Warfare School Joint Forces Staff College, NDU July 2003 [old version July 2002].

Joint Command, Control and Information Warfare School – Joint Forces Staff College (2003) *Joint Information Operations Planning Handbook*, Washington, DC: Joint Forces Staff College.

Joint Pub. 3–13 (20 January 2001) *Joint Doctrine for Information Operations*, Washington, DC: Joint Chiefs of Staff. Online, available at: http://www.dtic.mil/doctrine/ jel/new_pubs/jp3_13.pdf.

Jordan, T. (1999) 'New Space, New Politics: The Electronic Frontier Foundation and the Definition of Cyberpolitics', in T. Jordan (ed.), *Storming the Millennium: The New Politics of Change*, London: Lawrence & Wishart.

Jordan, T. (2002) *Activism! Direct Action, Hacktivism and the Future of Society*, London: Reaktion Books.

Jordan, T. (2007) 'Online Direct Action: Hacktivism and Radical Democracy', in L. Dahlberg and E. Siapera (eds), *Radical Democracy and the Internet*, Basingstoke: Palgrave Macmillan.

Jordan, T. and Taylor, P. (2004) *Hacktivism and Cyberwars: Rebels With a Cause*, London: Routledge.

Joustra, T. (2007) Jihadis and the Internet, National Coordinator for Counterterrorism.

Juris, J. S. (2005) 'Social Forums and their Margins: Networking Logics and the Cultural Politics of Autonomous Space', *Ephemera*, 5: 2, pp. 253–72.

Justus, Z. S. and Hess, A. (2006) 'One Message for Many Audiences: Framing the Death of Abu Musab al-Zarqawi', Report #0605, Consortium for Strategic Communication, Arizona State University. Online, available at: www.asu.edu/clas/communication/ about/csc/documents/CSCreport0605.pdf.

Kabay, M. E. (2 March 2004) ISCA White Paper on Computer Crime Statistics. Online, available at: http://www.ncsa.com/knowledge/research/comp_crime.htm.

Kagan, R. (2004) 'America's Crisis of Legitimacy', *Foreign Affairs*, 83: 2.

Kahn, J. (20 January 2006) 'China Shows Assertiveness in Weapons Test', *New York Times*.

Kahn, R. and Kellner, D. (2004) 'New Media and Internet Activism: From the "Battle of Seattle" to Blogging', *New Media & Society*, 6: 1, pp. 87–95.

Kalb, M. (February 2007) 'The Israeli Hezbollah War of 2006: The Media as a Weapon of Assymetrical Conflict', Harvard University. Online, available at: www.hks.harvard.edu/presspol/research_publications/papers/research_papers/R29.pdf.

Karasic, C. (n.d.) 'Electronic Disturbance Theater and FloodNet Scrapbook'. Online, available at: http://www.pixelyze.com/scrapbook/index.htm (accessed 10 January 2008).

Karatzogianni, A. (2006) *The Politics of Cyberconflict*, London and New York, NY: Routledge.

Karatzogianni, A. 'New Media Tools and Asymmetric Pressure in the Global Periphery', work in progress.

Karatzogianni, A. and Robinson, A. (2004) 'With or Without You: US Foreign Policy, Domination, Hegemony and Rhizomes of Resistance', Online, available at: http://vectors.usc.edu/thoughtmesh/publish/135.php or http://andyrobinsontheoryblog. blogspot.com/2004/11/with-or-without-you-foreign-policy.html.

Karatzogianni, A and Robinson, A. (following, 2009) *Power, Conflict and Resistance in the Contemporary World: Social Movements, Networks and Hierarchies*, London: Routledge.

Karim, H. K. (2003) 'Mapping Diaspora Media Scapes', in K. H. Karim (ed.), *Media of Diaspora*, London: Routledge.

Kartenberg, H. P. (2005) 'A Transparent and Civil Act of Disobedience'. Online, available at: http://post.thing.net/node/304 (accessed 10 January 2008).

Katz, J. E. and Rice, R. E. (2002) *Social Consequences of Internet Use*, Cambridge, MA: MIT Press.

Kaye, B. K. and Johnson, T. (2004) 'Blogs as a Source of Information about the War in Iraq', in R. D. Berenger (ed.), *Global Media go to War*, Spokane, WA: Marquette Books.

Kearney, J. (1997) *Postnationalist Ireland: Politics, Culture, Philosophy*, London: Routledge.

Kelsen, H. (1998) *US Naval War College Int'l Law Studies-Collective Security Under International Law*, Newport. RI: Naval War College Press.

Keohane, R. O. and Nye, J. S. (1989) *Power and Interdependence*, Glenview, IL: Scott, Foresman & Co.

Keohane, R. O. and Nye, J. S. (2000) 'Globalization: What's New? What's Not? (And So What?)', *Foreign Policy*, 118.

Khalizad, Z. M. and White, J. P. (eds) (4 July 1999) *Strategic Appraisal: The Changing Role of Information in Warfare*, Santa Monica, CA: Rand Corporation. Online, available at: http://www.rand.org/publications/MR/MR1016.

Khokhlova, V. (22 September 2006) 'Notes on Montenegro and Transnistria'. www.globalvoicesonline.org. Online, available at: http://www.globalvoicesonline.org/2006/09/22/notes-on-montenegro-and-transnistria/.

King, M. L. (2000) [1962] 'A Legacy of Creative Protest', in P. Tillich and H. N. Wieman, *Papers of Martin Luther King, Jr. 2*, pp. 339–544.

Kirk, P. Online, available at: http://galeria.origo.hu/szandelszky/szbeng.html, and pictures of the region at: http://galeria.origo.hu/szandelszky/szbeng.html.

Kivikuru, U. (2006) 'Tsunami Communication in Finland: Revealing Tensions in the Sender–Receiver Relationship', *European Journal of Communication*, 21: 4, pp. 499–520.

Klandermans, B. (1997) *The Social Psychology of Protest*, London: Blackwell.

Klein, N. (2002) *Fences and Windows: Dispatches from the Front Lines of the Globalization Debate*, New York, NY: Picador.

Kress, G. R. and van Leeuwen, T. (2001) *Multimodal Discourse*, London: Arnold.

Ko, S. (4 September 2003) 'Cabinet says Computers Under Attack', *Taipei Times*.

Kuehl, D. (2004) 'Wanted: a National Information Strategy for the Interconnected Age' at FISSEA conference, 11 March 2004.

Kunz, J. L. (1947) 'Individual and Collective Self-Defense in Art. 5 of the Charter of the United Nations', *American Journal of International Law*, 41.

Lague, D. (29 January 2004) 'Chen Launches his Missile Vote', *Far Eastern Economic Review.*

Lake, E. (2 August 2006) 'Israel War Effort Extends Even To Hezbollah TV', *New York Sun*. Online, available at: http://www.nysun.com/article/37140 (accessed 29 February 2008).

Lauter (2000) [1958] 'From Stride Toward Freedom', in P. Lauter (ed.), *Walden and Civil Disobedience*, Boston, MA: Houghton Mifflin.

Lauter (ed.) (2003) *Walden and Civil Disobedience*, Boston, MA: Houghton Mifflin, p. 433.

Lemon, S. (29 May 2007) 'China Accused of Information Warfare: Warfare by Virus', Techworld. Online, available at: http://www.techworld.com/security/news/index.cfm?NewsID=8959 (accessed 13 July 2007).

LeVine, P. and Scollon, R. (eds) (2004) *Discourse & Technology: Multimodal Discourse Analysis*, Washington, DC: Georgetown University Press.

Levy, S. (1984) *Hackers: Heroes of the Computer Revolution*, New York, NY: Anchor Press/Doubleday.

Lillich, R. B. (1976) *Economic Coercion and the New International Economic Order*, Charlottesville, VA: The Michie Company.

Lillich, R. B. and Paxman, J. E. S. (1961) 'Intervention in International Law: A Study of Some Cases', *Recueil des Cours de l'Academie de Droit International*, 103, pp. 343–63.

Lin, C. P. (1995) 'Red Fist: China's Army in Transition', *International Defense Review*, 28.

Lindberg, T. (1 June 2004) 'What is Going on in the Outlaw Region of Transnistria, Moldova? No one Really Seems to Know', *Hoover Digest*, 3, Washington, DC (appeared in the *Washington Times* on 1 June 2004). Online, available at: http://www.hoover.org/publications/digest/3020556.html.

Little, Mark (1999) 'Practical Anarchy: an Interview with Critical Art Ensemble', *Angelaki*, 4: 2, pp. 192–201.

Liu, H. (1993) 'Unswervingly March along the Road of Building a Modern Army with Chinese Characteristics', *Jiefangjun Bao*, 6 August, in FBIS-CHI, 20 November 1996.

Lovink, G. (2002) *Dark Fiber: Tracking Critical Internet Culture*, Cambridge, MA: MIT Press.

Lovink, G. and Schneider, F. (25 June 2001) 'New Rules of the New Actonomy', posted to the Nettime list. Online, available at: http://amsterdam.nettime.org/Lists-Archives/-nettime-l-0106/msg00114.html (accessed 10 January 2008).

MacBride, S. and International Commission for the Study of Communications Problems (1980) *Many Voices One World*, Paris: UNESCO. Online, available at: http://unesdoc.unesco.org/images/0004/000400/040066eb.pdf (accessed 4 November 2007).

McCullagh, D. (28 May 2002) 'Besieged ISP Restores Pearl vid', *Wired*. Online, available at: http://www.wired.com/politics/law/news/2002/05/52818.

MacLachlan, M. (9 March 1998) 'Security Market is Maturing but Needs Standards', TechWeb News. Online, available at: http://www.techweb.com/wire/story/0398iwld/TWB19980309S0015.

McLuhan, M. (1968) *The Medium Is the Massage*, New York, NY: John Wiley.

McLuhan, M. (2001) *Understanding Media*, London: Routledge.

McLuhan, M. and Fiore, Q. (1967) *The Medium is the Massage*, San Francisco, CA: Hardwired.

McLuhan, M. and Fiore, Q. (1968) *War and Peace in the Global Village*, New York, NY: Bantam.

McNair, Brian (2006) *Cultural Chaos: Journalism, News and Power in a Globalised World*, London: Routledge.

McNealy, T. D. (20 February 1997) 'Hackers, Crackers and Trackers, The American Legion Magazine at 34'. Online, available at: http://www.legion.org/pubs/1997/hackers.htm.

Mani, L. (1990) 'Multiple Mediations: Feminist Scholarship in the Age of Multinational Reception', *Feminist Review*, 35, pp. 24–41.

Manion, M. and Goodrum, A. (2000) 'Terrorism or Civil Disobedience: Toward a Hacktivist Ethic', *Computers and Society*, June, pp. 14–19.

Margolis, M. and Resnick, D. (2000) *Politics as Usual: The Cyberspace 'Revolution'*, Thousand Oaks, CA: Sage.

Marston, Q. (1988) Armed Intervention in the 1956 Suez Canal Crisis: the Legal Advice tendered to the British Government, *International and Comparative Law Quarterly*, 37, 773, 795, 800.

Martin, D. (15 May 2002) 'Terror, Lies and Videotape', CBS News. Online, available at: http://www.cbsnews.com/stories/2002/05/14/attack/main509059.shtml.

Masden, W., Sobel, D. L., Rotenberg, M. and Banisar, D. (5 September 1998) *Cryptography and Liberty: An International Survey of Encryption Policy*, Washington, DC: Electronic Privacy Information Center. Online, available at: http://www.epic.org/alert/EPIC_alert_8.05.html.

Massey, D. (1994) *Space, Place and Gender*, Cambridge: Polity Press.

Massey, D. (2005) *For Space*, London: Sage.

Matheson, D. (2004) 'Weblogs and the Epistemology of the News: Some Trends in Online Journalism', *New Media & Society*, 6: 4, pp. 443–68.

Matthews, J. T. (1997) 'Power Shift', *Foreign Affairs*, 76: 1.

Mayer, R. C., Davis, J. H. and Schoorman, F. D. (1995) 'An Integrative Model of Organizational Trust', *Academy of Management Review*, 20: 3, pp. 709–34.

MCI (9 October 1997) Information on DoSTracker. Online, available at: http://www.security.mci.net/dostracker/prelease.html.

Meikle, Graham (2002) *Future Active: Media Activism and the Internet*, New York, NY: Routledge.

Melucci, Alberto (1996) *Challenging Codes: Collective Action in the Information Age*, Cambridge: Cambridge University Press.

Mercer, P. (14 October 2005) 'Australia Winds Down Nauru Camp', BBCNews. Online, available at: http://news.bbc.co.uk/go/pr/fr/-/2/hi/asia-pacific/4341110.stm (accessed 5 May 2007).

Mercer, P. (17 February 2007) 'Cargo Cult Lives on in South Pacific', BBC News. Online, available at: http://news.bbc.co.uk/1/hi/world/asia-pacific/6370991.stm.

Mermin, J. (1999) *Debating War and Peace: Media Coverage of U.S. Intervention in the Post-Vietnam Era*, Princeton, NJ: Princeton University Press.

Meyrowitz, J. (1986) *No Sense of Place: The Impact of Electronic Media on Social Behavior*, Oxford: Oxford University Press.

Mieszkowski, K. (18 September 2000) 'Blowing up "The Anarchist Cookbook"'. Online, available at: http://dir.salon.com/story/tech/log/2000/09/18/anarchy/index.html (accessed 4 November 2007).

Mills, E. (31 January 2007) 'Google Fourth-quarter Profit Nearly Triples'. CNetnews.com. Online, available at: http://www.news.com/Google-fourth-quarter-profit-nearly-triples/2100-1030_3-6155180.html (accessed 4 November 2007).

Minnick, W. (9 June 2006) 'Taiwan Faces Increasing Cyber Assaults'. Online, available at: http://www.defensenews.com/story.php?F=1861031&C=asiapac (accessed 13 July 2007).

Mohanty, C. (1991) 'Under Western Eyes: Feminist Scholarship and Colonial Discourses', in A. R. Mohanty and L. Torres (eds), *Third World Women and the Politics of Feminism*, Bloomington and Indianapolis, IN: Indiana University Press.

Molander, R. C., Riddle, A. S. and Wilson, P. A. (1996) *Strategic Information Warfare: A New Face of War*, Santa Monica, CA: RAND Corporation.

Morgan, C. H. (2002) *Why Computer Crime is so Tough*, Colorado Springs, CO: United States Air Force – Air Force Office of Special Investigations.

Morgan, H. (2001) *Cyber Attacks and Computer Intrusion Investigations*, Colorado Springs, CO: Air Force Office of Special Investigations.

Morgenthau, H. J. (1970) *Truth and Power*, New York, NY: Praeger.

Moss, M. and Mekhennet, S. (28 May 2007) 'Militants Widen Reach as Terror Seeps Out of Iraq', *New York Times*.

Moss, M. and Mekhennet, S. (15 October 2007) 'An Internet Jihad Aims at U.S. Viewers', *New York Times*.

Mouffe, C. (2005) *On the Political*, London: Routledge.

Mulligan, T. and Wooters, D. (eds) (2002) *1000 Photo Icons: George Eastman House*, Köln: Taschen.

Mulvenon, J. (1999) 'The PLA and Information Warfare', in J. C. Mulvenon and R. Yang (eds), *The People's Liberation Army in the Information Age*, Santa Monica, CA: RAND Corporation.

Murilo, J. (2006) 'Lusosphere Blogs Report the Latest Political Twists in East Timor'. Global Voices. Online, available at: http://www.globalvoicesonline.org/2006/06/27/-lusosphere-blogs-report-the-latest-political-twists-in-east-timor/ (accessed 12 January 2008).

Naficy, H. (1991) 'Exile Discourse and Televisual Fetishization', *Quarterly Review of Film and Video*, 13, pp. 288–314.

Naraynan, U. (1997) *Dislocating Cultures: Identities, Traditions and Third World Feminist,* New York, NY: Routledge.

Naulilaa Case (1928) *Reports of International Arbitral Awards* 2, pp. 1011, 1026.

Nesser, P. (2004) Jihad in Europe – A Survey of the Motivations for Sunni Islamist Terrorism in Post-millennium Europe, forsvarets forskningsinstitutt Norwegian Defence Research Establishment.

Neurink, J. (2005) '"Mujahideen of the lowlands" on trial in the Netherlands', *Terrorism Monitor*, 3, pp. 6–8.

New York Times (13 October 2002) 'Guerrilla Warfare, Waged with Code on the Internet'.

Noble, G. (2005 'The Discomfort of Strangers: Racism, Incivility and Ontological Security in a Relaxed and Comfortable Nation', *Journal of Intercultural Studies*, 26, pp. 107–1290.

Office of the Undersecretary of Defense for Acquisition, Technology and Logistics (2001) 'Protecting the Homeland: Report of the Defense Science Board Task Force on Defensive Information Operations', *Memorandum for the Chairman, Defense Science Board* 1, Washington, DC: Department of Defense.

Office of the US Secretary of Defense (26 February 1999) 'The Security Situation in the Taiwan Strait'. Online, available at: www.defenselink.mil/pubs/twStrait_02261999.html (accessed 23 March 2003).

O'Hanlon, M. (2000) 'Why China Cannot Conquer Taiwan', *International Security*, 25: 2.

O'Neill, S. and McGrory, D. (2006) *The Suicide Factory: Abu Hamza and the Finsbury Park Mosque*, London: HarperPerennial.

OpenNet Initiative Online (14 April 2005) 'Internet Filtering in 2004–05'. Online, available at: http://www.opennetinitiative.net/studies/china/http://www.opennetinitiative.net/modules.php?op=modload&name=Archive&file=index&req=viewarticle&artid=1 (accessed 4 November 2007).

O'Reilly, T. (2005) 'What is Web 2.0: Design Patterns and Business Models for the Next Generation of Software', oreillynet.com. Online, available at: http://www.oreillynet.com/pub/a/oreilly/tim/news/2005/09/30/what-is-web-20.html.

Palser, B. (2002) 'Journalistic Blogging', *American Journalism Review*, 24: 6, 58–9.

Parks, L. (2003) 'Our World, Satellite Televisuality, and the Fantasy of Global Presence', in L. Parks and S. Kumar (eds), *Planet TV: A Global Television Reader*, New York: New York University Press, pp. 74–93.

Parks, L. and Kumar, S. (eds) (2003) *Planet TV: A Global Television Reader*, New York, NY: New York University Press.

Patai, D. (1994) *Professing Feminism: Cautionary Tales from the Strange World of Women's Studies*, New York. NY: Basic Books.

Patomäki, H. and Teivainen, T. (2004) 'The World Social Forum: An Open Space or a Movement of Movements?', *Theory, Culture and Society*, 21: 6, pp. 145–54.

Pavlik, J. V. (2001) *Journalism and New Media*, New York, NY: Columbia University Press.

PCCIP (23 January 1999) Report on the President's Commission on Critical Infrastructure Protection (a series of 12 reports). Online, available at: http://www.pccip.gov/report_index.html.

People in Need. Transnistria. Online, available at: http://www.clovekvtisni.cz/index2en.php?parent=544&sid=404&id=546 (accessed 5 May 2007).

Peters, R. (24 September 2007) Interview with author.

Petru, Clej (11 December 2006) 'Trans-Dniester Winner's Long Game', BBC News, Online, available at: http://news.bbc.co.uk/go/pr/fr/-/2/hi/europe/6169623.stm (accessed 5 May 2007).

Philo, G. and Berry, M. (2004) *Bad News from Israel*, Glasgow University Media Group.

Postman, N. (1984) *Amusing Ourselves to Death: Public Discourse in the Age of Show Business*, New York, NY: Penguin.

Practicalities Working Group (13 December 2003) 'Minutes of the Practicalities Working Group Meeting', London: City Hall.

Prunier, G. (1995) *The Rwanda Crisis, 1959–1994: The History of Genocide*, London: Hurst & Co.

Qin, J., Zhou, Y., Reid, E., Lain, G. and Chen, H. (2007) 'Analyzing Terror Campaigns on the Internet: Technical Sophistication, Content Richness, and Web Interactivity', *International Journal of Human-Computer Studies*, January 2007, 65: 1.

Qlinks.net (10 December 1997) Communiqué of the Meeting of Justice and Interior Ministers of the Eight. Online, available at: http://www.qlinks.net/comdocs/washcomm.htm.

Raban, J. (1974) *Soft City*, London: Hamish Hamilton.

Rafael, V. L. (2006) [2003] 'The Cell Phone and the Crowd: Messianic Politics in the Contemporary Philippines', in W. Chun and T. Keenan (eds), *New Media Old Media: A History and Theory Reader*, New York, NY: Routledge.

Rathmell, A., Overill, R., Valeri, L. and Gearson, J. (17 June 1997) The IW Threat from Sub-State Groups: An Interdisciplinary Approach Proceedings of the Third International Command & Control Research and Technology Symposium, National Defense University, Washington, DC, 17–20 June 1997, pp. 164–78; reprinted in *Journal of Financial Crime*, 6: 2, pp. 146–56 (1998) Online, available at: http://www.kcl.ac.uk/orgs/icsa/terrori.htm.

Rawnsley, G. D. (2000) 'Taiwan's Propaganda Cold War', *Intelligence and National Security*, 14: 4.

Rawnsley, G. D. (2007) 'Virtual China: The Internet as Threat or Opportunity?', *St. Antony's International Review*, 3: 1.

Rawnsley, G. D. and Rawnsley, M. Y. T. (eds) *Political Communications in Greater China: The Construction and Reflection of Identity*, London: RoutledgeCurzon.

Reid, J. (20 February 2006) 'The Uneven Playing Field', Lecture, King's College, London.

Reid, Tim. (8 September 2007) 'China's Cyber Army is Preparing to March on America, says Pentagon', *The Times*. Online, available at: http://technology.timesonline.co.uk/tol/news/tech_and_web/the_web/article2409865.ece (accessed 4 November 2007).

Renwick, N. and Cao, Q. (2003) 'Modern Political Communication in China', in G. D. Rawnsley and M. Y. T. Rawnsley (eds), *Political Communications in Greater China*, London: RoutledgeCurzon.

Reynolds, G. H. (2004) 'The Blogs of War', *National Interest*, 75, pp. 59–64.

Rheingold, Howard (2002) *Smart Mobs: the Next Social Revolution*, Cambridge, MA: Basic Books.

Rivlin, Alice M. (30 August – 1 September 2001) 'Commentary: The "New Economy": Background, Historical Perspective, Questions, and Speculations' in Federal Reserve Bank of Kansas City, Symposium: Economic Policy for the Information Economy, Jackson Hole, Wyoming. Online, available at: http://www.kc.frb.org/publicat/sympos/2001/papers/S02rivl.pdf; http://www.kc.frb.org/publicat/sympos/2001/sym01prg.htm (accessed 4 November 2007).

Roberts, A. and Guelff, R. (2000) *Documents on the Laws of War*, Oxford: Oxford University Press.

Robinson, S. (2002) *The CNN Effect: The Myth of News, Foreign Policy and Intervention*, London: Routledge.

Robinson, S. (2006) 'The Mission of the J-Blog: Recapturing Journalistic Authority Online', *Journalism*, 7: 1, pp. 65–83.

Ronfeldt, D. and Arquilla, J. (2001) 'What Next for Networks and Netwars?', in J. Arquilla and D. Ronfeldt (eds), *Networks and Netwars: The Future of Terror, Crime, and Militancy*, Santa Monica, CA: RAND Corporation.

Rosenau, J. (1990) *Turbulence in World Politics*, Princeton, NJ: Princeton University Press.

Rosenau, J. (2003) *Distant Proximities: Dynamics Beyond Globalization*, Princeton, NJ and Oxford: Princeton University Press.

Rosenau, J. and Johnson, D. (2002) 'Information Technologies and Turbulence in World Politics', in J. E. Allison (ed.), *Technology, Development, and Democracy: International Conflict and Cooperation in the Information Age*, Albany, NY: SUNY Press, pp. 55–78.

Rosenbloom, A. (2004) 'The Blogosphere: Introduction', *Communications of the ACM*, 47: 12, pp. 30–3.

Sageman, M. (2004) *Understanding Terror Networks*, Philadelphia, PA: University of Pennsylvania Press.

Sassen, S. (1998) *Globalization and its Discontents: Essays on the New Mobility of People and Money*, New York, NY: New Press.

Save the Children (2005) Forgotten Casualties of War: Girls in Armed Conflict. London: Save the Children.

Scalmer, Sean (2002) *Dissent Events: Protest, the Media and the Political Gimmick in Australia*, Sydney: UNSW Press.

Scarry, E. (1985) *The Body in Pain: The Making and Unmaking of the World*, New York, NY: Oxford University Press.

Schachter, O. (1960) 'The Enforcement of International Judicial and Arbitral Decisions', *American Journal of International Law*, 54.

Schachter, O. (1984) 'The Legality of Pro-Democratic Invasion', *American Journal of International Law*, 78.

Schachter, O. (1985) *International Law in the Hostage Crisis: Implications for Future Cases*, New Haven, CT and London: Yale University Press.

Schachter, O. (1986) 'In Defense of International Rules on the Use of Force', *University of Chicago Law Review*, 53.

Schachter, O. (1989a) 'Just War and Human Rights', *Pace Yearbook of International Law*, 1..

Schachter, O. (1989b) 'The Lawful Use of Force by A State against Terrorists in Another Country', *Israel Yearbook of Human Rights*, 19..

Schachter, O. (1991) *International Law in Theory and Practice*, New Haven, CT and London: Yale University Press.

Schachter, O. (1998) 'The Right of States to Use Armed Force', *Michigan Law Review.*

Schachter, O. and Joyner, C. C. (1995) *United Nations Legal Order*, Cambridge: Grotius.

Schechter, D. (2003) *Media Wars: News at a Time of Terror*, Lanham, MD: Rowman & Littlefield.

Schlesinger, Philip, Murdock, Graham and Elliott, Philip (1983) *Televising 'Terrorism': Political Violence in Popular Culture*, London: Comedia.

Schneider, Florian (2002) 'Virtual Sabotage', in E. Lubbers (ed.), *Battling Big Business: Countering Greenwash, Infiltration and Other Forms of Corporate Bullying*, Melbourne: Scribe Publications.

Scholte, J. (1996) 'The Geography of Collective Identities in a Globalizing World', *The Review of International Political Economy*, 73, pp. 427–52.

Schulman, D. (2005) 'State of Art: Their War', *Columbia Journalism Review*, 44: 13.

Schultz, K. A. (1999) 'Do Democratic Institutions Constrain or Inform? Contrasting Two Institutional Perspectives on Democracy and War', *International Organization*, 5: 2, pp. 233–66.

Schultz, K. A. (2001) *Democracy and Coercive Diplomacy*, Cambridge: Cambridge University Press.

Scollon, R. and Scollon, S. W. (2004) *Nexus Analysis: Discourse and the Emerging Internet*, London and New York, NY: Routledge.

Seipp, C. (2002) 'Online Uprising', *American Journalism Review*, 24, pp. 42–7.

Shapiro, J. (3 September 1999) *Information and War: Is it a Revolution?* Santa Monica, CA: Rand Corporation. Online, available at: http://www.rand.org/publications/MR/MR1016/MR1016.chap5.pdf.

Sharp, Gene (1973) *The Politics of Nonviolent Action* (three volumes), Boston, MA: Porter Sargent.

Sheridan, M. (2002) 'China's Net Warriors take on West', *Sunday Times*, 1 September.

Shijie Ribao (11 May 1990) 'Pingtong faxian Zhonggong qianting' ['Chinese Communist Submarines Discovered Outside Pingtong'].

Shijie Ribao (17 May 1990) 'Tai gushi you die' ['Taiwan's Stockmarket Crashes Again'].

Siklos, Richard (10 June 2007) 'Murdoch sees Journal as Hub for Empire', *International Herald Tribune.*

Simma, B. (2002) *The Charter of the United Nations: A Commentary*, Oxford: Oxford University Press.

Singh, A. (2006) 'Information Warfare: Reshaping Traditional Perceptions'. Online, available at: www.idsa-india.org/an-mar-4.html (accessed 31 January 2006).

Singh, J. P. (2002) 'Information Technologies and the Changing Scope of Global Power and Governance', in J. Rosenau and J. P. Singh (eds), *Information Technologies and Global Politics: The Changing Scope of Power and Governance*, Albany, NY: SUNY Press, pp. 1–38.

Smolkin, R. (2004) 'The Expanding Blogosphere', *American Journalism Review*, 26, pp. 38–43.

Sontag, S. (2001) *On Photography*, New York, NY: Picador.

Sorel, G. (2004) *Reflections on Violence*, Cambridge: Cambridge University Press.

Spangler, T. (8 December 1997) 'Rapid Consolidation in Security Market', Webweek. Online, available at: http://www.Internetworld.com/print/1997/12/08/news/19971208-rapid.html.

Spivak, G. (1999) *A Critique of Post-Colonial Reasons: Toward a History of the Vanishing Present*, Cambridge, MA: Harvard University Press.

Spyer, P. (2002) 'Fire without Smoke and other Phantom's of Ambon's Violence: Media Effects, Agency and the Work of the Imagination', Indonesia.

Sreberny, A. (2008) 'A Contemporary Persian Letter and its Global Purloining: the Shifting Spatialities of Contemporary Communication', in D. Hesmondhalgh and J Toynbee. (eds), *The Media and Social Theory*, London: Routledge.

Stein, T. L. (1982) 'Contempt, Crisis and the Court: The World Court and the Hostage Rescue Attempt', *American Journal of International Law*, 76, pp. 499, 500 n. 8.

Sterling, Bruce (1992) *The Hacker Crackdown*, London: Viking.

Szafranski, R. (1994) 'Neocortical Warfare? The Acme of Skill', *Military Review*, 74: 11.

Taboul, D. (2005) 'Francophone Internet Forums Shed Light on Concerns and Issues of Islamists in Europe', *The Project for the Research of Islamist Movements*, pp. 1–20.

Taipei Times (29 August 1999) 'Hacked China.com'.

Taipei Times (7 March 2000) 'NSB Websites Attacked'.

Taipei Times (3 January 2001) 'Taiwan's First Information Warfare Group Enters Service'.

Talbot, D. (2005) 'Terror's Server: Fraud, Gruesome Propaganda, Terror Planning: the Net Enables it all. The Online Industry can Help Fix it', *Technology Review*, February 2005. Online, available at: http://www.technologyreview.com/printer_friendly_article.aspx?id=14150.

Tarrow, S. 'The New Transnational Contention: Organizations, Coalitions, Mechanisms', paper presented at the American Political Science Association Annual Meeting, Chicago, August–September 2002.

Taylor, P. A. (2005) 'From Hackers to Hacktivists: Speed Bumps on the Global Superhighway?', *New Media & Society*, 7: 5, pp. 625–46.

Taylor, P. M. (1996) *Munitions of the Mind*, Manchester: Manchester University Press.

Taylor, P. M. (1998) *War and the Media: Propaganda and Persuasion in the Gulf War*, Manchester: Manchester University Press.

Thelwall, M. and Stuart, D. (2007) 'RUOK? Blogging Communication Technologies During Crises', *Journal of Computer-Mediated Communication*, 12: 2, pp. 523–48.

Thomas, T. L. (2000) *Like Adding Wings to the Tiger: Chinese Information War Theory and Practice* (local copy).

Thomas, R. D. (2 March 2001) 'The Nation's Cutting Edge Cyber Detective – A kind of Private Eye'. Online, available at: http://www.pimall.com/nais/n.seanor.html.

Thomas, T. (2000) 'China's Technology Strategems', *Jane's Intelligence Review*, December 2000.

Thomas, T. L. (2003) 'New Developments in Chinese Strategic Psychological Warfare', *Special Warfare*, April 2003.

Thompson, G. (2003) 'Blogs, Warblogs, the Public Sphere and Bubbles'. Online, available at: http://www4.svsu.edu/~glt/Transformations_piecerev.pdf (accessed 25 February 2007).

Thompson, John (1995) *The Media and Modernity*, Cambridge: Polity.

Thoreau, Henry David (2000) [1849, 1866] 'Civil Disobedience', in P. Lauter (ed.), *Walden and Civil Disobedience*, Boston, MA: Houghton Mifflin.

Thrift, N. (2004) *Knowing Capitalism*, London: Sage.

Thrift, N. (2007) *Non-Representational Theory: Space, Politics, Affect*, London: Routledge.

Tiraspol Times, The (30 November 2006) 'United Nations Petitioned by Pridnestrovie, Two Other Unrecognized Countries'. Online, available at: http://www.tiraspoltimes.com/node/366 (accessed 5 May 2007).

Tololyan, K. (2001) 'Cultural Narrative and the Motivation of the Terrorist', in D. Rapaport (ed.), *Inside the Terrorist Organization*, London: Frank Cass.

Tremayne, M. (2007) 'Introduction: Examining the Blog–Media Relationship', in M. Tremayne (ed.), *Blogging, Citizenship and the Future of Media*, New York, NY: Routledge.

Tuchman, G. (1978) *Making News: A Study in the Construction of Reality*, New York, NY: Free Press.

Turkle, Sherry (1984) *The Second Self*, Cambridge, MA: MIT Press.

Turkle, T. (1995) *Life on the Screen: Identity in the Age of the Internet*, New York, NY: Touchstone.

Ulasowski, N. (2007) 'A Literature Review: Difference and Diversity. Feminist Conception of Solidarity', unpublished MA dissertation, University of Queensland. Posted to the WiB list.

United Nations Manual on the Prevention and Control of Computer Related Crime (1 March 2000). Online, available at: http://www.ifs.univie.ac.at/~pr2gq1/rev434.html.

USA Today (28 May 2002) 'FBI wants Pearl Video off the Internet'. Online, available at: http://www.usatoday.com/tech/news/2002/05/28/pearl-internet.htm.

US Department of Defense (1991) *Instruction 5000.2, Defense Acquisition Management Policies and Procedures*, Washington, DC: Department of Defense.

US Department of Defense (1995) *TRADOC Pamphlet 525–69 – The Force XXI Army: Concept for Information Operations*, Washington, DC: Department of the Army.

US Department of Defense (1996) *Directive S-3600.1, Information Operations*, Washington, DC: Department of Defense.

US Department of Defense (1996) *Instruction 5000.1, Defense Acquisition*, Washington, DC: Department of Defense.

US Department of Defense (17 September 1997) *Joint Chiefs of Staff, Information Assurance: Legal, Regulatory, Policy and Organizational Considerations*, 3rd edn, Washington, DC: Joint Chiefs of Staff.

US Department of Defense (1998) *Active Defense against Peacetime Computer Intrusions*, Washington, DC: Department of Defense.

US Department of Defense (1998) *Joint Publication 3–13, Joint Doctrine for Information Operations*, Washington, DC: Department of Defense.

US Department of Defense (1999) *Office of the General Counsel: An Assessment of International Legal Issues in Information Operations*, Washington, DC: Department of Defense.

US Department of Defense (1 March 1999) *Dictionary of Military and Associated Terms*, Washington, DC: Department of Defense. Online, available at: http://www.dtic.mil/doctrine/jel/c_pubs.html.

US Department of Defense, (1999) *Joint Vision 2010*, Washington, DC: Department of Defense.

US Department of Defense (2001) *Protecting the Homeland* 85, Washington, DC: Department of Defense.

US Department of Defense, (2004) *Joint Vision 2020*, Washington, DC: Department of Defense.

US Department of Defense (2004) *Protecting the Homeland: Report of the Defense Science Board Task Force on Defensive Information Operations*, Washington, DC: Department of Defense.

US Department of Defense, Joint Chiefs of Staff, Joint Publication 3–13 (2000) *Joint Doctrine for Information Operations*, Washington, DC: Joint Chiefs of Staff.

US Department of Justice, (23 January 2000) *Computer Crime and Intellectual Property Section, International Aspects of Computer Crime*, Washington, DC: Department of Justice. Online, available at: http://www.usdoj.gov/criminal/cybercrime/intl.html.

US Navy, US Marines and US Coast Guard (October 2007). 'A Cooperative Strategy for 21st Century Seapower'. Online, available at: http://www.navy.mil/maritime/MaritimeStrategy.pdf.

Vaina, D. (2007) 'Newspapers and Blogs: Closer than we Think?' *Online Journalism Review*. Online, available at: http://www.ojr.org/ojr/stories/070423_vaina/ (accessed 17 September 2007).

Van Belle, D. A. (1997) 'Press Freedom and the Democratic Peace', *Journal of Peace Research*, 34: 4, pp. 405–14.

Van de Donk, W., Loader, B. D., Nixon, P. G. and Rucht, D. (2004) 'Introduction: Social Movements and ICTs', in W. van de Donk, B. D. Loader, P. G. Nixon and D. Rucht (eds), *Cyberprotest: New Media, Citizens and Social Movements*, London and New York, NY: Routledge.

Vatis, M. (2001) 'Cyber Terrorism and Information Warfare: Government Perspectives', in Y. Alexander and M. S. Swetnam (eds), *Cyber Terrorism and Information Warfare*, New York, NY: Transnational Publishers.

Vegh, S. (2003) 'Classifying Forms of Online Activism: the Case of Cyberprotests Against the World Bank', in M. McCaughey and M. D. Ayers (eds), *Cyberactivism: Online Activism in Theory and Practice*, New York, NY: Routledge.

Vegh, S. (2005) 'The Media's Portrayal of Hacking, Hackers and Hacktivism, before, after September 11', *First Monday*, 10: 2. Online, available at: http://www.firstmonday.org/issues/issue10_2/vegh/.

Vermaat, E. (2005) 'Terror on Trial', *FrontPageMagazine.*

Vermaat, E. (2006) 'The "Hofstadgroup" Terror Trial', *FrontPageMagazine.*

Vidino, L. (2006) *Al Qaeda in Europe: the New Battleground of International Jihad*, New York, NY: Prometheus Books.

Waever, O., Buzan, B. and Kelstrup, M. (1993) *Identity, Migration, and the New Security Agenda in Europe*, New York, NY: St. Martin's Press.

Wall, M. (2004) 'Blogs as Black Market Journalism: A New Paradigm for News', *The Journal of Education, Community and Values*, 4: 2.

Wall, M. (2005) 'Blogs of War: Weblogs as News', *Journalism*, 6: 2, pp. 153–172.

Waltz, E. (1998) *Information Warfare: Principles and Operations*, Norwood, MA: Artech House.

Wang, H. and Zhang, X. (eds) (2000) *Beijing Science of Campaigns*, Beijing: National Defense University Publishing House.

Wang, P. (1995) 'The Challenge of Information Warfare'. Online, available at: http://www.fas.org/irp/world/china/docs/iw_mg_wang.htm (accessed 20 October 2005).

Ward, M. (2002) 'Websites Spread al-Qaeda Message'. BBC News (12 December). Online, available at: http://news.bbc.co.uk/2/hi/technology/2566527.stm (accessed December 2002).

Wark, K. (1994) *A Hacker Manifesto*, New York, NY: St Martins Press.

Wark, K. (2003a) 'Toywars: Conceptual Art Meets Conceptual Business', *M/C Journal*, 6: 3/ Online, available at: http://journal.media-culture.org.au/0306/02-toywars.php (accessed 10 January 2008).

Wark, K. (2003b) 'The Media's Portrayal of Hacking, Hackers, and Hacktivism Before and After September 11', *First Monday*, 10: 2. Online, available at: http://firstmonday.org/issues/issue10_2/vegh/index.html (accessed 10 January 2008).

Wark, K. (2004) *A Hacker Manifesto*, Cambridge, MA: Harvard University Press.

Warner, M. (2002) 'Publics and Counterpublics', *Public Culture*, 14: 1, pp. 49–90.

War Room Research, LLC (20 December 1996) 1996 Information Systems Security Survey. Online, available at: http://www.warroomresearch.com/wrr/SurveysStudies/1996ISS_Survey_SummaryResults.htm.

War Room Research (23 January 1997) 1996 Information Systems Security Survey conducted by WarRoom Research, LC. Online, available at: http://www.infowar.com.

Wedgwood, R. (1999) 'Responding to Terrorism: The Strikes against Bin Laden', *Yale Journal of International Law*, 24.

Weimann, G. (2004) 'www.terror.net: How Modern Terrorism uses the Internet', United States Institute for Peace, Special Report 116. Online, available at: http://www.usip.org/pubs/specialreports/sr116.pdf.

Weimann, G. (2006) *Terror on the Internet: The New Arena, the New Challenges*, Washington, DC: United States Institute of Peace Press.

Wendt, A. (1999) *Social Theory of International Politics*, Cambridge: Cambridge University Press.

Whitaker, C. (2004) 'The WSF as Open Space', in J. Sen, A. Anand, A. Escobar and P. Waterman (eds), *World Social Forum: Challenging Empires*, Viveka Foundation.

Whitaker, M. (2006) 'Internet Counter Counter Insurgency: Tamilnet.com and Ethnic Conflict in Sri Lanka', in K. Landzelius (ed.), *Native on the Net: Indigenous and Diasporic Peoples in the Virtual Age*, London: Routledge.

White House, The, Office of the Press Secretary (2 October 1998) Fact Sheet: Summary of Presidential Decision Directives 62 and 63. Online, available at: http://www.pub.whitehouse.gov/uri-res/I2R?urn:pdi://oma.eop.gov.us/1998/5/22/6.text.1.

Wilkinson, I. (26 April 2006) 'Pakistan Waives 40-year Ban on Bollywood Films', *Telegraph*. Online, available at: http://www.telegraph.co.uk/news/main.jhtml?xml=/news/2006/04/26/wpak26.xml&sSheet=/news/2006/04/26/ixworld.html (accessed 4 November 2007).

Wingfield, T. C. (9 April 2003) Legal Aspects of Offensive Information Operations in Space. Online, available at: http://www.usafa.af.mil/dfl/documents/wingfield.doc.

Winterman, D. (13 July 2006) 'What's so Great about Living in Vanuatu?' BBC News Magazine. Online, available at: http://news.bbc.co.uk/go/pr/fr/-/2/hi/uk_news/magazine/5172254.stm (accessed 5 May 2007).

Wishart, A. and Bochsler, R. (2002) *Leaving Reality Behind*, London: Fourth Estate.

Wolfsfeld, G. (1997) *Media and Political Conflict: News from the Middle East*, Cambridge: Cambridge University Press.

Woodward, J. L. (17 May 2001) Statement to the House Armed Services Committee. Online, available at: http://www.globalsecurity.org/military/library/congress/2001_hr/01–05–17woodward.htm.

Wong, W. (24 February 2003) 'Security Software Companies continue Consolidation', Techweb News. Online, available at: http://www.techweb.com/wire/story/ TWB19980224S0011.

Wray, Stefan (1998) 'On Electronic Civil Disobedience'. Online, available at: http://www.thing.net/~rdom/ecd/oecd.html (accessed 10 January 2008).

Wray, Stefan (1999) 'The National Security Agency Performance' Online, available at: http://www.thing.net/~rdom/ecd/nsa_show1.html (accessed 10 January 2008).

WSF Charter of Principles (2006) Online, available at: http://www.wsf2007.org/process/- wsf-charter (accessed 20 May 2006).

Yahoo! Asia-News (7 March 2000) 'Gallup Hacked, Taiwan Cyber-attacked'. Online, available at: http://asia.dailynews.yahoo.com/headline (accessed 8 March 2000).

Yellen, Janet L. (30 August – 1 September 2001) 'Overview' in Federal Reserve Bank of Kansas City, Symposium: Economic Policy for the Information Economy, Jackson Hole, Wyoming. Online, available at: http://www.kc.frb.org/publicat/sympos/2001/ papers/S02yell.pdf; http://www.kc.frb.org/publicat/sympos/2001/sym01prg.htm (accessed 4 November 2007).

Yeltsin, B. (7 May 1996) The Russian Federation President's Inauguration Speech for the Official Installment of the New Minister of Defense.

Yiming, Sun and Yang, Liping (2005) 'Tactical Datalinks in Information Warfare', Beijing Post and Telecommunications Press.

You, J. (1999) 'The Revolution in Military Affairs and the Evolution of China's Strategic Thinking', *Contemporary Southeast Asia*, 21.

Young, I. M. (2002) *Inclusion and Democracy*, Oxford: Oxford University Press.

Yuri the Yaba (2001) 'Yabasta: Mobilizing Global Citizenship through Mass Direct Action', in N. Welton and L. Wolf (eds), *Global Uprising: Confronting the Tyrannies of the 21st Century*, Gabriola Island, B.C.: New Society Publishers.

Zelizer, B. (1998) *Remembering to Forget: Holocaust Memory through the Camera's Eye*, Chicago: University of Chicago Press.

Zourek, J. (1974) 'Enfin une Definition de l'Agression', *Annuaire francais de Droit International*, 20.

Index